Dylan™ Programming

Dylan™ Programming

An Object-Oriented and Dynamic Language

Neal Feinberg

Sonya E. Keene

Robert O. Mathews

P. Tucker Withington

Harlequin

The Late-Binding Company™

An imprint of Addison Wesley Longman, Inc.

Reading, Massachusetts • Menlo Park, California • New York • Harlow, England
Don Mills, Ontario • Sydney • Mexico City • Madrid • Amsterdam
Bonn • Singapore • Tokyo

Cover Image: *Jonathan Bachrach*
Cover Designer: *Eileen R. Hoff*
Copy Editor: *Lyn Dupré*
Proofreader: *Sarah Hallett Corey*

Library of Congress Cataloging-in-Publication Data
Dylan programming : an object-oriented and dynamic language /
Neal Feinberg . . . [et al.].
p. cm.
Includes index.
ISBN 0-201-47976-1
1. Dylan (Computer program language) 2. Object-oriented
programming (Computer science) I. Feinberg, Neal.
QA76.73.D95D95 1997
005. 13'3--dc20 96-12129
CIP

Many of the designations used by manufacturers and sellers to distinguish their products are claimed as trademarks. Where those designations appear in this book, and Harlequin and Addison-Wesley were aware of a trademark claim, the designations have been printed in initial caps or all caps.

Dylan is a trademark of Apple Computer, Inc.

The Late-Binding Company is a trademark of The Harlequin Group Limited.

The programs and applications presented in this book have been included for their instructional value only.

Access the latest information about Addison-Wesley books from our World Wide Web page:
`http://www.aw.com/cseng/`
Access the latest information about Harlequin from our World Wide Web page:
`http://www.harlequin.com/`

ISBN 0-201-47976-1
1 2 3 4 5 6 7 8 9 10—CRW—00 99 98 97 96

Contents

Preface

Dylan

Dylan (DYnamic LANguage) is a new programming language invented by Apple Computer and several partners. Dylan is dynamic, is object-oriented, and delivers efficient applications.

The Dylan language is defined by *The Dylan Reference Manual*, written by Andrew Shalit, and published by Addison-Wesley (1996). That manual is the definitive reference on Dylan. *The Dylan Reference Manual* is available on the World Wide Web; see Appendix A, *Resources on Dylan*, for details.

Dylan is up and running. You can get it from Harlequin, Carnegie Mellon University, Apple Computer, Digitool, and other organizations. Dylan implementations run on most of the popular computer platforms. Full-fledged implementations provide both a compiler and a development environment. You can obtain public-domain implementations. See Appendix A, *Resources on Dylan*.

Audience

This book is written for application programmers who have experience working in a conventional language, such as C, Pascal, COBOL, FORTRAN, or BASIC, or in an object-oriented language, such as C++, Java, Smalltalk, or Common LISP with CLOS. Familiarity with object-oriented programming and dynamic languages is not required. We do compare Dylan to C, C++, and Java in this book, but you can read and understand the book without any knowledge of C, C++, or Java.

Goals of this book

The primary goals of this book are to teach you how to program in Dylan, and how to write programs in an object-oriented style. Along the way, we hope to convince you to use Dylan. It is intended to be a practical, elegant, and fun language to use. This book is a tutorial on programming in Dylan, and it does the following:

- Begins with the most basic use of Dylan, and gradually expands to show the more powerful and advanced techniques.
- Gives the flavor of working with the Dylan language in a typical Dylan environment.
- Shows how to define classes and methods that work together to solve a problem.
- Shows how to use many of Dylan's classes, functions, and features to good effect within the context of an example application.
- Introduces the more advanced features of Dylan, including multiple inheritance, performance, exceptions, and macros.

This book does not attempt to be as complete as *The Dylan Reference Manual*, and does not provide the following kinds of material:

- Complete descriptions of all classes and functions provided by Dylan
- Complete descriptions of the detailed mechanisms in Dylan

To make full use of Dylan, programmers need *The Dylan Reference Manual*, as well as this book.

Organization of this book

We have divided the chapters of this book into four parts:

Part I, *Basic Concepts*, introduces the object-oriented and dynamic nature of Dylan.

Part II, *Intermediate Topics,* provides more details about Dylan's object-oriented techniques, and covers collections (that is, how to use strings, vectors, lists, and other kinds of collections), control flow, libraries, and modules.

Part III, *Sample Application,* contains a complete working application that illustrates the topics covered in Parts I and II.

Part IV, *Advanced Topics,* covers four areas that are sophisticated and powerful: multiple inheritance, performance versus flexibility, exceptions, and macros. The chapters in Part IV show how we can improve the example shown in Part III by applying advanced techniques.

Program examples

This book includes many program examples. Our approach is to show how evolutionary programming might work by presenting an example simply at first, and then expanding it gradually.

In Part I, *Basic Concepts,* we develop an example of a simple library that represents time and position. That library is needed for the sample airport application that we develop in Part III, *Sample Application*. The airport application simulates airplanes, runways, gates, flights, and airports. Its goal is to schedule gates for arriving and departing aircraft. To do scheduling, we need the library that represents and manipulates time and position.

Harlequin and Addison-Wesley provide World Wide Web pages containing the source code of the program examples. See Section A.1 in Appendix A, *Resources on Dylan*.

Dylan's core language is lean. It does not include input–output facilities, support for a user interface, or interfaces for communicating with programs written in other languages. These features are available in libraries supplied by vendors or in the public domain. We want this book to be applicable to the widest possible range of Dylan implementations, so we focus on the core Dylan language, and use only those library interfaces that are widely available.

Conventions used in this book

We use boldface when we introduce new terms, such as **library**.

We use bold typewriter font for code examples and names of Dylan functions and objects, such as **`define method`**. Code comments appear in oblique typewriter font — for example,

```
// Method that says a greeting
define method say-greeting (greeting :: <object>);
  format-out("%s\n", greeting);
end;
```

Many Dylan environments provide a **listener**, which enables you to type in expressions and to see their return values and output. We use a hypothetical Dylan listener to show the result of evaluating Dylan expressions:

```
? say-greeting("hi, there");
hi, there
```

In our hypothetical listener, the Dylan prompt is the question mark, `?`. The **`bold typewriter font`** shows what the user types. The ***`bold-oblique typewriter font`*** shows what the listener displays.

We use boxes to give information about Dylan's naming conventions, cautions, performance implications, comparisons to other languages such as C or C++, environment notes, and automatic-storage-management notes. Here is an example:

> **Environment note:** Our hypothetical development environment does not represent any particular Dylan development environment. Also note that the Dylan language does not require a development environment, so any given implementation may not provide one.

An image of Dylan

Jonathan Bachrach designed the image on the cover of this book. He played with the meaning that Dylan has for him by creating colorful tiles that appear to take off and fly. Each tile has its own vibrant color, unique personality, and individual strength. The tiles fly independently, but tend to flock with other tiles to achieve harmony within a community. Each tile could represent a Dylan component, or a Dylan programmer. Once Bachrach was satisfied with the still image, he took the next step, and built an animation of the tiles flying gracefully through space, flocking together, and creating a dynamic new world.

Bachrach wrote the animation and physical-modeling portions of the program in Dylan, using Open GL as the three-dimensional rendering substrate. Steve Rowley provided the physics equations. Bachrach demonstrated his animation at the Apple Worldwide Developers Conference in 1995.

Acknowledgments

We are fortunate to have at Harlequin a great pool of Dylan talent and expertise, including original inventors of the language, compiler gurus, and environment designers. A core group of Dylan experts and two expert C programmers gave us valuable technical advice and encouragement from the first to the final days of our project: Freeland Abbott, Jonathan Bachrach, Kim Barrett, Paul Butcher, Paul Haahr, Tony Mann, and Keith Playford. Other people reviewed our drafts along the way: Roman Budzianowski, Bob Cassels, Bill Chiles, Christopher Fry, David Gray, Eliot Miranda, Scott McKay, Nosa Omorogbe, Mike Plusch, and Andy Sizer. We are grateful to Harlequin people whose expertise lies in programming languages other than Dylan, for giving us their perspectives on our book: Judy Anderson, Wesley Dunnington, David Jones, Andy Latto, Peter Norvig, Kent Pitman, Steve Rowley, Craig Swanson, Jason Trenouth, Helen Vickers, and Evan Williams.

Andrew Shires carefully tested all our program examples. Brent Tennefoss gave us a great deal of help with graphics. Gary Palter shared his Macintosh expertise, and Leah Bateman shared her Windows expertise. Richard Brooksby let us steal time from other projects to write this book. Anne Altherr, Sharon Van Gundy, Clive Harris, and Sang Lee helped us to navigate the legal and business issues. Ken Jackson helped us to get the ball rolling, and gave it an extra push when needed. Jo Marks is one of Dylan's biggest fans — he urged us to write this book as a way to explain the power of Dylan to a wider audience.

We are grateful to Dylan experts outside of Harlequin who gave us thoughtful and thorough reviews of the book: Scott Fahlman, Robert Futrelle, David Moon, and Andrew Shalit.

Our editors at Addison-Wesley cheerfully and capably steered us through the process and helped to shape our book. We are grateful to Sarah Hallet Corey, Lyn Dupré, Nancy Fenton, and Helen Goldstein. Eileen Hoff designed the cover using Bachrach's image. It was, once again, a great pleasure to work with Peter Gordon.

We thank the people at Apple Computer who combined their vision of the future with hard work to make Dylan a reality. We thank the people at Carnegie Mellon University and Harlequin who continue to move Dylan forward with insight and creativity.

Part I. Basic Concepts

Chapter 1, *Introduction*, describes the goals of Dylan, and tells you where Dylan fits in the world of programming languages.

Chapter 2, *Quick Start*, is a practical guide for getting started using Dylan. It shows the look and feel of a hypothetical Dylan listener, introduces the most basic concepts of Dylan, and presents a complete Dylan program. You can type in these examples and experiment with Dylan.

Chapter 3, *Methods, Classes, and Objects*, introduces the concepts of methods, built-in classes, class inheritance, and explains what it means to be an object.

In Chapters 4 through 7, we start to develop an example of a library that represents different kinds of time and position. A **library** is a complete unit of code that can be used by many different clients. Our eventual goal in this book is to develop a sample application that handles the scheduling of aircraft that are arriving at, and departing from, an airport. For more information, see Chapter 15, *Design of the Airport Application*. The airport application will use the time and position library.

Also in Chapters 4 through 7, we show how to write object-oriented programs in Dylan. We explain class and method definition, class inheritance, method dispatch, and modularity.

Chapter 8, *A Simple Library* contains the code developed in Part I as a complete working library.

Part I Basic Concepts

1

Introduction

How many days did you spend in the past year tracking down elusive memory leaks and references to unallocated or freed memory?

How much time did you spend documenting which of the arguments to your functions are **input** and which are **output** arguments — and making sure all the callers of those functions agree?

Do you have trouble following your own programs' control flow because so much of it is devoted to checking and returning error codes?

How many conditional statements in your programs are there because you need to perform the same general operation in a different way for different kinds of data? How much time do you spend updating them to handle new types of data?

How often have you wished that you could leave the types of certain data unspecified while you develop an application — but later add the type information to improve error checking and performance?

How much time do you spend recompiling and relinking your application just to test a minor modification to the code?

Software development has progressed, but software productivity has failed to keep up with advances in hardware. Despite a proliferation of development tools and environments, programmers expend too much effort on tasks that the programming language and environment should make unnecessary.

1.1 Comparison of Dylan and other programming languages

Each language in wide use for applications has advantages and disadvantages. One way to compare languages is to imagine them arrayed along two axes. One axis ranges from **procedural** to **object-oriented** languages. The other axis ranges from **static** to **dynamic** languages. Figure 1.1 shows the comparison of several popular computer-programming languages on a graph.

- A program in a **procedural** language consists of **functions** operating on **data**. The programming task is to choose the best available representation for data, and the best algorithms for manipulating the data. Languages near the procedural end of the axis include C, FORTRAN, and COBOL.
- A program in an **object-oriented** language consists of **objects**, categorized by **class**, that combine data and behavior. The programming task is to define the best class relations to represent objects, and the best set of operations that objects of related classes support. Languages near the object-oriented end of the axis include C++, Java, Smalltalk, and the Common LISP Object System (CLOS).
- A **static** language requires most program structure — such as the types of variables and function arguments — to be determined at compile time. The compiler can detect errors and optimize performance at the cost of run-time flexibility. Languages near the static end of the axis include C, C++, and FORTRAN.
- A **dynamic** language allows you to make more run-time changes to program structure, such as passing arguments of different types to the same function and, in some languages, defining new types or classes. A dynamic environment might allow run-time definition and linking. Languages near the dynamic end of the axis include Common LISP and Smalltalk.

In reality, few languages in commercial use are purely procedural or object oriented, purely static or dynamic. In fact, the trend has been to add missing elements from one pole to languages that are close to the opposite pole. C++ adds object-oriented features to C; dynamic linking is becoming more common; LISP and Smalltalk vendors have made applications smaller and more efficient. This work, however, is hampered by the need to maintain compatibility with features of the language that were not designed with objects, dynamism, or performance in mind.

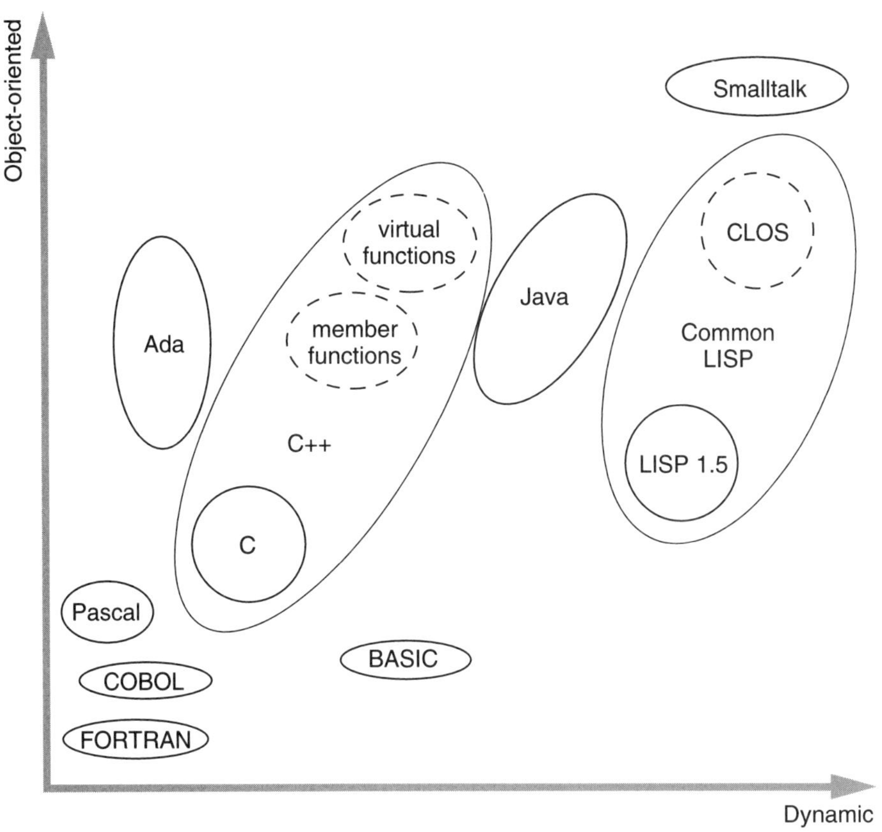

Figure 1.1 Object-oriented and dynamic extents of programming languages.

Dylan, in contrast, is a new language that integrates the best ideas from object-oriented, procedural, dynamic, and static languages, while avoiding many of the drawbacks. Figure 1.2 shows where Dylan fits on the graph.

Dylan's goals are simple:

- Promote modular, reusable, component-oriented programs.
- Support powerful and familiar procedural programming.
- Encourage rapid and productive development of programs.
- Permit delivery of safe, efficient, compact applications.

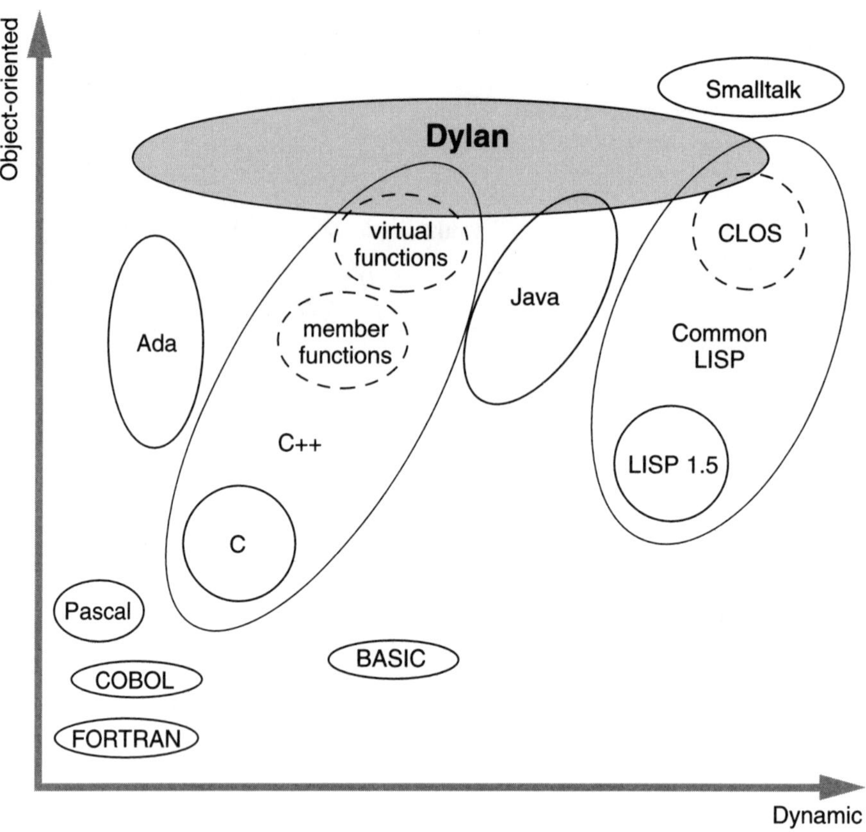

Figure 1.2 Object-oriented and dynamic extents of Dylan and other languages.

Let's take a brief look at features of Dylan that support these goals.

1.2 Modular, reusable, component-oriented programs

Dylan is an object-oriented language. Programs create and use objects, and they use classes to categorize and abstract attributes of objects. Classes play a number of key roles:

- They are data types, embodying subtype–supertype relationships between objects.

- They are the vehicle for abstraction of common attributes of objects.
- They organize sharing of attributes: Subclasses **inherit** the attributes of superclasses.
- They are the principal basis for specializing behavior of objects.

Objects contain *data* in **slots**, which are like structure members or fields in other languages. But the *behavior* of objects resides in generic functions and methods. A **generic function** is a function that embodies an operation common to different classes of the objects that are its arguments. A **method** is a function that acts as a specific implementation of a generic operation for objects of a particular class. A program calls a generic function, and Dylan determines the most appropriate method to invoke based on the arguments to the generic function. A program controls method selection, or **dispatch**, by means of class relationships, rather than via explicit conditional statements.

Abstraction of common attributes and methods in superclasses lets you reuse code, rather then reimplement it, for subclasses. By defining a subclass, you can add specialized data or behavior while having the subclass inherit attributes of superclasses, which may be defined in another component or library, or in Dylan itself.

Generic functions constitute abstract interfaces for specific operations. You can usually change the implementation of an operation or a data representation without changing the interface to the operation. In this way, you can change an implementation without changing the functions or objects that use the implementation. These functions or objects may be defined in another component or library.

Dylan provides large-scale variable namespaces, called **modules**. A module can include or use other modules, but only the variables explicitly exported from those modules are visible to it. Modules provide public and private global variables. Because functions and classes, as well as data, are variable values, modules define external interfaces for collections of classes and generic functions.

1.3 Powerful and familiar procedural programming

Dylan is not just an object-oriented language. It includes and extends the language features that you expect to find in a more purely procedural language. Dylan's syntax encourages clear and structured programming. It includes familiar, economical notation for infix operators and slot and array references. Dylan offers a choice of concise or expanded equivalents for many syntactic constructs to accommodate a range of programming styles, from terse to descriptive.

- You do not have to write a lot of intrusive code to support Dylan's object orientation. For example, the most common language expressions for defining a method automatically define a generic function if necessary. A method-defining expression looks much like a function-defining expression in other languages.
- You can define a function to take a variable number of arguments. You can also define a function to take arguments in the form of name–value pairs, thus supporting self-documenting function invocation.
- Functions can return more than one value. In fact, you can use a single expression to initialize multiple variables to the values returned by a single function call. You do not have to use a potentially confusing mechanism, such as output parameters, to obtain multiple values.
- Dylan has a rich set of variable-sized aggregate data types, called **collections**. Collection classes include strings, arrays, sets, queues, lists, stacks, and tables. Dylan has flexible iteration constructs and permits applications to extend them so that they operate on application-defined collection subclasses. In this way, a module that uses specialized collection classes can cooperate with another module that defines general collection operations.
- Dylan has a built-in exception-signaling and exception-handling system that permits both error handling and recovery. Exceptions are based on a class and object model that fits smoothly with the rest of the language and can be extended by the program. You do not have to return and check error codes from functions — an error-prone process in itself — to ensure that no exception has occurred.

1.4 Rapid and productive development of programs

Dylan promotes rapid development and incremental refinement of prototype programs. The language encourages you to spend time early in the programming cycle writing and experimenting with substantive, working code, and not worrying about distracting issues such as memory management and exact type specifications.

- Dylan allows flexible typing of variables, parameters, and return values. You can permit variables, parameters, and return values to be of a general type, so that their values can be objects of any subtype of the general type. Later in the development cycle, when the program specification is refined, you can add more specific type constraints.
- You can choose to allow run-time definition of new classes and methods. Even if you do not so choose, most Dylan development environments allow you to add or change definitions at run time without recompiling or relinking the program, while the program is under development.
- Like those of Java, Dylan implementations provide automatic storage management. You can create and use objects freely, even in complex algorithms, where control flow may make it difficult to tell when an object is no longer needed. You do not explicitly allocate or deallocate memory, and you do not have to worry about failing to free unused memory or referring to memory that has already been freed.
- Dylan includes a powerful **macro** language, based on pattern matching and replacement. Macros let you extend the base language by creating syntactic structures that more concisely match a particular problem domain. Macros can serve as shorthand for common idioms, and can create more abstract or problem-specific constructs that the compiler translates into Dylan.

1.5 Delivery of safe, efficient, compact applications

Languages that provide run-time flexibility have usually paid a price in decreased performance and large application size. Dylan's solution is to separate the development environment from the delivered run-time application. Dylan provides maximum flexibility during program development, but also lets you trade flexibility for performance in a delivered application. A Dylan compiler can often optimize such potentially expensive operations as slot access and method dispatch.

- You can declare type constraints for variables, parameters, return values, and slots. The more specific your type declarations, the better the compiler can detect type mismatches and optimize performance.
- By default, classes and generic functions are closed off, or **sealed**. No other library or application can define subclasses for a sealed class or define

methods for a sealed generic function. Sealing can help a compiler to optimize slot access and method dispatch.

- Dylan's core language is small. Extended components of the language, such as input–output and advanced mathematical operations, are provided by libraries. You can keep an application small by using only the libraries that the application needs. You can also create libraries of your own, and deliver them in compiled form.
- You can selectively open or **unseal** classes and generic functions to allow users of your application or library to specialize the interfaces that you provide. An open interface in Dylan includes link- and run-time information, so that an application that specializes the interface does not have to be recompiled to use a new version of the library.
- Most Dylan implementations provide support for operating in a multilanguage environment. A Dylan program can operate with code written in another language, and a program written in another language can operate with Dylan code. You can use a Dylan program as a component of a software system that includes code written in other languages.

Dylan's overall aim is to meet two needs that have often been in conflict:

1. To give programmers the freedom and power to develop applications rapidly
2. To deliver components and applications that can run efficiently on a wide range of machines and operating systems

This book introduces you to the features of Dylan that make those goals attainable. We think you will find Dylan to be a language that makes your programming time both productive and enjoyable.

2

Quick Start

We start by jumping right into Dylan. We show how to interact with a development environment, to use basic arithmetic functions, to define variables and constants, and to create a simple but complete Dylan program.

The Dylan language does not specify a development environment, but many Dylan implementations provide one. A **development environment** can contain many tools, such as an editor custom-tailored for Dylan code, a browser that helps you to examine objects, a debugger, and a **listener** that enables you to type in expressions and to see their return values and output. You can use a listener to test pieces of your program without compiling the whole program. When you start using Dylan, a good way to learn and explore is to use a listener. We use a hypothetical listener in this chapter to show the results of evaluating Dylan expressions. Of course, Dylan also supports the traditional approach of editing source files, compiling the program, and running the program.

2.1 Dialog with a Dylan listener

Here is a sample dialog between a user and a listener. The **`bold typewriter font`** shows what the user types. The ***`bold-oblique typewriter font`*** shows what the listener displays.

```
? 7 + 12;
19
```

In our hypothetical listener, the Dylan prompt is the question mark, `?`. The user types in `7 + 12;` and presses Enter. The listener executes the expression and displays the value returned by that expression, which is `19`. The listener displays any return values and output produced by the expression.

> **Environment note:** Our hypothetical development environment does not represent any particular Dylan development environment. The Dylan language does not require a development environment, so any given implementation may not provide one.

2.2 Simple arithmetic operations

We can do other simple arithmetic:

```
? 7 * 52;
364

? 7 - 12;
-5
```

> **Caution: Spaces are needed!** In Dylan, it is legal to use characters such as `+`, `-`, `*`, `<`, `>`, and `/` in names of variables. Therefore, in most cases, you must leave spaces around those characters in code, to make it clear that you are using them as functions, and that they are not part of the name of a variable. For example:
>
> `a + b` means add `a` and `b`.
>
> `a+b` means the name `a+b`.

We can multiply several numbers together:

```
? 24 * 7 * 52;
8736
```

2.2.1 True and false

We can compare the magnitude of two numbers:

```
? 1 = 1;
#t
```

```
? 3 < 30;
#t

? 15 > 16;
#f
```

The functions `=`, `<`, and `>` are **predicates**. A predicate returns true if the condition it is testing is true; otherwise, it returns false. As you might guess, `#t` means true and `#f` means false. False is represented by the unique value `#f` only, but any object that is not `#f` is true (thus, 0 is a true value).

> **Comparison with C and C++: Caution!** C and C++ use integers to represent Boolean values — 0 represents false, and any nonzero value is considered true. Dylan has an explicit `<boolean>` type with two instances: `#f` represents false, and `#t` represents the *canonical* true value. However, any value other than `#f` is also considered true in a Boolean test. Thus, in Dylan, 0 is considered true.

> **Comparison with Java**: Java has a separate type for Boolean values. Unlike Dylan, C, or C++, the Java `Boolean` class has only two values, `true` and `false`. This design allows the compiler to issue warnings for the common C error `if (a=b) ...`, because an assignment does not typically yield a Boolean result. An explicit conversion is required to test nonzero in Java: `if (a!=0) ...`.

2.2.2 Infix syntax and function-call syntax

The functions `+`, `-`, `*`, `<`, `>`, and `=` use **infix syntax**; that is, the function name appears between the arguments to the function. Most other Dylan functions use the function-call syntax shown in the following call to the `min` function, which returns the smallest of its arguments:

```
? min(2, 4, 6);
2
```

The function name appears first, followed by its arguments, which are surrounded by parentheses and separated by commas. Other examples of the function-call syntax follow:

```
? even?(3);
#f

? zero?(0);
#t
```

Convention: The names of most predicates end with a question mark — for example, **even?**, **odd?**, **zero?**, **positive?** and **negative?**. The question mark is part of the name, and does not have any special behavior. There are exceptions to this convention, such as the predicates named **=**, **<**, and **>**.

2.2.3 Case insensitivity

Dylan is case insensitive. Therefore, we can call the **max** function as follows:

```
? MAX(-1, 1);
1

? mAx(0, 55.3, 92);
92
```

2.3 Variables and constants

We can define variables for storing values:

```
? define variable *my-number* = 7;

? define variable *your-number* = 12;
```

In Dylan, these variables are called **module variables**. A module variable has a name and a value. For now, you can consider module variables to be like global variables in other languages. (See Section 13.2, page 189, for information about modules.) Module variables can have different values assigned to them during the execution of a program. When you define a module variable, you must **initialize** it; that is, you must provide an initial value for it. For example, the initial value of ***my-number*** is **7**.

Convention: Module variables have names that start and end with an asterisk — for example, ***my-number***. The asterisks are part of the name, and do not have any special behavior.

We can ask the listener for the values of module variables:

```
? *my-number*;
7

? *your-number*;
12
```

We can add the values stored in these variables:

```
? *my-number* + *your-number*;
19
```

We can multiply the values stored in these variables:

```
? *my-number* * *your-number*;
84
```

We can use the **assignment operator**, `:=`, to change the values stored in a variable:

```
? *my-number* := 100;
100
```

2.3.1 Assignment, initialization, and equality

People new to Dylan may find `=` and `:=` confusing, because the names are similar, and the meanings are related but distinct.

The meaning of `=` depends on whether it appears an expression, or in a definition of a variable or constant. In an expression, `=` is a function that tests for equality; for example,

```
? 3 = 3;
#t
```

In a definition of a variable or constant, `=` precedes the initial value of the variable or constant; for example,

```
? define variable *her-number* = 3;
```

After you initialize a variable with `=`, the `=` function returns true:

```
? *her-number* = 3;
#t
```

The assignment operator, `:=`, performs assignment, which is setting the value of an existing variable; for example,

```
? *her-number* := 4;
4
```

After you have assigned a value to a variable, the = function returns true:

```
? *her-number* = 4;
#t
```

Dylan offers an identity predicate, which we discuss in Section 3.3.1, page 35.

2.3.2 Variables that have type constraints

We defined the variables **`*my-number*`** and **`*your-number*`** without giving a **type constraint** on the variables. Thus, we can store any type of value in these variables. For example, here we use the assignment operator, **`:=`**, to store strings in these variables:

```
? *my-number* := "seven";
"seven"

? *your-number* := "twelve";
"twelve"
```

What happens if we try to add the string values stored in these variables?

```
? *my-number* + *your-number*;
ERROR: No applicable method for + with arguments ("seven", "twelve")
```

Dylan signals an error because the **+** function does not know how to operate on string arguments.

> **Environment note:** The Dylan implementation defines the exact wording of error messages, and what happens when an error is signaled. If your implementation opens a Dylan debugger when an error is signaled, you now have an opportunity to experiment with the debugger!

We can redefine the variables to include a type constraint, which ensures that the variables can hold only numbers. We specify that **`*my-number*`** can hold any integer, and that **`*your-number*`** can hold a single-precision floating-point number:

```
? define variable *my-number* :: <integer> = 7;
```

```
? define variable *your-number* :: <single-float> = 12.01;
```

What happens if we try to store a string in one of the variables?

```
? *my-number* := "seven";
ERROR: The value assigned to *my-number* must be of type <integer>
```

Both `<integer>` and `<single-float>` are **classes.** For now, you can think of a class as being like a datatype in another language. Dylan provides a set of built-in classes, and you can also define new classes.

> **Convention:** Class names start with an open angle bracket and end with a close angle bracket — for example, `<integer>`. The angle brackets are part of the name, and do not have any special behavior.

The `+` function can operate on numbers of different types:

```
? *my-number* + *your-number*;
19.01
```

2.3.3 Module constants

A **module constant** is much like a module variable, except that it is an error to assign a different value to a constant. Although you cannot assign a different value to a constant, you may be able to change the elements of the value, such as assigning a different value to an element of an array.

You use `define constant` to define a module constant, in the same way that you use `define variable` to define a variable. You must initialize the value of the constant, and you cannot change that value throughout the execution of a Dylan program. Here is an example:

```
? define constant $pi = 3.14159;
```

> **Convention:** Module constant names start with the dollar sign, `$` — for example, `$pi`. The dollar sign is part of the name, and does not have any special behavior.

Both module variables and module constants are accessible within a **module**.

(See Section 13.2, page 189, for information about modules.) Dylan also offers variables that are accessible within a smaller area, called **local variables**. There is no concept of a local constant; all constants are module constants. Therefore, throughout the rest of this book, we use the word *constant* as shorthand for module constant.

2.3.4 Local variables

You can define a local variable by using a `let` declaration. Unlike module variables, local variables are established dynamically, and they have **lexical scope**. During its lifetime, a local variable shadows any module variable, module constant, or existing local variable with the same name.

Local variables are scoped within the smallest body that surrounds them. You can use `let` anywhere within a body, rather than just at the beginning; the local variable is declared starting at its definition, and continuing to the end of the smallest body that surrounds the definition.

A **body** is a region of program code that delimits the scope of all local variables declared inside the body. When you are defining functions, usually there is an implicit body available. For example, `define method` creates an implicit body. (For information about method definitions, see Section 3.1, page 27.) Other control structures, such as `if`, create implicit bodies. Bodies can be nested. If there is no body handy, or if you want to create a body smaller than the implicit one, you can create a body by using `begin` to start it and `end` to finish it:

```
? begin
    let radius = 5;
    let circumference = 2 * $pi * radius;
    circumference;
  end;
31.4159
```

The local variables `radius` and `circumference` are declared, initialized, and used within the body. The value returned by the body is the value of the expression executed last in the body, which is `circumference`. Outside the lexical scope of the body, the local variables are no longer declared, and trying to access them is an error:

```
? radius
ERROR: The variable radius is undefined.
```

2.4 Formatted output

Throughout this book, we use the **format-out** function to print output. The syntax of **format-out** is

format-out *string arg1 ... argn*

The **format-out** function sends output to the standard output destination, which could be the window where the program was invoked, or a new window associated with the program. The standard output destination depends on the platform.

The *string* argument can contain ordinary text, formatting instructions beginning with `%`, and characters beginning with a backslash, `\`. Ordinary text in the format string is sent to the destination verbatim. You can use the backslash character in the *string* argument to insert unusual characters, such as `\n`, which prints the newline character.

```
? format-out("Your future is filled with wondrous surprises.\n")
Your future is filled with wondrous surprises.
```

Formatting instructions begin with a percent sign, `%`. For each `%`, there is normally a corresponding argument giving an object to output. The character after the `%` controls how the object is formatted. A wide range of formatting characters is available, but we use only the following formatting characters in this book:

`%d`	Prints an integer represented as a decimal number
`%s`	Prints the contents of its string argument unquoted
`%=`	Prints an implementation-specific representation of the object; you can use `%=` for any class of object

Here are examples:

```
? format-out
    ("Your number is %= and mine is %d\n", *your-number*, *my-number*);
Your number is 12.01 and mine is 7.

? format-out("The %s meeting will be held at %d:%d%d.\n", "Staff", 2, 3, 0);
The Staff meeting will be held at 2:30.
```

In Dylan, functions do not need to return any values. The **format-out** function returns no values. Thus, it is called only for its side effect (printing output).

> **Comparison with C:** **`format-out`** is similar to **`printf`**.

The **`format-out`** function is available from the **`format-out`** library, and is not part of the core Dylan language. We now describe how to make the **`format-out`** function accessible to our program, and how to set up the files that constitute the program. Many of the details depend on the implementation of Dylan, so you will need to consult the documentation of your Dylan implementation.

> **Usage note:** The Apple Technology Release does not currently provide the **`format-out`** function. For information about how to run these examples in the Apple Technology Release, see Harlequin's or Addison-Wesley's Web page for our book. See Section A.1. in Appendix A, *Resources on Dylan*.

2.5 A complete Dylan program

In this section, we show how to create a complete Dylan program. The Dylan program will print the following:

```
Hello, world
```

The Dylan expression that prints that output is

```
format-out("Hello, world\n");
```

A Dylan **library** defines a software component — a separately compilable unit that can be either a stand-alone program or a component of a larger program. Thus, when we talk about creating a Dylan program, we are really talking about creating a library.

A library contains **modules**. Each module contains definitions and expressions. The module is a **namespace** for the definitions and expressions. For example, if you define a module variable in one particular module, it is available to all the code in that module. If you choose to export that module variable, you can make it accessible to other modules that import it. In this chapter, we give the bare minimum of information about libraries and modules — just enough for you to get started quickly. For a complete description of libraries and modules, see Chapter 13, *Libraries and Modules*.

To create a complete Dylan program, we need

- To define the library that is our program; we shall create a library named **`hello`**
- To define a module (or more than one) in the library, to hold the definitions and expressions in our program; we shall create a module named **`hello`** in the **`hello`** library
- To write the program code, in the module; we shall put the **`format-out`** expression in the **`hello`** module of the **`hello`** library

2.5.1 Files of a Dylan program

Different Dylan environments store programs in different ways, but there is a file-based **interchange format** that all Dylan environments accept. In this interchange format, any program consists of a minimum of two files: a file containing the program itself, and a file describing the libraries and modules. The most trivial program consists of a single module in a single library, but it is still expressed in two files. Most Dylan implementations also accept a third file, which enumerates all the files that make up a program; this file is called a **library-interchange definition (LID)** file.

The details of how the files are named and stored depends on your Dylan implementation. Typically, however, you have a directory containing all the files of the program. As shown in Figure 2.1, we name our program directory **`hello`**, and name the files **`hello.lid`**, **`library.dylan`**, and **`hello.dylan`** (the latter is the program file).

```
hello
   hello.lid
   library.dylan
   hello.dylan
```

Figure 2.1 The **`hello`** directory and the three files that it contains.

> **Comparison with C:** The following analogies may help you to understand how the elements of Dylan programs correspond to elements of C programs:
> - The program files are similar to **.c** files in C.
> - The library file is similar to a C header file.
> - The LID file is similar to a **makefile**, which is used in certain C development environments.

2.5.2 Components of a Dylan program

We start with this simple Dylan expression:

```
format-out("Hello, world\n");
```

All Dylan expressions must be in a module. Therefore, we use a text editor to create a file that contains the expression within a module:

The program file: **hello.dylan**.

```
module: hello

format-out("Hello, world\n");
```

The **hello.dylan** file is the top-level file; you can think of it as the program itself. When you run this program, Dylan executes all the expressions in the file in the order that they appear in the file. There is only one expression in this program — the call to **format-out**.

The first line of this file declares that the expressions and definitions in this file are in the **hello** module. Before we can run (or even compile) this program, we need to define the **hello** module. All modules must be in a library, so we must also define a library for our **hello** module. We create a second file, called the library file, and define the **hello** module and **hello** library in the library file:

The library file: **`library.dylan`**.

```
module: dylan-user

define library hello
  use dylan;
  use format-out;
end library hello;

define module hello
  use dylan;
  use format-out;
end module hello;
```

The first line of **`library.dylan`** states that the expressions in this file are in the **`dylan-user`** module. Every Dylan expression and definition must be in a module, including the definitions of libraries and modules. The **`dylan-user`** module is the starting point — the predefined module that enables you to define the libraries and modules that your program uses.

In the file **`library.dylan`**, we define a library named **`hello`**, and a module named **`hello`**. We define the **`hello`** library to use the **`dylan`** library and the **`format-out`** library, and we define the **`hello`** module to use the **`dylan`** module and the **`format-out`** module.

One library **uses** another library to allow its modules to use the other library's exported modules. Most libraries need to use the **`dylan`** library, because it contains the **`dylan`** module. One module **uses** another module to allow its definitions to use the other module's exported definitions. Most modules need to use the **`dylan`** module in the **`dylan`** library, because that module contains the definitions of the core Dylan language. We also need to use the **`format-out`** module in the **`format-out`** library, because that module defines the **`format-out`** function, which we use in our program.

Finally, we create a LID file that enumerates the files that make up the library. This file does not contain Dylan expressions, but rather is simply a textual description of the library's files:

The LID file: **`hello.lid`**.

```
library: hello
files:   library
         hello
```

The LID file simply states that the library **hello** comprises two files, named **library** and **hello**. In other words, to build the **hello** library, the compiler must process the two files listed, in the order that they appear in the file. The order is significant, because a module must be defined before the code that is in the module can be analyzed and compiled.

You can consult the documentation of your Dylan implementation to find out how to build an executable program from these files, and how to run that program once it is built. Most Dylan environments produce executable programs that can be invoked in the same manner as any other program on the particular platform that you are using.

We incur a fair amount of overhead in setting up the files that make up a simple program. Most environments automate this process — some of the complexity shown here occurs because we are working with the lowest common denominator: interchange files. The advantages of libraries and modules are significant for larger programs. See Chapter 13, *Libraries and Modules*.

2.6 Summary

In this chapter, we covered the following:

- We entered Dylan expressions to a listener and saw their values or output.
- We used simple arithmetic functions: **+**, *****, **-**. We used predicates: **=**, **<**, **>**, **even?**, and **zero?**.
- We described certain naming conventions in Dylan; see Table 2.1.

Dylan element	Example of name
module variable	***my-number***
constant	**$pi**
class	**<integer>**
predicate	**positive?**

Table 2.1 Dylan naming conventions shown in this chapter.

Dylan element	Syntax example
string	`"Runway"`
true	any value that is not `#f`
canonical true value	`#t`
false	`#f`
infix syntax function call	`2 + 3;`
function call	`max(2, 3);`

Table 2.2 Syntax of Dylan elements.

- We described the syntax of some commonly used elements of Dylan; see Table 2.2.
- We defined module variables (with **`define variable`**), constants (with **`define constant`**), and local variables (with **`let`**).
- We set the value of variables by using **`:=`**, the assignment operator.
- We defined a simple but complete Dylan program, consisting of a LID file, a library file, and a program file.

Here, we summarize the most basic information about libraries and modules:

- A Dylan library defines a software component — a separately compilable unit that can be either a stand-alone program or a component of a larger program. Thus, when we talk about creating a Dylan program, we are really talking about creating a library.
- Each Dylan expression and definition must be in a module. Each module is in a library.
- One module uses another module to allow its definitions to use the other module's exported definitions. Most modules need to use the **`dylan`** module in the **`dylan`** library, because it contains the definitions of the core Dylan language.

- One library uses another library to allow its modules to use the other library's exported modules. Most libraries need to use the **`dylan`** library, because it contains the **`dylan`** module.

3

Methods, Classes, and Objects

In this chapter, we introduce the basic concepts of methods, classes, and objects. We define simple methods, and show that each method is intended for a certain class of argument. We discuss built-in classes in Dylan, and show that they are related by class inheritance. Finally, we discuss what it means to be an object.

Dylan's model of objects and classes differs significantly from the C++ model. If you are familiar with C++, we recommend that you read Appendix B, *Dylan Object Model for C and C++ Programmers*.

3.1 Method definitions

In Dylan, we define methods — a **method** is a kind of function. We define a simple method, **say-hello**, as follows:

```
define method say-hello ()
  format-out("hello, world\n");
end;
```

We call **say-hello** as follows:

```
? say-hello();
hello, world
```

We use **define method** to define a method named **say-hello**. Just after the name **say-hello**, we specify the method's **parameter list**, **()**. The parameter list of this method is empty, meaning that this method takes no arguments. The call to **say-hello** provides an empty argument list, meaning that there are no arguments in the call.

The body of the **say-hello** method has one expression — a call to **format-out**. A method returns whatever is returned by the expression executed last in its body. In general, a method can return a single value, multiple values, or no value at all. The **say-hello** method returns what **format-out** returns — no value at all. In the call to **say-hello**, we see the output of **format-out** in the listener; we see output and not a returned value (because no value is returned).

> **Usage note:** In this chapter, we define methods that call the **format-out** function. Because **format-out** is in the **format-out** module, we need to make that module available. There are two ways to do so. The first way is to work in files, as described in Section 2.5. The second way is to use a gesture or command in your Dylan environment to make the **format-out** module accessible. Then, you can simply enter the method definitions into the listener.

3.1.1 A method that takes an argument

We can define a method similar to **say-hello**, called **say-greeting**, that takes an argument:

```
define method say-greeting (greeting :: <object>);
  format-out("%s\n", greeting);
end;
```

The **say-greeting** method has one required parameter, named **greeting**. The type constraint of the required parameter indicates the type that the argument must be. The **greeting** parameter has the type constraint **<object>**, which is the most general class. All objects are of the type **<object>**, so using this class as the type constraint allows the argument to be any object. You can omit the type constraint of a required parameter; that omission has the same effect as specifying **<object>** as the type constraint.

We can call **say-greeting** on a string:

```
? say-greeting("hi, there");
hi, there
```

We can call **say-greeting** on an integer, although the integer does not give a particularly friendly greeting:

```
? define variable *my-number* :: <integer> = 7;

? say-greeting(*my-number*);
7
```

3.1.2 Two methods with the same name

For fun, we can change **say-greeting** to take a different action for integers, such as to print a message:

```
Your lucky number is 7.
```

To make this change, we define another method, also called **say-greeting**. This method has one required parameter named **greeting**, which has the type constraint **<integer>**.

```
define method say-greeting (greeting :: <integer>)
  format-out("Your lucky number is %s.\n", greeting);
end;

? say-greeting(*my-number*);
Your lucky number is 7.
```

A Dylan method is similar to a procedure or subroutine in other languages, but there is an important difference. You can define more than one method with the same name. Each one is a method for the same **generic function**. Figure 3.1 shows how you can picture a generic function.

When a generic function is called, it chooses the most appropriate method to call for the arguments. For example, when we call the **say-greeting** generic function with an integer, the method whose parameter is of the type **<integer>** is called:

```
? say-greeting(1000);
Your lucky number is 1000.
```

When we call the **say-greeting** generic function with an argument that is not an integer, the method whose parameter is of the type **<object>** is called:

```
? say-greeting("Buenos Dias");
Buenos Dias
```

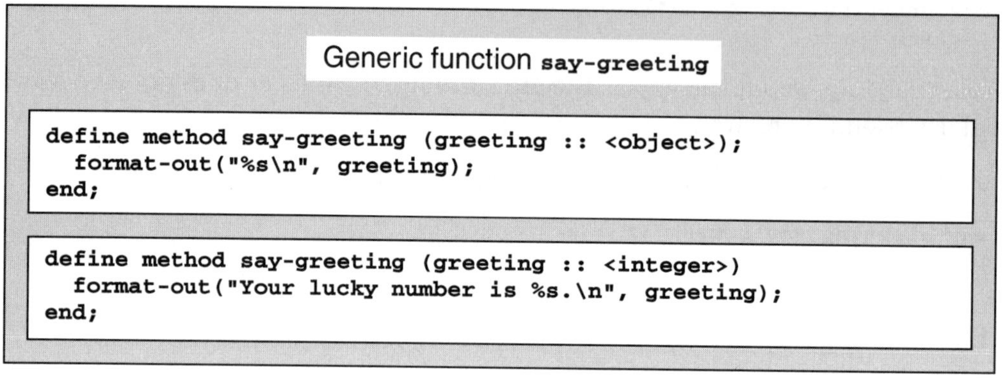

Generic function **say-greeting**

```
define method say-greeting (greeting :: <object>);
  format-out("%s\n", greeting);
end;
```

```
define method say-greeting (greeting :: <integer>)
  format-out("Your lucky number is %s.\n", greeting);
end;
```

Figure 3.1 The **say-greeting** generic function and its methods.

3.2 Classes

We have already seen examples of classes in Dylan: **<integer>**, **<single-float>**, **<string>**, and **<object>**.

Individual values are called **objects**. Each object is a **direct instance** of one particular class. You can use the **object-class** function to determine the direct class of an object. For example, in certain implementations, **7**, **12**, and **1000** are direct instances of the class **<integer>**:

```
? object-class(1000);
{class <integer>}
```

The value returned by **object-class** is the **<integer>** class itself. The appearance of a class, method, or generic function in a listener depends on the Dylan environment. We have chosen a simple appearance of classes for this book.

All the classes that we have seen so far are built-in classes, provided by Dylan. In Chapter 4, *User-Defined Classes and Methods*, we show how to define new classes.

3.2.1 Class inheritance

One important aspect of classes is that they are related to one another by **inheritance**. Inheritance enables classes that are logically related to one another to share the behaviors and attributes that they have in common. Each class inherits from one or more classes, called its **superclasses**. If no other class is appropriate, then the class inherits from the class **<object>**. This class is the **root** of all classes: All classes inherit from it, either directly or indirectly, and it does not have any direct superclasses.

> **Comparison with C++:** If you are familiar with the class concepts of C++, you might initially be confused by Dylan's class model. In Dylan, all base classes are effectively virtual base classes with "virtual" data members. When a class inherits another class more than once (because of multiple inheritance), only a single copy of that base class is included. Each of the multiple-inheritance paths can contribute to the implementation of the derived class. The Dylan class model favors this mix-in style of programming. For more information, see Section B.2 in Appendix B, *Dylan Object Model for C and C++ Programmers.*

In Dylan, we distinguish between two terms: *direct instance* and *general instance.* An object is a **direct instance** of exactly one class: the class that **object-class** returns for that object. An object is a **general instance** of its direct class, and of all classes from which its direct class inherits. The term *instance* is equivalent to *general instance.* You can use the **instance?** predicate to ask whether an object is an instance of a given class:

```
? instance?(1000, <integer>);
#t

? instance?("hello, world", <integer>);
#f
```

All objects are instances of the class **<object>**:

```
? instance?(1000, <object>);
#t

? instance?("hello, world", <object>);
#t
```

Figure 3.2 shows the inheritance relationships among several of the built-in classes. If class A is a superclass of class B, then class B is a **subclass** of class A. For example, **<object>** is a superclass of **<string>**, and **<string>** is a subclass of **<object>**. For simplicity, Figure 3.2 omits certain classes that intervene between the classes shown.

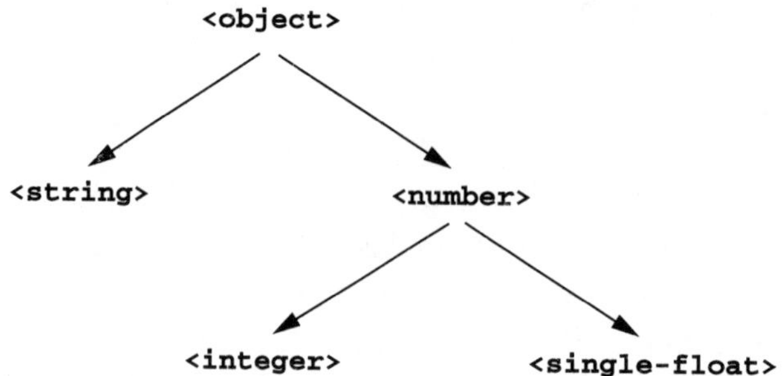

Figure 3.2 Classes and subclasses. Each arrow points from a class to a subclass.

A typical Dylan environment provides a browser to explore inheritance relationships among classes; certain environments show the relationships graphically.

The Dylan language includes functions that provide information about the inheritance relationships among classes. We can use **subtype?** to ask whether one class inherits from another class:

```
? subtype?(<integer>, <number>);
#t

? subtype?(<integer>, <object>);
#t

? subtype?(<single-float>, <object>);
#t

? subtype?(<string>, <integer>);
#f
```

It may be confusing that we use a function called **subtype?** here, but Dylan does not provide a function called **subclass?**. Every class is a **type**, but certain types are not classes (see Section 9.1, page 109). The **subtype?** function works for both classes and other types.

We can ask for all the superclasses of a given class:

```
? all-superclasses(<string>);
#[{class <string>}, {class <mutable-sequence>}, {class <sequence>},
{class <mutable-collection>}, {class <collection>}, {class <object>}]

? all-superclasses(<integer>);
#[{class <integer>}, {class <rational>}, {class <real>}, {class <number>},
{class <object>}]
```

```
? all-superclasses(<single-float>);
#[{class <single-float>}, {class <float>}, {class <real>}, {class <number>},
{class <object>}]
```

The **`all-superclasses`** function returns a vector containing the class itself and all that class's superclasses. The **`#[...]`** syntax represents a **vector**, which is a one-dimensional array. (For information about vectors, see Chapter 11, *Collections and Control Flow*.)

3.2.2 Relationship between classes and methods

The relationship between classes and methods in Dylan is different from that in C++ and Smalltalk, among other languages.

> **Comparison to C++ and Smalltalk:** In C++ and Smalltalk, a class contains the equivalent of methods. In Dylan, a class does not contain methods; instead, a method belongs to a generic function. This design decision enables these powerful features of Dylan:
>
> - You can define methods on built-in classes (because you do not have to modify the class definition to define a method intended for use on the class). For an example, see Section 6.1, page 75. More generally, you can define a method for a class that you did not define.
> - You can write multimethods. In a **multimethod**, the method dispatch is based on the classes of more than one argument to a generic function. For an introduction to method dispatch, see Section 5.5, page 63. For information about multimethods, see Chapter 6, *Multimethods*.
> - You can restrict generic functions to operate on specific classes of objects.

In Dylan, a method belongs to a generic function, as shown in Figure 3.1, page 30. Although methods are independent of classes, methods operate on instances of classes. A method states the types of objects for which it is applicable by the type constraint of each of its required parameters. Consider the **`say-greeting`** method defined earlier:

```
define method say-greeting (greeting :: <integer>);
  format-out("Your lucky number is %s.\n", greeting);
end;
```

This method operates on instances of the **<integer>** class. Notice how easy and convenient it is to define a method intended for use on the built-in class **<integer>**.

3.3 Objects

In Dylan, everything is an **object**. Characters, strings, numbers, arrays, and vectors are all objects. The canonical true and false values, **#t**, and **#f**, are objects. Methods, generic functions, and classes are objects. What does it mean to be an object?

- Most important, an object has a unique identity. You can use the **==** predicate to test whether two operands are the same object. See Section 3.3.1.
- An object is a direct instance of a particular class. You can use the **object-class** predicate to determine the direct class of an object.
- You can give an object a name. For example, if you define a variable or constant to contain an object, you have given that object a name. See Section 3.3.2.
- You can pass an object as an argument or return value — because generic functions and methods are objects, you can manipulate them just as you can any other object. See Section 12.3, page 180.

> **Comparison to C++ and Smalltalk:** In Dylan and Smalltalk, everything is an object (an instance of a class); we say that Dylan and Smalltalk have "objects all the way down." In contrast, in C++, some values are not objects; they have primitive types that are not classes. For example, in Dylan, 7 is an instance of **<integer>**. In C++, 7 is not an instance; it has the type **int**. This design decision enables Dylan users to define methods on built-in classes in the same way that they define methods on user-defined classes — a technique that cannot be done in C++.

Comparison to Java: Java recognizes the need for object representation of all classes with the **`Number`** class and its subclasses. However, Java still requires the programmer to work with nonobjects when writing mathematical statements. The **`Number`** classes can be used to "wrap" an object cloak around the primitive **`integer`**, **`float`**, and other numeric types, to allow object-based programming. Dylan does not separate the mathematical manipulation of numbers from their other object properties. Programmers need only to think in terms of numerical objects, and can rely on the compiler to implement mathematical operations efficiently. Similarly, the **`Boolean`** class is used to encapsulate primitive **`boolean`** values as objects, and programmers must convert back and forth, depending on the context.

3.3.1 Predicates for testing equality

Dylan provides two predicates for testing equality: `=` and `==`. The `=` predicate determines whether two objects are **similar**. Similarity is defined differently for different kinds of objects. When you define new classes, you can define how similarity is tested for those classes by defining a method for `=`.

The `==` predicate determines whether the operands are **identical** — that is, whether the operands are the same object. The `==` predicate (identity) is a stronger test: two values may be similar but not identical, and two identical values are always similar.

If two numbers are mathematically equal, then they are similar:

```
? 100 = 100;
#t

? 100 = 100.0;
#t
```

Two numbers that are similar, and have the same type, are the same object:

```
? 100 == 100;
#t
```

Two numbers that are similar, but have different types, are not the same object:

```
? 100 == 100.0;
#f
```

Characters are enclosed in single quotation marks. If two characters look the same, they are similar and identical:

```
? 'z' = 'z';
#t

? 'z' == 'z';
#t
```

Strings are enclosed in double quotation marks. Strings that have identical elements are similar, but may or may not be identical. That is, strings can have identical elements, but not be the same string. For example, these strings are similar:

```
? "apple" = "apple";
#t
```

Just by looking at two strings, you cannot know whether or not they are the identical string. The only way to determine identity is to use the **==** predicate. The following expression could return **#t** or **#f**:

```
? "apple" == "apple";
```

A string is always identical to itself:

```
? begin
    let yours = "apple";
    let mine = yours;
    mine == yours;
  end;
#t
```

3.3.2 Bindings: Mappings between objects and names

A **binding** is a mapping between an object and a name. The name can be a module variable, module constant, or local variable.

Here, we give the object **3.14159** the name **$pi**, where **$pi** is a module constant:

```
? define constant $pi = 3.14159;
```

Here, we give the object **"apple"** the name ***my-favorite-pie***, where ***my-favorite-pie*** is a module variable:

```
? define variable *my-favorite-pie* = "apple";
```

More than one variable can contain a particular object, so, in effect, an object can have many names. Here, we define a new variable that contains the very same pie:

```
? define variable *your-favorite-pie* = *my-favorite-pie*;

? *your-favorite-pie* == *my-favorite-pie*;
#t
```

When you define a method, **`define method`** creates a binding between a name and a method object:

```
? define method say-greeting (greeting :: <object>);
    format-out("%s\n", greeting);
  end;
```

All the bindings that we have created in this section so far are accessible within a module. (For information about modules, see Chapter 13, *Libraries and Modules*.) Figure 3.3 shows how you can picture each binding as a link between a name and another object.

Local variables are also bindings, but they are accessible only within a certain body of code; for example,

```
? begin
    let radius = 5.0;
    let circumference = 2.0 * $pi * radius;
    circumference;
  end;
```

Bindings can be constant or variable. You can use the assignment operator to change a variable binding, but you cannot change a constant binding. Module constants are constant bindings; module variables and local variables are variable bindings.

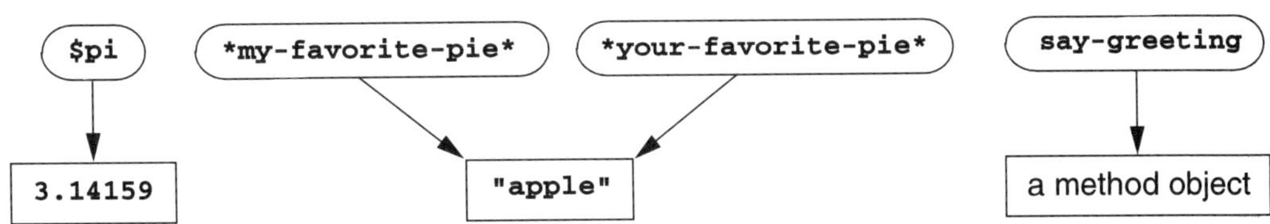

Figure 3.3 Bindings as links (shown as arrows) between names (enclosed in ovals) and objects (enclosed in rectangles) within a module.

3.4 Summary

In this chapter, we covered the following:

- A generic function can contain more than one method, where each method has parameters of different types, and thus is intended for different arguments. The **`say-greeting`** generic function has two methods.
- Dylan provides built-in classes, including **`<integer>`**, **`<single-float>`**, **`<string>`**, and **`<object>`**. These classes are related by inheritance.
- In Dylan, almost everything is an object. Each object has a unique identity.
- The `=` predicate tests for similarity; the `==` predicate tests for identity.
- A binding is an association between an object and a name.

4

User-Defined Classes and Methods

In this chapter, we show the most basic techniques for writing object-oriented code in Dylan. We define a class, make instances of the class, initialize slots of the instances, and get and set the values of slots. We define methods, and call them on the instances. One method returns multiple values — and that is an extremely useful technique. Another method uses local variables.

In this chapter, we start to develop an example of a library that represents different kinds of time. A library is a complete unit of code that can be used by many different clients, where a client can be another library or an application program. In Chapters 5 and 6, we expand and refine the example that we begin in this chapter. Chapter 8, *A Simple Library*, shows the result: a complete and working library.

4.1 Requirements of the time and position classes and methods

Our eventual goal in this book is to develop a sample application based on an airport theme. The sample application handles the scheduling of aircraft that are arriving into and departing from an airport. For more information, see Chapter 15, *Design of the Airport Application*.

We know that, for our airport application, we need to represent time. There are several ways to represent time. We could say that an event happened 2 hours ago (a time offset). We could say that an event happened at 21:30 (a time of day).

We must represent both kinds of time in our time library, and we must provide a way to print representations of both. In this chapter, we define a class named **`<time-of-day>`**, and we define a method that prints a representation of **`<time-of-day>`**. In Chapter 5, *Class Inheritance*, we define the **`<time-offset>`** class, and a method that prints a representation of **`<time-offset>`**.

The airport application also requires us to represent physical objects (such as aircraft), and the positions (locations) of physical objects. In Chapter 7, *Modularity*, we define classes that represent physical objects and positions.

Eventually, we need to be able to add times, to compare times for similarity, and to determine which of two times is greater than the other. We implement those operations in Chapter 6, *Multimethods*.

We package the result of all our work into a complete and working library, in Chapter 8, *A Simple Library*. Later, we refine this library to achieve greater modularity and extensibility. The final result is given in Chapter 14, *Four Complete Libraries*.

4.2 User-defined classes

A **user-defined class** is like a structure or a record type in other languages. When you define a class, you specify its name, its direct superclasses, and its **slots**. A slot has a name and a type. Normally, each instance stores its own value for the slot. A class inherits the slots defined by its superclasses, and it can define more slots if it needs them.

4.2.1 The `<time-of-day>` class

We start by defining a class to represent the concept of a time of day, such as 21:30. The definition of the **`<time-of-day>`** class is as follows:

```
// A specific time of day from 00:00 (midnight) to below 24:00 (tomorrow)
define class <time-of-day> (<object>)                                  // 1
  slot total-seconds :: <integer>;                                     // 2
end class <time-of-day>;                                               // 3
```

The top line is a **comment**. The `//` characters begin a comment, which continues to the end of the line. We also provide comments that number the lines of code after the first comment. The line numbers are useful only for discussing the code examples in the book, and would not be used in source files. You can also have multiline comments that start with **`/*`** and end with **`*/`**.

On line 1, the words **define class** start the class definition. The name of the class is **<time-of-day>**. The list following the name of the class is a list of the direct superclasses of this class. The **<time-of-day>** class has one direct superclass, which is the class **<object>**. Each user-defined class must have at least one direct superclass. If no other class is appropriate, the class must have **<object>** as its superclass.

Line 2 contains the only slot definition of this class. This class has one slot, named **total-seconds**. The slot's type constraint is **<integer>**. The double colon, **::**, specifies the type constraint of a slot, just as it specifies the type constraint of a module variable or of a method's parameter.

Line 3 is the end of the class definition. The text after the word **end** and before the semicolon is an optional part of the definition; it documents which definition is ending. Any text appearing after the **end** must match the definition ending, such as **end class <time-of-day>**, or **end class**. You do not need to put any text after the **end** — however, such text is useful for long or complex definitions, where it can be difficult to see which language construct is ending.

4.2.2 The type constraint of a slot

The type constraint of the **total-seconds** slot is **<integer>**. This slot can hold instances of **<integer>**, and cannot hold any other kind of object.

The type constraint of a slot is optional. Specifying a slot with no explicit type constraint is equivalent to specifying **<object>** as the type constraint. A slot whose type constraint is **<object>** can hold any object. The ability to have slots with the type constraint **<object>** provides flexibility that can be valuable; for more information, see Chapter 19, *Performance and Flexibility*.

4.3 Use of make to create an instance

We want to make an instance of **<time-of-day>**, but first we need a place to store it. We define a module variable called ***my-time-of-day***, and initialize it to contain a new instance of **<time-of-day>**:

```
? define variable *my-time-of-day* = make(<time-of-day>);
```

The **make** function creates an instance of **<time-of-day>**. The argument to **make** is the class to create. The **make** function returns the new instance.

The instance stored in **`*my-time-of-day*`** has a **`total-seconds`** slot with no value. The next logical step is to store a value in that slot.

4.4 Getters and setters of slot values

We can store a value in the **`total-seconds`** slot of the **`<time-of-day>`** instance by using the assignment operator, **`:=`**, as follows:

```
? *my-time-of-day*.total-seconds := 180;
180
```

We can examine the value of the slot in the instance:

```
? *my-time-of-day*.total-seconds;
180
```

Although these expressions may look like they are accessing the slots directly, they are not. They are abbreviations for function calls to a getter and a setter. A **getter** is a method that retrieves the current value of a slot in an object. A **setter** is a method that stores a value in a slot. Each slot in a class automatically has a getter and a setter defined for it. You can see the function-call syntax, and other information about getters and setters, in Chapter 10, *Slots*.

4.5 Initialization of slots when instances are made

So far, we have made an instance and set the value of its slot. We might like to combine those two steps and to set the slot's value while making the instance — in other words, to **initialize** the slot when we make the instance. One way to do that is to provide a **keyword argument** to **`make`**. (Dylan offers several techniques for initializing slots; see Chapter 10, *Slots*.)

4.5.1 Keyword arguments in function calls

We would like to be able to call **`make`** as follows:

```
? make(<time-of-day>, total-seconds: 120);
```

We will be able to make this call after we have done a bit of homework, as we shall show in Section 4.5.2. In the preceding call to **`make`**, we provided a keyword argument, consisting of a keyword, **`total-seconds:`**, followed by a value, **`120`**.

The **<time-of-day>** instance returned by **make** has its **total-seconds** slot set to **120**.

A **keyword argument** consists of a keyword followed by the keyword's value. A **keyword** is a name followed by a colon, such as **total-seconds:**. The colon after a keyword is not a convention; it is a required part of the keyword. There must be no space between the name and the colon.

You can define functions to accept keyword arguments. When a function accepts keyword arguments, you can provide them in any order. Keyword arguments can be useful for functions that take many arguments — when you call the function, you do not need to remember the order of the arguments. Keyword arguments are optional arguments, so they are useful for parameters that have a default value that you may want to override at times. For more information about keyword arguments, see Section 12.2.3, page 172.

How does **make** know that the value of the **total-seconds:** keyword should be used to initialize the **total-seconds** slot? The keyword and the slot happen to have the same name, but that is not how it knows. Before you can use the **total-seconds:** keyword argument to **make**, you must associate that keyword with the **total-seconds** slot in the class definition.

4.5.2 Init keywords: Keywords that initialize slots

The **total-seconds:** keyword is an **init keyword** — a keyword that we can give to **make** to provide an initial value for a slot. To make it possible to give an init keyword to **make**, we need to use the **init-keyword:** slot option when we define the class. A **slot option** lets us specify a characteristic of a slot. Slot options appear after the optional type specifier of a slot.

Here, we redefine the **<time-of-day>** class to use the **init-keyword:** slot option:

```
// A specific time of day from 00:00 (midnight) to below 24:00 (tomorrow)
define class <time-of-day> (<object>)                               // 1
  slot total-seconds :: <integer>, init-keyword: total-seconds:;    // 2
end class <time-of-day>;                                            // 3
```

The preceding definition **redefines** the class **<time-of-day>**. That is, this new definition of **<time-of-day>** replaces the old definition of **<time-of-day>**.

In line 2, the **init-keyword:** slot option defines **total-seconds:** as a keyword parameter that we can give to **make** when we make an instance of this class. Now that we have defined **total-seconds:** as an init keyword, we can provide the keyword argument as follows:

```
? *my-time-of-day* := make(<time-of-day>, total-seconds: 120);
{instance of <time-of-day>}
```

The preceding expression creates a new instance of **<time-of-day>**, and stores that instance in the variable ***my-time-of-day***. The value of the **total-seconds** slot of this instance is initialized to **120**. The assignment operator returns the new value stored; in the preceding call, the new value is the newly created instance of **<time-of-day>**, which the listener displays as ***{instance of <time-of-day>}***.

We can use the getter to verify that the slot has an initial value:

```
? *my-time-of-day*.total-seconds;
120
```

If you call **make** and provide a keyword that has not been declared as a valid keyword for the class, you get an error; for example,

```
? make(<time-of-day>, seconds: 120);
ERROR: seconds: is not a valid keyword argument to make for {class <time-of-
day>}
```

Automatic storage-management note: Dylan provides automatic storage management (also called garbage collection). Thus, you do not need to deallocate memory explicitly. When an object becomes inaccessible, Dylan's automatic storage management will recycle the storage used by that object. In this section, there are two examples of objects that become inaccessible:

- We redefined the **<time-of-day>** class. The storage used by the old class definition can be recycled.
- We stored a new instance in ***my-time-of-day***. The storage used by the instance previously stored in that variable can be recycled.

Although redefinition is not part of the Dylan language, most Dylan development environments support redefinition.

Comparison with Java: Java recognizes that manual memory management can be the source of program errors and often can be exploited to breach security measures. Like Dylan, Java has an automatic garbage collector that correctly and efficiently recovers unused objects in a program — freeing the programmer of that mundane but difficult chore.

4.6 Methods for handling time

We decided to represent the time of day with a single slot named **`total-seconds`**. An alternate choice would be to give the class three slots, named **`hours`**, **`minutes`**, and **`seconds`**. People naturally think of time in terms of hours, minutes, and seconds. We chose to store the total seconds instead, because we envisioned needing to operate on times, such as adding a time of day to a time offset. For example, if it is 9:00 now, and a meeting is to be held 2.5 hours from now, then the meeting will be held at 11:30. It is easier to operate on a single value, rather than on three values of hours, minutes, and seconds. On the other hand, it is convenient to see times expressed as hours, minutes, and seconds. We can represent the instances with a single slot, and can provide methods that let users create and see **`<time-of-day>`** instances as being hours, minutes, and seconds.

4.6.1 Method for `encode-total-seconds`

We can provide a method that converts from hours, minutes, and seconds to total seconds:

```
define method encode-total-seconds                                          // 1
    (hours :: <integer>, minutes :: <integer>, seconds :: <integer>) // 2
 => (total-seconds :: <integer>)                                            // 3
  ((hours * 60) + minutes) * 60 + seconds;                                  // 4
end method encode-total-seconds;                                            // 5
```

Line 2 contains the parameter list of the method **`encode-total-seconds`**. The method has three required parameters, named **`hours`**, **`minutes`**, and **`seconds`**, each of type **`<integer>`**. This method is invoked when **`encode-total-seconds`** is called with three integer arguments.

Line 3 contains the **value declaration**, which starts with the characters **=>**. It is a list declaring the values returned by the method. Each element of the list contains a descriptive name of the return value and the type of the value (if the type is omitted, it is **<object>**). In this case, there is one value returned, named **total-seconds**, which is of the type **<integer>**. The name of a return value is used purely for documentation purposes. Although methods are not required to have value declarations, there are advantages to supplying those declarations. When you provide a value declaration for a method, the compiler signals an error if the method tries to return a value of the wrong type, can check receivers of the results of the method for correct type, and can usually produce more efficient code. These advantages are significant, so we use value declarations throughout the rest of this book. For more information about value declarations, see Section 12.2.4, page 175.

Line 4 is the only expression in the body. It uses arithmetic functions to convert the hours, minutes, and seconds into total seconds. All methods return the value of the expression executed last in the body. This method returns the result of the arithmetic expression in line 4.

In line 5, we could have simply used **end;**. We provided **end method decode-total-seconds;** for documentation purposes. Throughout the rest of this book, we provide the extra words after the **end** of a definition.

We can call **encode-total-seconds** with arguments representing 8 hours, 30 minutes, and 59 seconds:

```
? encode-total-seconds(8, 30, 59);
30659
```

We find it convenient to call **encode-total-seconds** to initialize the **total-seconds** slot when we create an instance of **<time-of-day>**, or when we store a new value in that slot. Here, for example, we create a new instance:

```
? define variable *your-time-of-day*
    = make(<time-of-day>, total-seconds: encode-total-seconds(8, 30, 59));
```

We examine the value of the **total-seconds** slot:

```
? *your-time-of-day*.total-seconds;
30659
```

The result reminds us that it would be useful to convert in the other direction as well — from total seconds to hours, minutes, and seconds.

4.6.2 Method for `decode-total-seconds`

We define **decode-total-seconds** to convert in the other direction — from total seconds to hours, minutes, and seconds:

```
define method decode-total-seconds                                         // 1
    (total-seconds :: <integer>)                                           // 2
 => (hours :: <integer>, minutes :: <integer>, seconds :: <integer>)       // 3
  let(total-minutes, seconds) = truncate/(total-seconds, 60);              // 4
  let(hours, minutes) = truncate/(total-minutes, 60);                      // 5
  values(hours, minutes, seconds);                                         // 6
end method decode-total-seconds;                                           // 7
```

We can use **decode-total-seconds** to see the value of the **total-seconds** slot:

```
? decode-total-seconds(*your-time-of-day*.total-seconds);
8
30
59
```

The value declaration on line 3 specifies that **decode-total-seconds** returns three separate values: the hours, minutes, and seconds. This method illustrates how to return multiple values, and how to use **let** to initialize multiple local variables. We describe these techniques in Sections 4.6.3 and 4.6.4.

4.6.3 Multiple return values

The method for **decode-total-seconds** returns three values: the hours, the minutes, and the seconds. To return the three values, the method uses the **values** function as the expression executed last in the body. The **values** function simply returns all its arguments as separate values. The ability to return multiple values allows a natural symmetry between **encode-total-seconds** and **decode-total-seconds**, as shown in Table 4.1.

Method	Parameter(s)	Return value(s)
encode-total-seconds	**hours, minutes, seconds**	**total-seconds**
decode-total-seconds	**total-seconds**	**hours, minutes, seconds**

Table 4.1 Symmetry of **encode-total-seconds** and **decode-total-seconds**.

Lines 4 and 5 of the **`decode-total-seconds`** method contain calls to **`truncate/`**. The **`truncate/`** function is a built-in Dylan function. It takes two arguments, divides the first by the second, and returns two values: the result of the truncating division, and the remainder.

> **Comparison with C:** In C, / on integers produces a truncated result. In Dylan, / on integers is implementation defined, and is not recommended for portable code. The Dylan functions named **`floor`**, **`ceiling`**, **`round`**, and **`truncate`** convert a rational or floating-point result to an integer with the appropriate rounding. The Dylan functions named **`floor/`**, **`ceiling/`**, **`round/`**, and **`truncate/`** take two arguments. Those generic functions divide the first argument by the second argument, and return two values: the rounded or truncated result, and the remainder.

4.6.4 Use of `let` to declare local variables

When a function returns multiple values, you can use **`let`** to store each returned value in a local variable, as shown in lines 2 and 3 of the **`decode-total-seconds`** method in Section 4.6.2. On line 2, we use **`let`** to declare two local variables, named **`total-minutes`** and **`seconds`**, and to initialize their values to the two values returned by the **`truncate/`** function. Similarly, on line 3, we use **`let`** to declare the local variables **`hours`** and **`minutes`**.

The local variables declared by **`let`** can be used within the method until the method's **`end`**. Although there is no **`begin`** to define explicitly the beginning of a body for local variables, **`define method`** begins a body, and its **`end`** finishes that body. Local variables are scoped within the smallest body that surrounds them, so you can use **`begin`** and **`end`** within a method to define a smaller body for local variables, although doing so is usually not necessary.

4.6.5 Second method for `decode-total-seconds`

The **`decode-total-seconds`** method is called as follows:

```
? decode-total-seconds(*your-time-of-day*.total-seconds);
```

If we envision calling **decode-total-seconds** frequently to see the hours, minutes, and seconds stored in a **<time-of-day>** instance, we can make it possible to decode **<time-of-day>** instances, as well as integers. For example, we can make it possible to make this call:

```
? decode-total-seconds(*your-time-of-day*);
```

We can implement this behavior easily, by defining another method for **decode-total-seconds**, which takes a **<time-of-day>** instance as its argument:

```
define method decode-total-seconds
    (time :: <time-of-day>)
 => (hours :: <integer>, minutes :: <integer>, seconds :: <integer>)
  decode-total-seconds(time.total-seconds);
end method decode-total-seconds;)
```

Figure 4.1 shows the two methods for the **decode-total-seconds** generic function.

Generic function **decode-total-seconds**

```
// Method on <integer>
define method decode-total-seconds
    (total-seconds :: <integer>)
 => (hours :: <integer>, minutes :: <integer>, seconds :: <integer>)
  let(total-minutes, seconds) = truncate/(total-seconds, 60);
  let(hours, minutes) = truncate/(total-minutes, 60);
  values(hours, minutes, seconds);
end method decode-total-seconds;
```

```
// Method on <time-of-day>
define method decode-total-seconds
    (time :: <time-of-day>)
 => (hours :: <integer>, minutes :: <integer>, seconds :: <integer>)
  decode-total-seconds(time.total-seconds);
end method decode-total-seconds;
```

Figure 4.1 The **decode-total-seconds** generic function and its methods.

Looking at Figure 4.1, we analyze what happens in this call:

```
? decode-total-seconds(*your-time-of-day*);
```

1. The argument is an instance of **<time-of-day>**, so the method on **<time-of-day>** is called.
2. The body of the method on **<time-of-day>** calls **decode-total-seconds** on an instance of **<integer>**, the value of the **total-seconds** slot of the **<time-of-day>** instance. In this call, the argument is an integer, so the method on **<integer>** is called.
3. The method on **<integer>** returns three values to its caller — the method on **<time-of-day>**. The method on **<time-of-day>** returns those three values.

The purpose of the method on **<time-of-day>** is simply to allow a different kind of argument to be used. The method extracts the integer from the **<time-of-day>** instance, and calls **decode-total-seconds** with that integer.

4.6.6 Method for say-time-of-day

We can provide a way to ask an instance of **<time-of-day>** to describe the time in a conventional format, such as 8:30. For the application that we are planning, there is no need to view the seconds. We want the method to print the description in a window on the screen. We define a method named **say-time-of-day**:

```
define method say-time-of-day (time :: <time-of-day>) => ()                // 1
  let(hours, minutes) = decode-total-seconds(time);                         // 2
  format-out                                                                // 3
    ("%d:%s%d", hours, if (minutes < 10) "0" else "" end, minutes);        // 4
end method say-time-of-day;                                                 // 5
```

On line 1, we provide an empty value declaration, which means that this method returns no values.

On line 2, we use **let** to initialize two local variables to the first and second values returned by **decode-total-seconds**. Remember that **decode-total-seconds** returns three values (the third value is the seconds). For the application that we are planning, the **say-time-of-day** method does not need to show the seconds, so we do not use the third value. It is not necessary to receive the third value of **decode-total-seconds**; here we do not provide a local variable to receive the third value, so that value is simply ignored.

On line 4, we use **`if`** to print a leading 0 for the minutes when there are fewer than 10 minutes, such as **`2:05`**.

> **Comparison to C:** In C, **`if`** does not return a value. In Dylan, **`if`** returns the value of the body that is selected, if any is.

> **Note on `format-out`:** We have purposely used a limited subset of the **`format-out`** function's features to allow our examples to run on as many Dylan implementations as possible. The printing of times could be done much more elegantly if we used the full power of the **`format-out`** function.

We can call **`say-time-of-day`**:

```
? say-time-of-day(*your-time-of-day*);
8:30

? say-time-of-day(*my-time-of-day*);
0:02
```

The listener displays the output (printed by **`format-out`**), but displays no values, because **`say-time-of-day`** does not return any values.

4.7 Summary

In this chapter, we covered the following:

- We defined a class (with **`define class`**).
- We created an instance (with **`make`**).
- We read the value of a slot by calling a getter.
- We set the value of a slot by using **`:=`**, the assignment operator.
- We defined a method that returns multiple values (with **`values`**), and showed how to initialize multiple local variables (with **`let`**).
- We showed the syntax of some commonly used elements of Dylan; see Table 4.2.

Dylan element	Syntax example
calling a getter	***my-time-of-day*.total-seconds;**
calling a setter	***my-time-of-day*.total-seconds := 180;**
keyword	**total-seconds:**
single-line comment	**// Text of comment**
multiline comment	**/* Text of comment that spans more than one line */**
value declaration	**=> (total-seconds :: <integer>)**

Table 4.2 Syntax of Dylan elements.

5

Class Inheritance

In this chapter, we continue to develop the time library by defining another kind of time to represent time offsets, such as 2 hours ago, and 30 minutes from now. We find an opportunity to use inheritance to good advantage, so we redefine some classes and a method to take advantage of inheritance. We also show how to define a generic function explicitly.

5.1 The `<time-offset>` class and methods

In this section, we define a class to represent time offsets, and a method that describes a time offset. We start by defining the `<time-offset>` class:

```
// A relative time between -24:00 and +24:00
define class <time-offset> (<object>)
  slot total-seconds :: <integer>, init-keyword: total-seconds:;
end class <time-offset>;
```

5.1.1 Reasons for defining two similar classes

The `<time-offset>` class is similar to the `<time-of-day>` class. They both define a `total-seconds` slot. Why do we need to have two classes that are so similar?

- A `<time-of-day>` is conceptually different from a `<time-offset>`. If the `total-seconds` slot of a `<time-of-day>` is `180`, that means the time of day at 0:03 (that is, 3 minutes past midnight). If the `total-seconds` slot of a

<time-offset> is **180**, that means 3 minutes in the future. If you ask what time it is, the answer is a **<time-of-day>**. If you ask how long it takes to wash the dog, the answer is a **<time-offset>**.

- A **<time-offset>** can represent time in the past by having a negative value of **total-seconds**. A **<time-of-day>**, in contrast, should not have a negative value of **total-seconds**. Later in this book, we provide methods that guarantee that the **total-seconds** slot of **<time-of-day>** instances is not negative; see Section 10.2.2, page 120, and Section 10.3, page 123.
- We need different methods for describing instances of **<time-offset>** and instances of **<time-of-day>**. The **<time-of-day>** method prints **8:30**, and the **<time-offset>** method should print **minus 8:30** or **plus 8:30**.
- Eventually, we will need to be able to add a **<time-of-day>** to a **<time-offset>**. For example, we can add the **<time-of-day>** 9:03 to the **<time-offset>** 2:50 and get the **<time-of-day>** 11:53. We will also need to add two **<time-offset>** instances. For example, 2 minutes plus 8 minutes is equal to 10 minutes. But we cannot add two **<time-of-day>** instances, because it does not make sense to add three o'clock to four o'clock.

5.1.2 Creation of instances of <time-offset>

We can create an instance of **<time-offset>** representing 15:20:10 in the future:

```
? define variable *my-time-offset* :: <time-offset>
    = make(<time-offset>, total-seconds: encode-total-seconds(15, 20, 10));
```

We can create an instance of **<time-offset>** representing 6:45:30 in the past, by using the unary minus function, **-**, which returns the negative of the value that follows it:

```
? define variable *your-time-offset* :: <time-offset>
    = make(<time-offset>, total-seconds: - encode-total-seconds(6, 45, 30));
```

5.1.3 Methods on <time-offset>

Because a **<time-offset>** can represent future time or past time, it will be useful to provide a convenient way to determine whether a **<time-offset>** is in the past. We define a new predicate named **past?** as follows:

```
define method past? (time :: <time-offset>) => (past? :: <boolean>)
  time.total-seconds < 0;
end method past?;
```

The **past?** method returns an instance of **<boolean>**, which is **#t** if the time offset is in the past, and otherwise is **#f**. Here is an example:

```
? past?(*my-time-offset*)
#f

? past?(*your-time-offset*)
#t
```

We need a method to describe instances of **<time-offset>**. The output should look like this:

```
? say-time-offset(*my-time-offset*);
plus 15:20

? say-time-offset(*your-time-offset*);
minus 6:45
```

We might define the method in this way:

```
define method say-time-offset (time :: <time-offset>) => ()
  let(hours, minutes) = decode-total-seconds(time);
  format-out("%s %d:%s%d",
             if (past?(time)) "minus" else "plus" end,
             hours,
             if (minutes < 10) "0" else "" end,
             minutes);
end method say-time-offset;
```

If we test this method in a listener, however, the result is different:

```
? say-time-offset(*my-time-offset*);
ERROR: No applicable method for decode-total-seconds with argument {instance
<time-offset>}
```

"No applicable method" means that there is no method for this generic function that is appropriate for the arguments. To understand this error, we can look at the methods for **decode-total-seconds** in Figure 4.1, page 49. One method takes an argument of the type **<integer>**. Another method takes an argument of the type **<time-of-day>**. There is no method for instances of **<time-offset>**, so Dylan signals an error. There are three possible approaches to solving this problem.

As a first approach, we could define the **say-time-offset** method to call **decode-total-seconds** with an integer.

```
// First approach: Call decode-total-seconds with an integer
define method say-time-offset (time :: <time-offset>) => ()               // 1
  let(hours, minutes) = decode-total-seconds(abs(time.total-seconds)); // 2
  format-out("%s %d:%s%d",                                              // 3
             if (past?(time)) "minus" else "plus" end,                  // 4
             hours,                                                     // 5
             if (minutes < 10) "0" else "" end,                         // 6
             minutes);                                                  // 7
end method say-time-offset;                                             // 8
```

We changed only the call to **decode-total-seconds** on line 2. Here, we call it with the absolute value (returned by the **abs** function) of the **total-seconds** slot.

This approach works, but it is awkward because we need to remember what kinds of arguments **decode-total-seconds** can take. The convenient calling syntax that we introduced for calling **decode-total-seconds** with an instance of **<time-of-day>** is not available for other kinds of time.

As a second approach, we could to define a third method for **decode-total-seconds** that takes as its argument an instance of **<time-offset>**:

```
// Second approach: Define a method on <time-offset>
define method decode-total-seconds (time :: <time-offset>) => ()
  decode-total-seconds(abs(time.total-seconds));
end method decode-total-seconds;
```

The method for **say-time-offset** can then call **decode-total-seconds**, as we did in the first place:

```
define method say-time-offset (time :: <time-offset>) => ()
  let(hours, minutes) = decode-total-seconds(time);
  format-out("%s %d:%s%d",
             if (past?(time)) "minus" else "plus" end,
             hours,
             if (minutes < 10) "0" else "" end,
             minutes);
end method say-time-offset;
```

This approach works, and it preserves the flexibility of calling **decode-total-seconds** on instances of **<integer>**, **<time-of-day>**, and **<time-offset>**. However, the body of the method on **<time-offset>** (defined in this section) is nearly identical to the body of the method on **<time-of-day>** (defined in Section 4.6.5, page 48). The only difference is that we use **abs** in the method on **<time-offset>**

but not in the method on **<time-of-day>**. If we used it in the method on **<time-of-day>**, it would be harmless. Duplication of code is ugly, adds maintenance overhead, and is particularly undesirable when programming in an object-oriented language, where it may indicate a flaw in the overall design.

The best solution to the problem lies in a third approach — to rethink the classes and methods in a more object-oriented style, using inheritance. We show this solution in the next section.

5.2 Class inheritance

We have defined two simple classes, **<time-of-day>** and **<time-offset>**. We repeat the definitions here:

```
// A specific time of day from 00:00 (midnight) to before 24:00 (tomorrow)
define class <time-of-day> (<object>)
  slot total-seconds :: <integer>, init-keyword: total-seconds:;
end class <time-of-day>;

// A relative time between -24:00 and +24:00
define class <time-offset> (<object>)
  slot total-seconds :: <integer>, init-keyword: total-seconds:;
end class <time-offset>;
```

There is commonality between the two classes:

- Both classes represent a kind of time — they have a conceptual basis in common.
- Both classes have a **total-seconds** slot — they have structure in common.
- Both classes need a **decode-total-seconds** method to convert the **total-seconds** slot to hours, minutes, and seconds — they have behavior in common.

We can use inheritance to model the shared aspects of these two classes directly. We need to define a new class, such as **<time>**, and to redefine the two classes to inherit from **<time>**. The **<time>** class will contain the slot **total-seconds,** and the other two classes will inherit that slot. We shall redefine the **decode-total-seconds** method such that its parameter is of the **<time>** type, which means that it can be called for instances of **<time-of-day>** and of **<time-offset>**.

5.2.1 New definitions of the time classes

We define the new class **<time>**:

```
define class <time> (<object>)
  slot total-seconds :: <integer>, init-keyword: total-seconds:;
end class <time>;
```

We redefine **<time-of-day>** and **<time-offset>** to inherit from **<time>**:

```
// A specific time of day from 00:00 (midnight) to before 24:00 (tomorrow)
define class <time-of-day> (<time>)
end class <time-of-day>;

// A relative time between -24:00 and +24:00
define class <time-offset> (<time>)
end class <time-offset>;
```

> **Dynamic feature — no need to recompile:** In C++, a complete recompile of the program would be necessary to change the superclass of a class. Most Dylan development environments support a mode that requires only that you compile the new class definitions. The difference between compiling only a few class definitions and compiling the whole program can be a time saver for complex applications.

5.2.2 Slot inheritance

A class inherits the slots of its superclasses, and can define more slots if they are needed. For example, the **<time-of-day>** and **<time-offset>** classes inherit the **total-seconds** slot from their superclass, **<time>**. A class inherits the slot options from its superclasses as well. A class cannot remove or replace any slots defined by its superclasses. It is an error for a class to define a slot with the same name as a slot inherited from one of that class's superclasses.

5.2.3 Existing instances of the classes

The variables ***my-time-of-day***, ***your-time-of-day***, ***my-time-offset***, and ***your-time-offset*** all contain instances of classes that have now been redefined. Some environments might be able to update instances of the old class definitions to conform to the new class definitions, but we will be conservative and assume that our environment does not update instances. Therefore, we create the instances again:

```
? *my-time-offset*
    := make(<time-offset>, total-seconds: encode-total-seconds(15, 20, 10));

? *your-time-offset*
    := make(<time-offset>, total-seconds: - encode-total-seconds(6, 45, 30));

? *my-time-of-day* := make(<time-of-day>, total-seconds: 120);

? *your-time-of-day*
    := make(<time-of-day>, total-seconds: encode-total-seconds(8, 30, 59));
```

5.2.4 Relationships of the time classes

It is helpful to look at the relationships among the time classes. We show them in Figure 5.1.

Referring to Figure 5.1, we introduce terminology by example:

- The `<time-of-day>` class is a **direct subclass** of the `<time>` class.
- The `<time-of-day>` class is a **subclass** of the `<object>` class.
- The `<time>` class is a **direct superclass** of the `<time-of-day>` class.
- The `<object>` class is a **superclass** of the `<time-of-day>` class.
- When you make an instance of the `<time-of-day>` class, the result is a **direct instance** of that class.

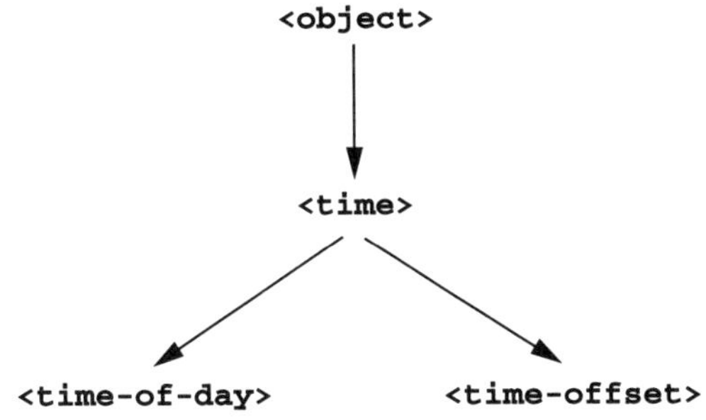

Figure 5.1 Inheritance relationships of the time classes.

- A direct instance of **<time-of-day>** is an **indirect instance** of **<time>** and **<object>**.
- An object is a **general instance** of a class if it is either a direct or an indirect instance of that class. The term **instance** is equivalent to general instance. A direct instance of **<time-of-day>** is both a general instance and an instance of **<time-of-day>**, **<time>**, and **<object>**.
- The **<time-of-day>** class is a **subtype** of the **<time>** and **<object>** classes. A class is also a subtype of itself. All classes are types.
- The **<object>** class is a **supertype** of all the other classes shown. All classes are subtypes of the **<object>** class. All objects are instances of the **<object>** class.

5.3 Methods for classes that use inheritance

Figure 5.2 shows the methods that we now have defined for the **decode-total-seconds** generic function; Figure 5.3 shows the methods that we want to have.

Generic function **decode-total-seconds**

```
// Method on <integer>
define method decode-total-seconds
    (total-seconds :: <integer>)
 => (hours :: <integer>, minutes :: <integer>, seconds :: <integer>)
  let(total-minutes, seconds) = truncate/(total-seconds, 60);
  let(hours, minutes) = truncate/(total-minutes, 60);
  values(hours, minutes, seconds);
end method decode-total-seconds;
```

```
// Method on <time-of-day>
define method decode-total-seconds
    (time :: <time-of-day>)
 => (hours :: <integer>, minutes :: <integer>, seconds :: <integer>)
  decode-total-seconds(time.total-seconds);
end method decode-total-seconds;
```

Figure 5.2 Existing methods for **decode-total-seconds**.

Generic function **decode-total-seconds**

```
// Method on <integer>
define method decode-total-seconds
    (total-seconds :: <integer>)
 => (hours :: <integer>, minutes :: <integer>, seconds :: <integer>)
  let(total-minutes, seconds) = truncate/(total-seconds, 60);
  let(hours, minutes) = truncate/(total-minutes, 60);
  values(hours, minutes, seconds);
end method decode-total-seconds;
```

```
// Method on <time>
define method decode-total-seconds
    (time :: <time>)
 => (hours :: <integer>, minutes :: <integer>, seconds :: <integer>)
  decode-total-seconds(abs(time.total-seconds));
end method decode-total-seconds;
```

Figure 5.3 Desired methods for **decode-total-seconds**.

To take advantage of the redefined classes, we want to remove the method on **<time-of-day>**, and to add a method on **<time>**. The method on **<time>** is appropriate for instances of both **<time-of-day>** and **<time-offset>**.

There are two important points to cover. We first discuss how to remove the method on **<time-of-day>** and how to add the method on **<time>** in Section 5.4. We then describe how the **decode-total-seconds** generic function works in Section 5.5.

5.4 Redefinition of a method

It is important to understand that when you define a method, Dylan will do one of the following:

- Add that method to the generic function (without affecting existing methods), if the parameter list of the new method is different from the parameter lists of all the existing methods.

- Redefine an existing method of the generic function, if the parameter list of the new method is equivalent to the parameter list of one of the existing methods. (Although the concept of redefinition is not in the Dylan language, most Dylan development environments support redefinition.)

Two parameter lists are equivalent if the types of each required parameter are the same. A parameter with no type is the same as a parameter whose type is **<object>**. For example, the following parameter lists are equivalent:

```
(a :: <string>, b :: <integer>, c)
(str :: <string>, num :: <integer>, any-old-thing :: <object>)
```

Assume that we are working in a listener, and already have defined the methods shown in Figure 5.2. Consider what happens when we define the method on **<time>**. The parameter list of the new method is not equivalent to the parameter list of any of the existing methods, so the new method is added to the generic function. Thus, **decode-total-seconds** has three methods: a method on **<integer>**, a method on **<time-of-day>**, and a method on **<time>**. The environment may offer a way to remove a method from a generic function. When we remove the definition of the method on **<time-of-day>** using the environment, the **decode-total-seconds** generic function contains only the desired methods, as shown in Figure 5.3. A typical browser will help you to find the methods to remove.

If, however, we are working in source files rather than in a listener, we simply need to remove the method on **<time-of-day>** with the editor, and to type in the method on **<time>**. When we next compile the file, the generic function will contain only the desired methods, as shown in Figure 5.3.

We can now call **decode-total-seconds** on instances of **<time-of-day>** and on instances of **<time-offset>**:

```
? decode-total-seconds(*your-time-of-day*);
8
30
59

? decode-total-seconds(*your-time-offset*);
6
45
30
```

The result is as expected — **decode-total-seconds** returns the hours, minutes, and seconds. We now describe how this generic function works.

5.5 Method dispatch

When a generic function is called, it chooses the **most specific applicable method** and calls that method. The process of choosing the most specific method and calling it is **method dispatch**. This process has three steps:

1. Find all the **applicable methods** for the argument to the generic function.
2. Sort the applicable methods by **specificity**.
3. Call the most specific method.

Dylan does the method dispatch automatically, but it is important that you understand the semantics of the method dispatch. When you understand how Dylan determines the applicability of methods and how it sorts them by specificity, you can design classes and methods that work together correctly. Method dispatch is at the heart of object-oriented programming.

5.5.1 Step 1: Find the applicable methods

Start with the set of methods defined for the generic function that was called. A method is **specialized** on a required parameter that has a type constraints. The type constraint of the required parameter is called the **parameter specializer** of the parameter. A method is **applicable** if the argument to the generic function is an instance of the parameter specializer of the method.

For example, consider the `decode-total-seconds` generic function. Table 5.1 shows which method is applicable for certain arguments.

Argument	Argument's type	Applicable methods
`*my-time-of-day*`	`<time-of-day>`	method on `<time>`
`*my-time-offset*`	`<time-offset>`	method on `<time>`
`1000`	`<integer>`	method on `<integer>`
`"hello, world"`	`<string>`	none

Table 5.1 Applicable methods for arguments to `decode-total-seconds`.

The first row of the table shows that, when the argument is a direct instance of **<time-of-day>**, the method on **<time>** is applicable, because the argument is an instance of **<time>** (the method's parameter specializer). The final row of the table shows that, when the argument is **"hello, world"**, none of the defined methods are applicable, because **"hello, world"** is not an instance of **<time>** or **<integer>**.

For **decode-total-seconds**, there is either no or one applicable method for any argument. If there is one applicable method, it is called. If there is no applicable method, the "No applicable method" error is signaled. There is no need to continue to step 2.

In other cases, there can be several applicable methods. Consider the generic function **say-greeting**, shown in Figure 5.4. Table 5.2 shows that, for certain arguments, one method is applicable, but that, for an integer argument, two methods are applicable.

When the argument is **7**, a direct instance of **<integer>**, the method on **<object>** is applicable, because **7** is an instance of **<object>** (the method's parameter specializer); the method on **<integer>** also is applicable, because **7** is an instance of **<integer>** (the method's parameter specializer).

Generic function **say-greeting**

```
define method say-greeting (greeting :: <object>)
  format-out("%s\n", greeting);
end;
```

```
define method say-greeting (greeting :: <integer>)
  format-out("Your lucky number is %s.\n", greeting);
end;
```

Figure 5.4 The **say-greeting** generic function and its methods.

Argument	Applicable method(s)
`7`	method on `<object>` method on `<integer>`
`$pi`	method on `<object>`
`"hello, world"`	method on `<object>`

Table 5.2 Applicable methods for different arguments to **`say-greeting`**.

5.5.2 Step 2: Sort applicable methods by specificity

Start with the set of applicable methods. Compare the parameter specializers of the methods. If one type is a subtype of the other, the method whose parameter is of the subtype is **more specific** than the other method. Sort the list of applicable methods from most specific to least specific.

Let's continue with the example of calling **`say-greeting`** with an argument of `7`. The parameter specializers of the two methods are **`<object>`** and **`<integer>`**. Because **`<integer>`** is a subtype of **`<object>`**, the method on **`<integer>`** is more specific than the method on **`<object>`**.

5.5.3 Step 3: Call the most specific method

The generic function calls the most specific method.

5.5.4 Precedence in method dispatch

This conceptual description of how method dispatch works should help you to understand how to design methods. The most important concept to realize is that method dispatch should feel natural — it gives precedence to the methods that are more closely related to the argument, rather than to the methods that are more general. This precedence ordering lets you adjust the behavior of a class with respect to that class's superclasses.

> **Performance note:** The Dylan compiler and run-time system ensure that the method-dispatch rules are followed for every call to a generic function. Given accurate type declarations, however, a compiler can usually compute the result of the dispatch rules at compile time, so the executed code is just as efficient as a normal function call in a language without generic functions and methods. See Chapter 19, *Performance and Flexibility*.

5.6 Definition of a generic function

We repeat the definitions of the methods for **say-time-of-day** and **say-time-offset** here:

```
define method say-time-of-day (time :: <time-of-day>) => ()
  let(hours, minutes) = decode-total-seconds(time);
  format-out
    ("%d:%s%d", hours, if (minutes < 10) "0" else "" end, minutes);
end method say-time-of-day;

define method say-time-offset (time :: <time-offset>) => ()
  let(hours, minutes) = decode-total-seconds(time);
  format-out("%s %d:%s%d",
             if (past?(time)) "minus" else "plus" end,
             hours,
             if (minutes < 10) "0" else "" end,
             minutes);
end method say-time-offset;
```

Now that **decode-total-seconds** has an applicable method for instances of **<time-offset>** and **<time-of-day>**, both these methods work correctly:

```
? say-time-of-day(*my-time-of-day*);
0:02

? say-time-of-day(*your-time-of-day*);
8:30

? say-time-offset(*my-time-offset*);
plus 15:20

? say-time-offset(*your-time-offset*);
minus 6:45
```

We have defined two methods: **say-time-offset** and **say-time-of-day**. A method defined with **define method** cannot exist without a **generic function**. When you define a method, and no generic function of that name exists, Dylan automatically creates a generic function. When we defined these two methods, there were no generic functions with those names defined, so Dylan created module variables named **say-time-of-day** and **say-time-offset**, created the generic functions, stored the generic functions in the module variables, and added the methods to the generic functions.

These two methods are logically related to each other, but have no explicit relationship in the code, other than in the similarity of their names. A cleaner approach is to abstract the concept of what these methods are trying to do — that is, to describe an object. To introduce this abstraction, we define a new generic function.

We use **define generic** to define the generic function explicitly:

```
// Given an object, print a description of the object
define generic say (any-object :: <object>) => ();
```

This generic function has a name: **say**. It receives one argument: the object to describe. That argument must be of the type **<object>**. All objects are of the type **<object>**, so this generic function does not restrict the type of its argument.

Our definition for the generic function **say** is similar to that of the generic function that Dylan would have created automatically if we had defined a method for **say** before we defined the generic function **say**. (The only difference is that the automatically defined generic function would have a more general value declaration.) However, defining the generic function explicitly enables us to formalize its purpose, to name the parameter, to specify a type constraint on the parameter, to specify the return values and their types, and to give comments about the generic function as a whole. The generic function defines the **contract** that all methods for this generic function must obey. The contract of the **say** generic function is as follows:

> The **say** generic function receives one required argument, which must be of the type **<object>**. It prints a description of the object. The **say** generic function returns no values.

Dylan requires all the methods for a generic function to have congruent parameter lists and values declarations. See Section 12.2.5, page 176.

Now, we define two methods for **say**. The method for **say** on **<time-of-day>** fulfills the same purpose (and has the same body) as the **say-time-of-day** method, which we remove from the library with an editor or a gesture in the environment.

```
define method say (time :: <time-of-day>) => ()
  let (hours, minutes) = decode-total-seconds(time);
  format-out
    ("%d:%s%d", hours, if (minutes < 10) "0" else "" end, minutes);
end method say;
```

Similarly, the method for **say** on **<time-offset>** is intended to replace **say-time-offset**, which we remove.

```
define method say (time :: <time-offset>) => ()
  let(hours, minutes) = decode-total-seconds(time);
  format-out("%s %d:%s%d",
             if (past?(time)) "minus" else "plus" end,
             hours,
             if (minutes < 10) "0" else "" end,
             minutes);
end method say-time-offset;
```

Figure 5.5 shows that the generic function **say** has two methods defined for it.

Generic function **say**

```
define method say (time :: <time-of-day>) => ()
  let (hours, minutes) = decode-total-seconds(time);
  format-out
    ("%d:%s%d", hours, if (minutes < 10) "0" else "" end, minutes);
end method say;
```

```
define method say (time :: <time-offset>) => ()
  let(hours, minutes) = decode-total-seconds(time);
  format-out("%s %d:%s%d",
             if (past?(time)) "minus" else "plus" end,
             hours,
             if (minutes < 10) "0" else "" end,
             minutes);
end method say-time-offset;
```

Figure 5.5 Methods for the **say** generic function.

We can call **say**:

```
? say(*my-time-of-day*);
0:02
```

In the preceding call, the argument is of the type **<time-of-day>**, so the method on **<time-of-day>** is the only applicable method. That method is invoked.

```
? say(*my-time-offset*);
plus 15:20
```

In the preceding call, the argument is of the type **<time-offset>**, so the method on **<time-offset>** is the only applicable method. That method is invoked.

5.7 Use of next-method to call another method

Notice that there is duplication of code in the two methods for **say**, as shown in Figure 5.5. Both methods call **decode-total-seconds** to get the hours and minutes, and call **format-out** to print the hours and minutes. Both methods print a leading zero for the minutes, if appropriate. These two tasks are all that the method on **<time-of-day>** does. The method on **<time-offset>** does a bit more; it prints either **minus** or **plus**, depending on the value of the **past?** slot. We can eliminate this duplication by defining another method that does the shared work. This method will be on the **<time>** class, so it will be applicable to instances of **<time-of-day>** and **<time-offset>**. The method for **<time-of-day>** is no longer needed, because the new method does the same work. However, a revised method for **<time-offset>** is needed, to do the extra work of printing **minus** or **plus**, and to call the method on **<time>**, which is the next most specific method.

You can use the **next-method** function to call the next most specific method. Recall that the result of Dylan's method dispatch procedure is a list of applicable methods, sorted by specificity. When one method calls the **next-method** function, Dylan consults the list of sorted methods and invokes the next most specific method on the list. (It is an error to call **next-method** from the least specific method.)

We remove the definitions of the existing **say** methods, and define these new methods:

```
define method say (time :: <time>) => ()
  let (hours, minutes) = decode-total-seconds(time);
  format-out
    ("%d:%s%d", hours, if (minutes < 10) "0" else "" end, minutes);
end method say;

define method say (time :: <time-offset>)
  format-out("%s ", if (past?(time)) "minus" else "plus" end);
  next-method();
end method say;
```

We can call **say**:

```
? say(*my-time-of-day*);
0:02
```

In the preceding call, the argument is of the type **<time-of-day>**, so the method on **<time>** is the only applicable method. That method is invoked.

```
? say(*my-time-offset*);
plus 15:20
```

In the preceding call, the argument is of the type **<time-offset>**, so two methods are applicable. The method on **<time-offset>** is more specific than is the method on **<time>**, so the method on **<time-offset>** is called. That method on **<time-offset>** prints **minus** or **plus**, and calls **next-method**. The **next-method** function calls the method on **<time>**, which prints the hours and minutes.

Using **next-method** is convenient in cases such as this, where a method on a superclass can do most of the work, but a method on a subclass needs to do additional work.

When **next-method** is called with no arguments, as it is in the method on **<time-offset>**, Dylan calls the next most specific method with the same arguments provided to the method that calls **next-method**.

You can provide arguments to **next-method**. For example, you could provide a keyword argument with a value that each method can manipulate (such as adding a value to a number, or appending an element to a list). If you provide arguments to **next-method**, the arguments must be compatible with the generic function, as described in Section 12.2.5, page 176. In addition, you cannot supply required arguments that have classes different from those of the original required arguments to the generic function, if doing so would have changed the method dispatch in any way. Providing arguments to **next-method** is an advanced technique; see Section 12.2.3, page 172, and Section 17.2.2, page 260.

5.8 The time library (so far)

In the course of introducing methods, classes, and generic functions, we have created elements of a library dealing with two kinds of time. Now, we construct a simple library containing those elements (we will continue to develop the time library throughout this book). We represent the time library in four files: a LID file, a library file, a library implementation file, and a test file. We could have expressed this library in three files, by combining into a single file the library implementation file and the test file, but we decided that it would be clearer to separate the underlying implementation (the definitions of classes, methods, and generic functions) from the test (where we create instances and call **say** on them).

The LID file: **time.lid**.

```
library: time

files:   library
         library-implementation
         test
```

The library file defines the **time** library and the **time** module.

The library file: **library.dylan**.

```
module: dylan-user

define library time
  use dylan;
  use format-out;
end library time;

define module time
  use dylan;
  use format-out;
end module time;
```

The library implementation file defines the classes, methods, and generic functions.

The implementation file: `library-implementation.dylan`.

```
module: time

// Class definitions

define class <time> (<object>)
  slot total-seconds :: <integer>, init-keyword: total-seconds:;
end class <time>;

// A specific time of day from 00:00 (midnight) to before 24:00 (tomorrow)
define class <time-of-day> (<time>)
end class <time-of-day>;

// A relative time between -24:00 and +24:00
define class <time-offset> (<time>)
end class <time-offset>;

// Method for determining whether a time offset is in the past
define method past? (time :: <time-offset>) => (past? :: <boolean>)
  time.total-seconds < 0;
end method past?;

// Methods for encoding and decoding total seconds

define method encode-total-seconds
    (hours :: <integer>, minutes :: <integer>, seconds :: <integer>)
 => (total-seconds :: <integer>)
  ((hours * 60) + minutes) * 60 + seconds;
end method encode-total-seconds;

define method decode-total-seconds
    (time :: <time>)
 => (hours :: <integer>, minutes :: <integer>, seconds :: <integer>)
  decode-total-seconds(abs(time.total-seconds));
end method decode-total-seconds;

define method decode-total-seconds
    (total-seconds :: <integer>)
 => (hours :: <integer>, minutes :: <integer>, seconds :: <integer>)
  let(total-minutes, seconds) = truncate/(total-seconds, 60);
  let(hours, minutes) = truncate/(total-minutes, 60);
  values(hours, minutes, seconds);
end method decode-total-seconds;
```

The implementation file: `library-implementation.dylan`. *(continued)*

```
// The say generic function and its methods

// Given an object, print a description of the object
define generic say (any-object :: <object>) => ();

define method say (time :: <time>) => ()
  let (hours, minutes) = decode-total-seconds(time);
  format-out
    ("%d:%s%d", hours, if (minutes < 10) "0" else "" end, minutes);
end method say;

define method say (time :: <time-offset>)
  format-out("%s ", if (past?(time)) "minus" else "plus" end);
  next-method();
end method say;
```

The test file creates instances and calls **say** on the instances. The test file can access variables defined in the implementation file, because both files are in the **time** module.

The test file: `test.dylan`.

```
module: time

define variable *my-time-offset* :: <time-offset>
  = make(<time-offset>, total-seconds: encode-total-seconds(15, 20, 10));

define variable *your-time-offset* :: <time-offset>
  = make(<time-offset>, total-seconds: - encode-total-seconds(6, 45, 30));

define variable *my-time-of-day*
  = make(<time-of-day>, total-seconds: encode-total-seconds(0, 2, 0));

define variable *your-time-of-day*
  = make(<time-of-day>, total-seconds: encode-total-seconds(8, 30, 59));

say(*my-time-offset*);

say(*your-time-offset*);

say(*my-time-of-day*);

say(*your-time-of-day*);
```

When we run the **`test.dylan`** file, Dylan creates two instances of **`<time-offset>`** and two instances of **`<time-of-day>`**. It calls **`say`** on all four instances. The output of the test is

```
plus 15:20
minus 6:45
0:02
8:30
```

5.9 Summary

In this chapter, we covered the following:

- We showed how to use class inheritance.
- We introduced the terminology of classes: direct subclass, subclass, direct superclass, superclass, direct instance, indirect instance, instance, subtype, and supertype.
- We showed how method dispatch works for a generic function with one argument, when there is more than one applicable method.
- We created a generic function explicitly (with **`define generic`**).
- We used **`next-method`** to call the next most specific method.

6

Multimethods

In this chapter, we show two important techniques. First, we define methods for built-in generic functions — in this case, for the functions **+**, **<**, and **=**. Second, we define multimethods. We describe how method dispatch works for multimethods.

6.1 Methods for the + generic function

We need to make it possible to add one time to another. We could define a method with a name such as **`add`** or **`plus`**. However, the concept of adding times is the same as the concept of adding numbers. Dylan already provides the + generic function for adding numbers. Instead of inventing a new name for the addition operation, we define new methods on the built-in generic function **+**. We can extend **+** by defining new methods for it. In certain languages, this technique is called **operator overloading**.

Comparison with C++ and Java: In C++, operator overloading means customizing the action of any built-in operator for classes that you define. In Dylan, operators are just generic functions, and you can add methods to those generic functions for your classes. In C++, the meaning of an overloaded operator is resolved at compile time — the types of the operands must be known at compile time. Because Dylan operators are generic functions, the method is chosen dynamically according to the argument types —at run time, if the types may vary at run time.

Java does not allow operator overloading. The Java designers believe that overloading of operators results in inscrutable code (because the meaning of the operator can vary). Dylan and C++ designers believe that, judiciously used, operator overloading permits clearer, more concise code.

6.1.1 Method for adding two time offsets

We now define a method for **+**. The method adds two time offsets and returns the sum, which is also a time offset:

```
// Method on <time-offset>, <time-offset>
define method \+                                                      // 1
    (offset1 :: <time-offset>, offset2 :: <time-offset>)              // 2
 => (sum :: <time-offset>)                                            // 3
  let sum = offset1.total-seconds + offset2.total-seconds;            // 4
  make(<time-offset>, total-seconds: sum);                            // 5
end method \+;                                                        // 6
```

On line 1, notice that the method is defined on **\+**, rather than simply on **+**. When we define a method on **+** or on another infix function, we need to use a backslash before the function name. The backslash clarifies that we mean the value of the variable + (which is a generic function), and that we are not trying to call the function.

On line 4, we add the values stored in the **total-seconds** slots of the two instances. On line 5, we make and return a new instance of **<time-offset>**. We initialize the **total-seconds** slot to contain the sum calculated in line 4.

To test the method, we need to create two instances of **<time-offset>**:

```
define variable *minus-2-hours* =
  make(<time-offset>, total-seconds: - encode-total-seconds (2, 0, 0));

define variable *plus-15-20-45* =
  make(<time-offset>, total-seconds: encode-total-seconds (15, 20, 45));
```

We can add the time offsets:

```
? *minus-2-hours* + *plus-15-20-45*;
{instance <time-offset>}
```

The result is a new instance of `<time-offset>`. We did not save the value returned. (Many environments offer a way to access values returned by the listener.) We can add the time offsets again, and view the `total-seconds` slot of the result:

```
? decode-total-seconds(*minus-2-hours* + *plus-15-20-45*);
13
20
45
```

6.1.2 Methods for adding a time of day to a time offset

These methods implement addition between a time offset and a time of day:

```
// Method on <time-offset>, <time-of-day>
define method \+
    (offset :: <time-offset>, time-of-day :: <time-of-day>)
 => (sum :: <time-of-day>)
  make(<time-of-day>,
       total-seconds: offset.total-seconds + time-of-day.total-seconds);
end method \+;
```

The method on `<time-offset>`, `<time-of-day>` is invoked when the first argument is a time offset and the second argument is a time of day. It does the work of creating a new `<time-of-day>` instance with the `total-seconds` slot initialized to the sum of the `total-seconds` slots of the two arguments.

```
// Method on <time-of-day>, <time-offset>
define method \+
    (time-of-day :: <time-of-day>, offset :: <time-offset>)
 => (sum :: <time-of-day>)
  offset + time-of-day;
end method \+;
```

The method on **<time-of-day>**, **<time-offset>** is invoked when the first argument is a time of day and the second argument is a time offset. It simply calls **+** with the order of the arguments switched — this call invokes the method on **<time-offset>**, **<time-of-day>**.

To test these methods, we can use one of the time offsets created in Section 6.1.1, and define the ***8-30-59*** variable, which contains a **<time-of-day>** instance, which we define as follows:

```
define variable *8-30-59* =
  make(<time-of-day>, total-seconds: encode-total-seconds(8, 30, 59));
```

We add the time offset and the time of day:

```
? decode-total-seconds(*minus-2-hours* + *8-30-59*);
6
30
59
```

We add the time of day and the time offset:

```
? decode-total-seconds(*8-30-59* + *minus-2-hours*);
6
30
59
```

6.1.3 Method for adding other kinds of times

We have already defined methods for adding the kinds of time that it makes sense to add together. It is not logical to add one time of day to another time of day — what would three o'clock plus two o'clock mean? Someone could create another concrete subclass of **<time>**, without providing any methods for adding that time to other times. If someone tries to add times that we do not intend them to add, the result will be a "No applicable method" error.

We could provide a method whose sole purpose is to give more information to the user than "No applicable method" when + is called on two times that cannot be added, because there is no applicable method for adding them. We define such a method here:

```
// Method on <time>, <time>
define method \+ (time1 :: <time>, time2 :: <time>)
  error("Sorry, we can't add a %s to a %s.",
        object-class(time1), object-class(time2));
end method \+;
```

This method is called only when the arguments are both general instances of **<time>**, and none of the more specific methods are applicable to the arguments. The **error** function signals an error. For more information about signaling and handling errors, see Chapter 20, *Exceptions*.

Note: This method is useful for explaining how method dispatch works for multimethods, but it does not really give the user any more useful information than that supplied by the "No applicable method" error. Therefore, we define the method in this chapter, but do not include it as part of the final library.

6.2 Method dispatch for multimethods

A method is **specialized** on the required parameters that have explicit types. The type of the required parameter is called that parameter's **specializer**. A **multimethod** is a method that specializes more than one of its parameters. The methods that we defined in Section 6.1 specialize two required parameters, and therefore are multimethods.

> **Comparison with C++ and Java:** Neither C++ nor Java supports multimethods. In both languages, method dispatch is based on the first argument of virtual functions.

The method dispatch considers all the required parameters, and sorts the applicable methods by specificity as follows: For each required parameter, construct a separate list of the applicable methods, sorted from most specific to least specific for that parameter. Then, combine the separate sorted lists into an overall list of methods, sorted by specificity. In the overall method ordering, a method is more specific than another if it satisfies two constraints:

1. The method is *no less specific* than the other method for *all* required parameters. (The two methods might have the same types for some parameters.)

2. The method is *more specific* than the other method for *some* required parameter.

One method might be more specific than another for one parameter, but less specific for another parameter. These two methods are **ambiguous** in specificity and cannot be ordered. If the method-dispatch procedure cannot find any method that is more specific than all other methods, Dylan signals an error.

Type of first argument	Type of second argument	Applicable methods, ordered by specificity
`<time-offset>`	`<time-offset>`	1. method on `<time-offset>`, `<time-offset>` 2. method on `<time>`, `<time>`
`<time-of-day>`	`<time-offset>`	1. method on `<time-of-day>`, `<time-offset>` 2. method on `<time>`, `<time>`
`<time-offset>`	`<time-of-day>`	1. method on `<time-offset>`, `<time-of-day>` 2. method on `<time>`, `<time>`
`<time-of-day>`	`<time-of-day>`	method on `<time>`, `<time>`
`<integer>`	`<time-offset>`	none

Table 6.1 Applicable methods for different arguments to +, ordered by specificity.

Table 6.1 shows the applicable methods for various arguments to +. If two methods are applicable, we number the more specific method 1, and the less specific method 2.

We call + on two instances of **<time-offset>**:

```
? *minus-2-hours* + *plus-15-20-45*;
{instance of <time-offset>}
```

When both arguments are instances of **<time-offset>**, the first row of the table applies. Two methods are applicable. The method on **<time-offset>**, **<time-offset>** is more specific than the method on **<time>**, **<time>**. The parameter specializers of the method on **<time-offset>**, **<time-offset>** are subtypes of the parameter specializers of the method on **<time>**, **<time>**. That is, for the first parameter, **<time-offset>** is a subtype of **<time>**; for the second parameter, **<time-offset>** is a subtype of **<time>**.

6.3 Methods for comparison of times

We need to compare times to see whether they are the same, and to see whether one is greater (later) than another. These methods do the comparisons we need:

```
define method \< (time1 :: <time-of-day>, time2 :: <time-of-day>)
  time1.total-seconds < time2.total-seconds;
end method \<;

define method \< (time1 :: <time-offset>, time2 :: <time-offset>)
  time1.total-seconds < time2.total-seconds;
end method \<;

define method \= (time1 :: <time-of-day>, time2 :: <time-of-day>)
  time1.total-seconds = time2.total-seconds;
end method \=;

define method \= (time1 :: <time-offset>, time2 :: <time-offset>)
  time1.total-seconds = time2.total-seconds;
end method \=;
```

We can call these methods:

```
? *plus-15-20-45* = *minus-2-hours*;
#f
```

To compare times, we need only to define methods for < and =. All other numerical comparisons in Dylan are based on these two methods. So, we can call `>`, `>=`, `<=`, and `~=` (the not-equal-to function). Here are examples:

```
? *plus-15-20-45* ~= *minus-2-hours*;
#t

? *plus-15-20-45* > *minus-2-hours*;
#t
```

6.4 Summary

In this chapter, we covered the following:

- We defined new methods on the built-in generic functions +, `<`, and `=`.
- We discussed how method dispatch works for multimethods.

7

Modularity

Object-oriented programming can lead to modular code. When you are experienced with an object-oriented programming style, you might be able to define classes and methods with the right modularity from the start. Novices, however — and even experienced object-oriented programmers who are attacking large problems — may find that they discover opportunities for sharing as they begin to implement classes and methods. The dynamic aspects of Dylan support an evolutionary approach to programming, so it is easy to continue to refine your implementation and to design as you go.

In this chapter, we show an evolutionary approach to programming, as we define classes that represent different kinds of positions. We start out with one approach, and gradually refine it to achieve greater modularity. We illustrate one new Dylan feature: abstract classes.

Starting in this chapter, and continuing throughout the rest of the book, we take the approach of editing and compiling source code. Now and then, we use a listener to call a function and show the function's output. Whenever we use a listener, we show the ? prompt.

7.1 Requirements of the position classes

To predict when an aircraft will arrive at the airport, we need to know the speed of the aircraft relative to the ground, and the distance the aircraft is from the airport. Thus, we need to represent the positions of objects, such as airports and aircraft, to compute distances.

We shall use two ways to express the position of an object. First, we use latitude and longitude to indicate the **absolute position** of the object. Second, we describe the position of the object relative to a second object. For example, a particular aircraft might be 200 miles west of a given airport. This kind of description is a **relative position**.

We shall define the classes **`<absolute-position>`** and **`<relative-position>`**. The slots of **`<absolute-position>`** will store information about the latitude or longitude of that position. The slots of **`<relative-position>`** will include a distance (such as 200 miles), and a direction (such as south).

We need to provide **`say`** methods for absolute and relative positions. The following sample calls show the output that we want to achieve:

```
? say(*my-absolute-position*);
42 degrees 19 minutes 34 seconds North latitude
70 degrees 56 minutes 26 seconds West longitude

? say(*her-relative-position*);
30 miles away at heading 90 degrees
```

7.2 Initial class definitions

We start with these simple, initial class definitions:

```
// Superclass of all position classes
define class <position> (<object>)
end class <position>;

define class <absolute-position> (<position>)
  slot latitude;
  slot longitude;
end class <absolute-position>;

define class <relative-position> (<position>)
  slot distance;
  slot angle;
end class <relative-position>;
```

These initial definitions show the inheritance relationships among the classes, and the names of the slots show the information that the classes must provide. At this point, we omit the type declarations of the slots, which is equivalent to specifying the type **<object>**. We will fill in the implementation later, by deciding on the types of the slots, and providing the **say** methods.

Our requirements mention only **<absolute-position>** and **<relative-position>**, but we choose to define a superclass of both of them, named **<position>**.

> **Modularity note:** The benefits of defining the **<position>** class are these:
>
> - The **<position>** class creates an explicit relationship between the other position classes, which are related conceptually.
> - We can use the **<position>** class as the type of a slot or other object, in cases where either an absolute or relative position is appropriate.

7.3 Abstract classes

We intend that the **<position>** class will not have direct instances. Any position objects should be direct instances of **<absolute-position>** and **<relative-position>**. In Dylan, a class that is intended to be a superclass and not to have direct instances is an **abstract** class. A class that is intended to have direct instances is a **concrete** class.

By default, a user-defined class is concrete. To define an abstract class, you declare it to be abstract in the **define class** form. For example:

```
// Superclass of all position classes
define abstract class <position> (<object>)
end class <position>;
```

The **<time>** class is another one that we intend to have no direct instances, so we redefine it to be abstract:

```
define abstract class <time> (<object>)
  slot total-seconds :: <integer>, init-keyword: total-seconds:;
end class <time>;
```

If we tried to make an instance of **<position>** or **<time>** now, **make** would signal an error. For more information about abstract classes, see Section 7.7.

7.4 Absolute position

The **<absolute-position>** class represents latitude and longitude. One way to represent latitude and longitude is with degrees, minutes, seconds, and a direction. We can use the approach of combining degrees, minutes, and seconds into a total-seconds slot as we did for **<time>**. We can also define a class that represents total seconds and a direction, and call it **<directed-angle>**:

```
define abstract class <directed-angle> (<object>)
  slot total-seconds :: <integer>, init-keyword: total-seconds:;
  slot direction :: <string>, init-keyword: direction:;
end class <directed-angle>;
```

We use the **<directed-angle>** class in the definition of **<absolute-position>**:

```
define class <absolute-position> (<position>)
  slot latitude :: <directed-angle>, init-keyword: latitude:;
  slot longitude :: <directed-angle>, init-keyword: longitude:;
end class <absolute-position>;
```

> **Modularity note:** The **<directed-angle>** class represents the characteristics that latitude and longitude have in common.

> **Comparison to C:** If you are familiar with a language that uses explicit pointers, such as C, you may be confused by Dylan's object model. Although there is no pointer-to operation in Dylan, there are pointers in the implementation. If you are trying to imagine how Dylan objects are implemented, think in terms of always manipulating a pointer to the object — a Dylan variable (or slot) stores a pointer to an object, rather than a copy of the object's slots. Similarly, assignment, argument passing, and identity comparison are in terms of pointers to objects. See Appendix B, *Dylan Object Model for C and C++ Programmers*.

> **Comparison to Java:** Java recognizes that pointers make it extremely difficult to enforce safety and for a compiler to reason about a program for optimization. Java supports an object model similar to that of Dylan, where pointers are used in the implementation of objects, but are not visible to Java programs.

We could define the **say** method as follows:

```
define method say (position :: <absolute-position>) => ()
  format-out("%d degrees %d minutes %d seconds %s latitude\n",
             decode-total-seconds(position.latitude));
  format-out("%d degrees %d minutes %d seconds %s longitude\n",
             decode-total-seconds(position.longitude));
end method say;
```

The preceding method depends on **decode-total-seconds** having a method that is applicable to **<directed-angle>** (the type of the objects returned by **position.latitude** and **position.longtude**). We define such a method in Section 7.6.

> **Modularity note:** The preceding **say** method does not take advantage of the similarity between latitude and longitude. One clue that there is a modularity problem is that the two calls to **format-out** are nearly identical.

The **say** method on **<absolute-position>** should not call **format-out** directly on the two instances of **<directed-angle>** stored in the latitude and longitude slots. Instead, we can define a **say** method on **<directed-angle>**, and can call it in the method on **<absolute-position>**:

```
define method say (angle :: <directed-angle>) => ()
  let(degrees, minutes, seconds) = decode-total-seconds(angle);
  format-out("%d degrees %d minutes %d seconds %s",
             degrees, minutes, seconds, angle.direction);
end method say;
```

```
define method say (position :: <absolute-position>) => ()
  say(position.latitude);
  format-out(" latitude\n");
  say(position.longitude);
  format-out(" longitude\n");
end method say;
```

Modularity note: Our modularity is improved, now that the **<directed-angle>** class is responsible for describing its instances. This division of labor reduces duplication of code.

There is still a problem with this approach, because the **say** method on **<absolute-position>** must print "latitude" and "longitude" after calling **say** on the directed angles stored in its two slots. The modularity is still flawed, because the method on **<absolute-position>** acts on the knowledge that the method on **<directed-angle>** does not print "latitude" or "longitude."

We defined the **<directed-angle>** class to represent what latitude and longitude have in common. It is useful to recognize that latitude and longitude have differences as well as similarities. We represented latitude and longitude by the names of slots in **<absolute-position>**, and their implementations as instances of **<directed-angle>**. We can elevate the visibility of latitude and longitude by providing classes that represent each of them:

```
define class <latitude> (<directed-angle>)
end class <latitude>;

define class <longitude> (<directed-angle>)
end class <longitude>;
```

We redefine **<absolute-position>** to use **<latitude>** and **<longitude>**:

```
define class <absolute-position> (<position>)
  slot latitude :: <latitude>, init-keyword: latitude:;
  slot longitude :: <longitude>, init-keyword: longitude:;
end class <absolute-position>;
```

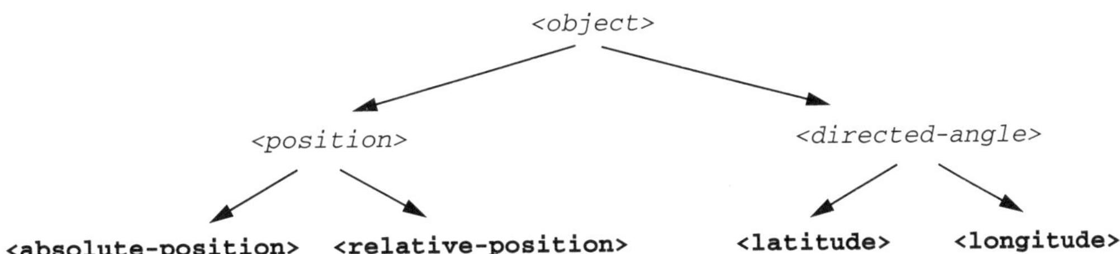

Figure 7.1 Inheritance relationships among the position and angle classes. Abstract classes are shown in *oblique typewriter font*.

Figure 7.1 shows the inheritance relationships among the position and angle classes.

We define these new **say** methods:

```
define method say (latitude :: <latitude>) => ()
  next-method();
  format-out(" latitude\n");
end method say;

define method say (longitude :: <longitude>) => ()
  next-method();
  format-out(" longitude\n");
end method say;
```

The calls to **next-method** in the methods on **<latitude>** and **<longitude>** will call the method on **<directed-angle>**, shown on page 87.

We redefine the **say** method on **<absolute-position>**:

```
define method say (position :: <absolute-position>) => ()
  say(position.latitude);
  say(position.longitude);
end method say;
```

Modularity note: The approach of defining the classes **<latitude>** and **<longitude>** provides the following benefits:

- Each class is responsible for describing its instances. Each method depends on **say** working for all the classes. No method on one class must understand the details of a method on another class.
- We guard against any attempt to store a latitude in a slot designated for a longitude, and vice versa. This type checking will be useful when we introduce more differences between the classes. For example, the direction of a latitude is north or south, and the direction of a longitude is west or east. We can provide methods that ensure that the directions stored in a **<latitude>** instance are appropriate for latitude — and we can do the same for longitude. We show two techniques for implementing that type checking: See Section 10.6, page 128, and Section 19.5, page 318.
- You can ask an object what its class is by using the **object-class** function. In this case, you can find out that an object is a latitude or longitude, rather than just a directed angle. The data does not stand alone; it is an instance that carries with it its type, its identity, and the methods appropriate to it.

7.5 Relative position

We define the **<relative-position>** class as follows:

```
define class <relative-position> (<position>)
  // distance is in miles
  slot distance :: <single-float>, init-keyword: distance:;
  slot angle :: <relative-angle>, init-keyword: angle:;
end class <relative-position>;
```

The **distance** slot stores the distance to the other object, and the **angle** slot stores the direction to the other object. Unfortunately, the angle needed here is different from the **<directed-angle>** class, because the **<directed-angle>** class has a direction, such as south, which is not needed for the angle of **<relative-position>**.

We need to provide a class of angle without direction, which we can use for the **angle** slot of the **<relative-position>** class). Therefore, we define two new classes, and redefine **<directed-angle>**:

```
// Superclass of all angle classes
define abstract class <angle> (<object>)
  slot total-seconds :: <integer>, init-keyword: total-seconds:;
end class <angle>;

define class <relative-angle> (<angle>)
end class <relative-angle>;

define abstract class <directed-angle> (<angle>)
  slot direction :: <string>, init-keyword: direction:;
end class <directed-angle>;
```

> **Modularity note:** Why provide both the classes **<angle>** and **<relative-angle>**, when the **<relative-angle>** class has no additional slots? We need a class that has only the **total-seconds** slot, and no others. We need to use such a class as the type of the **angle** slot of **<relative-angle>**. We might consider making the **<angle>** class concrete, and using that class, which has only the **total-seconds** slot. However, that approach would not prevent someone from storing a **<directed-angle>** instance in the **angle** slot of **<relative-angle>**, because **<directed-angle>** instances are also instances of **<angle>**.
>
> In Dylan, by defining classes as specifically as possible, you enhance the reliability of your program, because the compiler (or run-time system) can verify that only correct values are used. In contrast, you could write a program in Dylan or C in which you represented everything as an integer — in that style of program, someone could far too easily introduce a programming error in which a time was stored where a latitude was needed.

The **<angle>** class looks remarkably similar to the **<time>** class defined earlier:

```
// Superclass of all angle classes
define abstract class <angle> (<object>)
  slot total-seconds :: <integer>, init-keyword: total-seconds:;
end class <angle>;

// Superclass of all time classes
define abstract class <time> (<object>)
  slot total-seconds :: <integer>, init-keyword: total-seconds:;
end class <time>;
```

We would like to call **decode-total-seconds** on instances of **<angle>**, but currently the method is defined to work on **<time>**. The next step is to take advantage of the similarity between **<angle>** and **<time>**.

7.6 Meeting of angles and times

We can create a new superclass to combine times and angles. Sometimes, the trickiest part of defining superclasses that model characteristics shared by other classes is thinking of the right name for the superclass. Here, we use **<sixty-unit>** to name the class that has **total-seconds** that can be converted to either hours, minutes, and seconds, or to degrees, minutes, and seconds. In the methods for decoding and encoding total seconds, we use the name **max-unit** to refer to the unit that is hours for time, and degrees for positions.

```
define abstract class <sixty-unit> (<object>)
  slot total-seconds :: <integer>, init-keyword: total-seconds:;
end class <sixty-unit>;

define method decode-total-seconds
    (sixty-unit :: <sixty-unit>)
 => (max-unit :: <integer>, minutes :: <integer>, seconds :: <integer>)
  decode-total-seconds(abs(sixty-unit.total-seconds));
end method decode-total-seconds;

define method encode-total-seconds
    (max-unit :: <integer>, minutes :: <integer>, seconds :: <integer>)
 => (total-seconds :: <integer>)
  ((max-unit * 60) + minutes) * 60 + seconds;
end method encode-total-seconds;
```

We redefine the time and angle classes and methods to take advantage of the new **<sixty-unit>** class:

```
define abstract class <time> (<sixty-unit>)
end class <time>;
```

```
define abstract class <angle> (<sixty-unit>)
end class <angle>;

define method say (angle :: <angle>) => ()
  let(degrees, minutes, seconds) = decode-total-seconds(angle);
  format-out("%d degrees %d minutes %d seconds",
             degrees, minutes, seconds);
end method say;

// definition unchanged, repeated for completeness
define abstract class <directed-angle> (<angle>)
  slot direction :: <string>, init-keyword: direction:;
end class <directed-angle>;

define method say (angle :: <directed-angle>) => ()
  next-method();
  format-out(" %s", angle.direction);
end method say;

// definition unchanged, repeated for completeness
define class <relative-angle> (<angle>)
end class <relative-angle>;

// we need to show degrees for <relative-angle>, but do not need to show
// minutes and seconds,so we override the method on <angle>
define method say (angle :: <relative-angle>) => ()
  format-out(" %d degrees", decode-total-seconds(angle));
end method say;

define method say (position :: <relative-position>) => ()
  format-out("%d miles away at heading ", position.distance);
  say(position.angle);
end method say;
```

To see the complete library, and the test code that creates position instances and calls **say** on them, see Chapter 8, *A Simple Library*.

Figure 7.2 shows the inheritance relationships of the classes. When one class inherits from another, the relationship is sometimes called the **is-a relationship**. For example, a direct instance of **<time-offset>** *is a* **<time>** as well, and it *is a* **<sixty-unit>**.

The classes have another kind of relationship as well — one class can use another class as the type of a slot, in what is called the **has-a relationship**. Figure 7.3 shows both the inheritance relationships, and the relationships of one class using another class as the type of a slot.

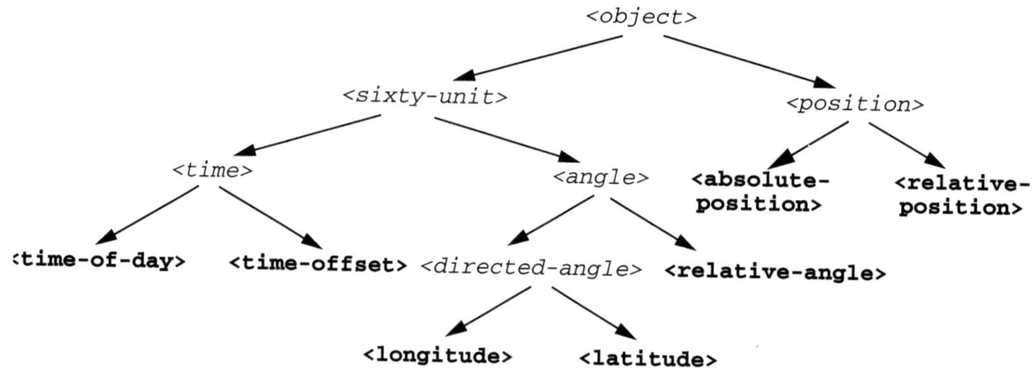

Figure 7.2 Is-a relationships (inheritance) among classes, shown by arrows. Abstract classes are shown in *`oblique typewriter font`*.

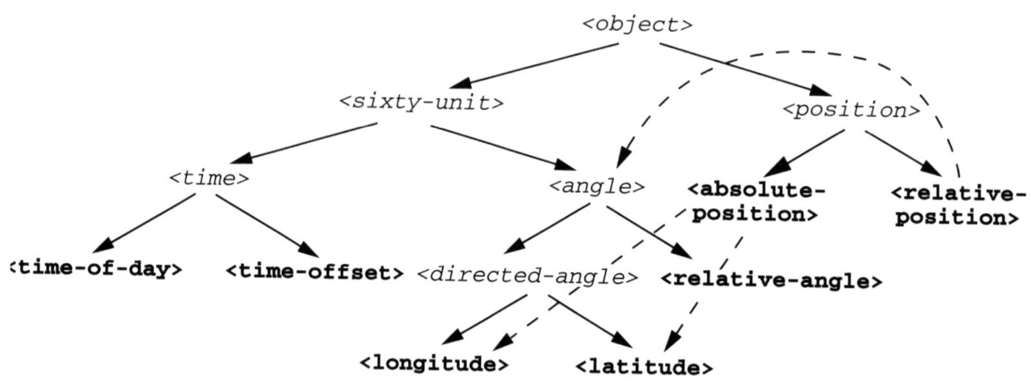

Figure 7.3 Has-a relationships among classes, shown by dashed arrows.

7.7 Abstract, concrete, and instantiable classes

A class is either abstract or concrete. Abstract classes are intended to be superclasses. There are never any direct instances of an abstract class. All superclasses of an abstract class must also be abstract. Concrete classes are intended to have direct instances.

When you define a class with **`define class`**, the result is a concrete class. When you define a class with **`define abstract class`**, the result is an abstract class.

7.7.1 Instantiable classes

A class that can be used as the first argument to **`make`** is an **instantiable** class. All concrete classes are instantiable. When you define an abstract class, Dylan does not provide a method for **`make`** that enables you to create direct instances of that class. Thus, if you call **`make`** on an abstract class, you get an error.

Even though an abstract class does not have direct instances, it is sometimes possible to use an abstract class as the first argument to **`make`**. In this case, the **`make`** function creates and returns a direct instance of a concrete subclass of the abstract class. In other words, **`make`** can return either a direct or an indirect instance of its first argument.

To make it possible for an abstract class to be provided as the first argument to **`make`**, you define the abstract class, and define one or more concrete subclasses of it. You then define a method for **`make`** that specializes its first parameter on the abstract class, and that returns an instance of one of its concrete subclasses. To define **`make`** methods, you need to use the **`singleton`** function to create a type whose only instance is the class itself; see Chapter 9, *Nonclass Types*. Definition of **`make`** methods is an advanced topic that we do not cover in this book.

What is the reason for enabling users to call **`make`** on an abstract class? This flexibility allows a program that needs a general kind of object, represented by a superclass, to ask for an instance of the superclass without specifying the direct class of the instance. For example, a program might need to store data in a vector, but might not be concerned about the specific implementation of the vector that it uses. Such a program can create a vector by calling **`make`** with the argument **`<vector>`**, and **`make`** will create an instance of a concrete subclass. The built-in **`<vector>`** class is abstract, but is instantiable.

7.7.2 Design considerations for abstract classes

The built-in Dylan classes follow a design principle in which concrete classes do not inherit from other concrete classes, but rather inherit from abstract classes only. In other words, the branches of the tree are abstract classes, and the leaves of the tree are concrete classes. We follow that design principle in this book as well. Figure 7.2 shows our classes graphically; the branches of the tree (abstract classes) appear in *oblique typewriter font*, and the leaves (concrete classes) appear in **bold typewriter font**.

Abstract classes can fill two roles. First, they act as an interface. For example, the **<sixty-unit>** class is an interface. If an object is of the **<sixty-unit>** type, you can expect certain behaviors from that object. Those behaviors are the generic functions that are specialized on **<sixty-unit>**, including **decode-total-seconds**, and **total-seconds**.

Abstract classes can also act as a partial implementation, if they define slots. The slots in an abstract class are useful for the classes that inherit from that class. For example, the **<sixty-unit>** class defines the **total-seconds** slot, which is useful for **<time>** and **<position>**.

7.8 Summary

In this chapter, we covered the following:

- A class can represent characteristics and behavior in common across other classes. For example, the **<directed-angle>** class represents the degrees-minutes-seconds aspects that are common to latitude and longitude. Also, the **<sixty-unit>** class represents the **total-seconds** that are common to **<time>** and **<angle>**.

- Classes can be used to represent differences between two similar kinds of objects. For example, the **<latitude>** and **<longitude>** classes are similar in that both classes inherit from **<directed-angle>**, and neither class defines additional slots. However, by providing the two classes, **<latitude>** and **<longitude>**, we make it possible to identify objects as being of type **<latitude>** or **<longitude>**, and we make it possible to customize the behavior of operations on **<latitude>** and **<longitude>** as needed.

- In many object-oriented libraries and programs, certain classes are not intended to have direct instances. You can define those classes as abstract classes to document their purpose.
- When you have two related classes and both will have direct instances, it is good practice to define a third class to be the superclass of the two other classes. The superclass is abstract, and the other two classes are concrete. We used this style in the time classes, the angle classes, and the position classes. People can use the abstract superclasses, such as **`<position>`**, as the type of objects that can be any kind of position.
- In proper modularity, a method on a particular class should not depend on information that is private to second class. If someone changes the representation of the second class, the method could break. We showed an example of breaking this rule when one version of the **`say`** method on **`<absolute-position>`** printed "latitude" and "longitude" after calling **`say`** on the directed angles stored in its two slots. The method on **`<absolute-position>`** acted on the knowledge that the method on **`<directed-angle>`** does not print "latitude" or "longitude."

One of the challenges of modular design is for you to decide which attributes to generalize (by moving them up to higher, or more general, classes in the inheritance graph), and which attributes to specialize (by moving them down the inheritance graph into more specific classes). Another challenge is deciding when to split a class into multiple behaviors, and when to introduce more abstract classes to hold shared behavior. No computer language can make these decisions for you, but dynamic languages typically allow more freedom to explore these relationships. Generic functions and multimethods allow more freedom in defining behavior than does attaching a method to a single class.

8

A Simple Library

In this chapter, we create a complete library that represents time and position. The **`timespace`** library provides the **`say`** generic function for all concrete classes, the mathematical function `+` on certain kinds of time, and the comparison functions `<` and `=`, which enable users to call all other numerical comparisons, `>`, `>=`, `<=`, and `~=`. Our library consists of four files:

- The LID file lists all the files in the **`timespace`** library.
- The library file defines the **`timespace`** library and the **`timespace`** module.
- The implementation file defines the classes, methods, and generic functions.
- The test file creates instances, calls **`say`** on them, and adds time instances.

We provide the test file so that you can experiment with the library. Because the test code has a purpose different from that of the implementation code, we separate them into two files. Normally, a finished library would not contain both the implementation and the test code — the test code would be in a separate library. However, when you are starting to implement your program or library, it is convenient to put all the code in one library, as we do here.

We shall continue to develop the time and position library in Part II. The complete version is given in Chapter 14, *Four Complete Libraries*.

8.1 The LID file

The LID file: `timespace.lid`.

```
library: timespace
files:   library
         library-implementation
          test
```

8.2 The library file

The library file: `library.dylan`.

```
module: dylan-user

define library timespace
  use dylan;
  use format-out;
end library timespace;

define module timespace
  use dylan;
  use format-out;
end module timespace;
```

8.3 The implementation file

The implementation file: `library-implementation.dylan`.

```
module: timespace

// The sixty-unit class

define abstract class <sixty-unit> (<object>)
  slot total-seconds :: <integer>, init-keyword: total-seconds:;
end class <sixty-unit>;
```

The implementation file: `library-implementation.dylan`. *(continued)*

```
// decode-total-seconds

define method decode-total-seconds
    (sixty-unit :: <sixty-unit>)
 => (max-unit :: <integer>, minutes :: <integer>, seconds :: <integer>)
  decode-total-seconds(abs(time.total-seconds));
end method decode-total-seconds;

define method decode-total-seconds
    (total-seconds :: <integer>)
 => (hours :: <integer>, minutes :: <integer>, seconds :: <integer>)
  let(total-minutes, seconds) = truncate/(total-seconds, 60);
  let(hours, minutes) = truncate/(total-minutes, 60);
  values(hours, minutes, seconds);
end method decode-total-seconds;

// encode-total-seconds

define method encode-total-seconds
    (max-unit :: <integer>, minutes :: <integer>, seconds :: <integer>)
 => (total-seconds :: <integer>)
  ((max-unit * 60) + minutes) * 60 + seconds;
end method encode-total-seconds;

// The say generic function

// Given an object, print a description of the object
define generic say (any-object :: <object>) => ();

// The time classes and methods

define abstract class <time> (<sixty-unit>)
end class <time>;

define method say (time :: <time>) => ()
  let (hours, minutes) = decode-total-seconds(time);
  format-out
    ("%d:%s%d", hours, if (minutes < 10) "0" else "" end, minutes);
end method say;

// A specific time of day from 00:00 (midnight) to before 24:00 (tomorrow)
define class <time-of-day> (<time>)
end class <time-of-day>;

// A relative time between -24:00 and +24:00
define class <time-offset> (<time>)
end class <time-offset>;
```

The implementation file: `library-implementation.dylan`. *(continued)*

```
// Method for determining whether a time offset is in the past
define method past? (time :: <time-offset>) => (past? :: <boolean>)
  time.total-seconds < 0;
end method past?;

define method say (time :: <time-offset>)
  format-out("%s ", if (past?(time)) "minus" else "plus" end);
  next-method();
end method say;

// Methods for adding times

define method \+
    (offset1 :: <time-offset>, offset2 :: <time-offset>)
 => (sum :: <time-offset>)
  let sum = offset1.total-seconds + offset2.total-seconds;
  make(<time-offset>, total-seconds: sum);
end method \+;

define method \+
    (offset :: <time-offset>, time-of-day :: <time-of-day>)
 => (sum :: <time-of-day>)
  make(<time-of-day>,
       total-seconds: offset.total-seconds + time-of-day.total-seconds);
end method \+;

define method \+
    (time-of-day :: <time-of-day>, offset :: <time-offset>)
 => (sum :: <time-of-day>)
  offset + time-of-day;
end method \+;

// Methods for comparing times

define method \< (time1 :: <time-of-day>, time2 :: <time-of-day>)
  time1.total-seconds < time2.total-seconds;
end method \<;

define method \< (time1 :: <time-offset>, time2 :: <time-offset>)
  time1.total-seconds < time2.total-seconds;
end method \<;

define method \= (time1 :: <time-of-day>, time2 :: <time-of-day>)
  time1.total-seconds = time2.total-seconds;
end method \=;
```

The implementation file: `library-implementation.dylan`. *(continued)*

```
define method \= (time1 :: <time-offset>, time2 :: <time-offset>)
  time1.total-seconds = time2.total-seconds;
end method \=;

// The angle classes and methods

define abstract class <angle> (<sixty-unit>)
end class <angle>;

define method say (angle :: <angle>) => ()
  let(degrees, minutes, seconds) = decode-total-seconds(angle);
  format-out
    ("%d degrees %d minutes %d seconds",
     degrees, minutes, seconds);
end method say;

define class <relative-angle> (<angle>)
end class <relative-angle>;

// We need to show degrees for <relative-angle> but we do not need to
// show minutes and seconds, so we override the method on <angle>
define method say (angle :: <relative-angle>) => ()
  format-out(" %d degrees", decode-total-seconds(angle));
end method say;

define abstract class <directed-angle> (<angle>)
  slot direction :: <string>, init-keyword: direction:;
end class <directed-angle>;

define method say (angle :: <directed-angle>) => ()
  next-method();
  format-out(" %s", angle.direction);
end method say;

// The latitude and longitude classes and methods

define class <latitude> (<directed-angle>)
end class <latitude>;

define method say (latitude :: <latitude>) => ()
  next-method();
  format-out(" latitude\n");
end method say;

define class <longitude> (<directed-angle>)
end class <longitude>;
```

The implementation file: `library-implementation.dylan`. *(continued)*

```
define method say (longitude :: <longitude>) => ()
  next-method();
  format-out(" longitude\n");
end method say;

// The position classes and methods

define abstract class <position> (<object>)
end class <position>;

define class <absolute-position> (<position>)
  slot latitude :: <latitude>, init-keyword: latitude:;
  slot longitude :: <longitude>, init-keyword: longitude:;
end class <absolute-position>;

define method say (position :: <absolute-position>) => ()
  say(position.latitude);
  say(position.longitude);
end method say;

define class <relative-position> (<position>)
  // Distance is in miles
  slot distance :: <single-float>, init-keyword: distance:;
  slot angle :: <angle>, init-keyword: angle:;
end class <relative-position>;

define method say (position :: <relative-position>) => ()
  format-out("%d miles away at heading ", position.distance);
  say(position.angle);
end method say;
```

8.4 The test file

The test file: `test.dylan`.

```
module: timespace

format-out("Creating an instance of <absolute-position>:\n");

define variable *my-absolute-position*
  = make(<absolute-position>,
         latitude: make(<latitude>,
                        total-seconds: encode-total-seconds(42, 19, 34),
                        direction: "North"),
         longitude: make(<longitude>,
                         total-seconds: encode-total-seconds(70, 56, 26),
                         direction: "West"));

say(*my-absolute-position*);

format-out("\n");

format-out("Creating an instance of <relative-position>:\n");

define variable *her-relative-position*
  = make(<relative-position>,
         distance: 30,
         angle: make(<angle>,
                     total-seconds: encode-total-seconds(90, 5, 0)));

say(*her-relative-position*);

format-out("\n");

format-out("Creating an instance of <time-offset> in *minus-2-hours*.\n");

define variable *minus-2-hours*
  = make(<time-offset>, total-seconds: - encode-total-seconds (2, 0, 0));

format-out("Creating an instance of <time-offset> in *plus-15-20-45*.\n");

define variable *plus-15-20-45*
  = make(<time-offset>, total-seconds: encode-total-seconds (15, 20, 45));

format-out("Creating an instance of <time-of-day> in *8-30-59*.\n");

define variable *8-30-59*
  = make(<time-of-day>, total-seconds: encode-total-seconds (8, 30, 59));
```

The test file: **test.dylan**. *(continued)*

```
format-out("Adding <time-offset> + <time-offset>: *minus-2-hours* + *plus-
15-20-45*:\n");

decode-total-seconds(*minus-2-hours* + *plus-15-20-45*);

format-out("Adding <time-offset> + <time-of-day>: *minus-2-hours* + *8-30-
59*:\n");

decode-total-seconds(*minus-2-hours* + *8-30-59*);

format-out("Adding <time-of-day> + <time-offset>: *8-30-59* + *minus-2-
hours* :\n");

decode-total-seconds(*8-30-59* + *minus-2-hours*);
```

When we run the test file, we see the following output and values:

```
Creating an instance of <absolute-position>:
42 degrees 19 minutes 34 seconds North latitude
70 degrees 56 minutes 26 seconds West longitude

Creating an instance of <relative-position>:
30 miles away at heading 90 degrees

Creating an instance of <time-offset> in *minus-2-hours*.
Creating an instance of <time-offset> in *plus-15-20-45*.
Creating an instance of <time-of-day> in *8-30-59*.
Adding <time-offset> + <time-offset>: *minus-2-hours* + *plus-15-20-45":
13
20
45
Adding <time-offset> + <time-of-day>: *minus-2-hours* + *8-30-59":
6
30
59
Adding <time-of-day> + <time-offset>: *8-30-59* + *minus-2-hours*:
6
30
59
```

8.5 Summary

In this chapter, we created the four files that constitute the **timespace** library.

Part II. Intermediate Topics

Chapter 9, *Nonclass Types*, discusses types that are not classes, including singleton types, limited types, and union types.

Chapter 10, *Slots*, focuses on slot getters and setters, techniques for initializing slots, different kinds of allocation of slots, virtual slots, and symbols.

Chapter 11, *Collections and Control Flow*, describes how to use collections, including strings, lists, vectors, tables, and arrays. It also shows how to use control-flow operators to alter the natural (sequential) order of statement execution, including performing iteration.

Chapter 12, *Functions*, describes the syntax of function calls, the function-calling protocol, and the uses of functions as objects.

Chapter 13, *Libraries and Modules*, shows how you can package your code into a reusable software component by designing libraries and modules.

Chapter 14, *Four Complete Libraries*, pulls together the techniques shown in Part II in the context of a set of complete working libraries.

9

Nonclass Types

Every class is a type, but not every type is a class. In this chapter, we describe how to create nonclass types, and how to make use of them.

9.1 Functions that create nonclass types

There are three functions that create types that are not classes: **`singleton`**, **`type-union`**, and **`limited`**.

`singleton` Takes any instance, and creates a type whose only member is that instance. You can define a singleton type to be used as the parameter specializer of a method that should be chosen for a particular instance.

`type-union` Takes one or more classes or types, and creates a new type whose members include all the members of the types that are its arguments.

`limited` Takes a type and creates a new type, which is a more restricted version of the type that is its argument (the **base type**). For example, you can define a new type that is based on **`<integer>`**, but has a given minimum or maximum value. Another example is to define a new collection type that specifies the type of elements, such as a type that is a list of integers. The main reasons for defining types with **limited** are to perform type checking and to increase efficiency. For information about the performance of limited types, see Section 19.4, page 315.

> **Convention:** Type names, like class names, are surrounded with angle brackets — for example, **<nonnegative-integer>**.

9.2 Examples of types that are not classes

Later in our development of the time library, we shall find it useful to define a new type that represents nonnegative integers:

```
// Define nonnegative integers as integers that are >= zero
define constant <nonnegative-integer> = limited(<integer>, min: 0);
```

We can use a nonclass type as a parameter specializer of a method, or as the type of a return value:

```
define method encode-total-seconds
    (max-unit :: <nonnegative-integer>,
     minutes :: <nonnegative-integer>,
     seconds :: <nonnegative-integer>)
 => (total-seconds :: <nonnegative-integer>)
  ((max-unit * 60) + minutes) * 60 + seconds;
end method encode-total-seconds;
```

To see how we use **<nonnegative-integer>** in the time library, see Section 10.2.2, page 120.

We can define a type whose only member is the false value, **#f**:

```
singleton(#f);
```

We can define a type that is the union of the false value and **<integer>**:

```
type-union(singleton(#f), <integer>);
```

We can make it convenient for people to create new types like the one defined in the preceding code. The new type is the union of the false value and the argument to the method:

```
define method false-or (other-type :: <type>) => (combined-type :: <type>)
  type-union(singleton(#f), other-type);
end method false-or;
```

False-or types are useful as the type of slots. Note that a slot can be uninitialized. Once a slot receives a value, however, it will always have a value: There is no way to return a slot to the uninitialized state. Sometimes it is useful to store in a slot a value that means none. Later on in our development of the airport example, we use a false-or type as the type of a slot that stores "the next vehicle, if there is one." If there is no next vehicle, the slot contains **#f**. We create the type by calling **false-or(<vehicle>)**, and use the result as the type of the slot. Note that, if the type of the slot were just **<vehicle>**, we could not store **#f** in the slot, and there would be no way to represent none.

You can use **type-union** and **singleton** together to define a type that is an enumeration of multiple-choice objects. For example,

```
define constant <latitude-direction>
  = type-union(singleton(#"north"), singleton(#"south"));
```

The **<latitude-direction>** type has two valid values: the keywords **#"north"** and **#"south"**. For an explanation of how we could use that type to enforce the correct values of a latitude slot, and for information about the performance of enumerations, see Section 19.5, page 318.

9.3 Method dispatch and nonclass types

In this section, we describe the implications for method dispatch of using nonclass types as parameter specializers. This advanced topic is included as reference material; you can skip it safely if you prefer. The description that we give here is meant to provide a general understanding, and does not cover all cases. For exact details, you should consult *The Dylan Reference Manual*.

Recall that, when a generic function is called, Dylan determines which method to invoke by comparing the required **arguments** passed to the generic function with the types of the corresponding **parameters** of the generic function's methods. Dylan uses the following procedure, assuming that there is only one required argument:

1. Find all the applicable methods. A method is applicable if the required argument is an instance of the type of the specialized parameter.

2. Sort the applicable methods in order of specificity. One method is more specific than another if the type of its specialized parameter is a **proper subtype** of the type of the other method's specialized parameter. For definitions of "proper subtype" in various situations, see Sections 9.3.1 through 9.3.5.

   (In the presence of multiple inheritance, the specificity rule is more complex. For more information, see Section 18.4, page 300.)

3. Call the most specific method.

(If there is more than one required argument, Dylan constructs the sorted list of methods by combining separate sorted lists for all required arguments.)

For any given argument and any given set of parameter types, Dylan has to answer two questions:

1. Is the argument an instance of a given type? The answer determines method applicability.
2. Is one type a proper subtype of another type? The answer determines method specificity.

9.3.1 Method dispatch and classes

We have already seen that, when all types are classes, Dylan uses the following rules:

1. An object is an instance of a class if it is a general instance of that class (a direct instance of the class or of one of that class's subclasses).
2. One class is a proper subtype of another if the first class is a subclass of the second.

For example, suppose that we have these definitions:

```
// Method 1
define method say (x :: <number>) ... end method say;

// Method 2
define method say (x :: <integer>) ... end method say;
```

Now, if `say` is called with an argument of `100`, both methods are applicable, and method 2 is more specific than method 1.

9.3.2 Method dispatch and singletons

When a type is a singleton, Dylan uses the following rules:

1. An object is an instance of a singleton only if the object is identical to the object used as the argument in the call to **singleton** that created the singleton.
2. A singleton is a proper subtype of any other type that the object belongs to. Thus, a singleton is more specific than any other type of which an object is an instance. In particular, a singleton is more specific than the object's class.

For example, suppose that we have these definitions:

```
// Method 1
define method say (x :: <integer>) ... end method say;

// Method 2
define method say (x == 0) ... end method say;
```

Note that method 2 illustrates a convenient syntax for defining a method on a singleton without calling **singleton** explicitly.

Now, if **say** is called with an argument of **0**, both methods are applicable, and method 2 is more specific than method 1. If **say** is called with an argument that is any other integer, only method 1 is applicable.

9.3.3 Method dispatch and unions

When a type is a union, Dylan uses the following rules:

1. An object is an instance of a union if it is an instance of any of the types that make up that union.
2. If none of the types that make up a union is a subtype of any other, then
   - A nonunion type is a proper subtype of a union if the nonunion type is a subtype of any of the types that make up the union.
   - A union is a proper subtype of a nonunion type if all types that make up the union are subtypes of the nonunion type, and if all the types that make up the union, taken together, are not equivalent to the nonunion type.

- A union is a proper subtype of another union if *each* of the types that make up the first union is a subtype of *one* of the types that make up the other union, and if the two unions are not equivalent.

For example, suppose that we have these definitions:

```
define constant <false-or-integer> = type-union(<integer>, singleton(#f));

// Method 1
define method say (x :: <false-or-integer>) ... end method say;

// Method 2
define method say (x :: <integer>) ... end method say;
```

Now, if **say** is called with an argument that is an integer, both methods are applicable, and method 2 is more specific than method 1. If **say** is called with an argument of **#f**, only method 1 is applicable.

9.3.4 Method dispatch and limited integers

When a type is a limited-integer type, Dylan uses the following rules:

1. An object is an instance of a limited-integer type if it is an instance of **<integer>** and if it is (inclusively) within the specified range.
2. A limited-integer type is a proper subtype of **<integer>**, as long as it is not equivalent to **<integer>**.

   One limited-integer type is a proper subtype of another limited-integer type if the range of the first type is entirely within the range of the second type, and if the two types are not equivalent.

For example, suppose that we have these definitions:

```
define constant <nonnegative-integer> = limited(<integer>, min: 0);

// Method 1
define method say (x :: <integer>) ... end method say;

// Method 2
define method say (x :: <nonnegative-integer>) ... end method say;
```

Now, if **say** is called with an argument of **1**, both methods are applicable, and method 2 is more specific than method 1. If **say** is called with an argument of **-1**, only method 1 is applicable.

Now suppose that, instead, we have the following definitions:

```
define constant <limited-integer-1> = limited(<integer>, min: -2, max: 2);

define constant <limited-integer-2> = limited(<integer>, min: 0, max: 4);

// Method 1
define method say (x :: <limited-integer-1>) ... end method say;

// Method 2
define method say (x :: <limited-integer-2>) ... end method say;
```

Now, if **say** is called with an argument of **1**, both methods are applicable, and neither method is more specific than the other; the two methods are **ambiguous**. If no more specific method exists, Dylan signals an error when we call **say** with an argument of **1**.

9.3.5 Method dispatch and limited collections

When a type is a limited-collection type, Dylan uses the following rules:

1. An object is an instance of a limited-collection type *<L1>* if the object was created via **make** (or a similar constructor) applied to limited-collection type *<L2>*, and if *<L2>* is a subtype of *<L1>*. An instance of a limited-collection type is also an instance of the collection's base type.
2. A limited-collection type is a proper subtype of its base type, as long as it is not equivalent to the base type.

   Generally, one limited-collection type is a proper subtype of another limited-collection type if all the following are true: the base type of the first is a subclass of the base type of the second; the two element types are equivalent; the size or dimensions of the first limited type are no less restricted than those of the second type; and the first limited type is not equivalent to the second.

For example, suppose that we have these definitions:

```
define constant <limited-vector-of-3-integers>
  = limited(<vector>, of: <integer>, size: 3);

define constant <limited-vector-of-3-numbers>
  = limited(<vector>, of: <number>, size: 3);

define constant $v1 = make(<limited-vector-of-3-integers>, size: 3, fill: 1);

define constant $v2 = vector(1, 1, 1);
```

```
// Method 1
define method say (x :: <vector>) ... end method say;

// Method 2
define method say (x :: <limited-vector-of-3-integers>) ... end method say;

// Method 3
define method say (x :: <limited-vector-of-3-numbers>) ... end method say;
```

Now, if **say** is called with an argument of **$v1**, both method 1 and method 2 are applicable, and method 2 is more specific than method 1. Note that **$v1** is an instance of **<limited-vector-of-3-integers>** but is not an instance of **<limited-vector-of-3-numbers>**, because the element type of **$v1** is not equivalent to the element type of **<limited-vector-of-3-numbers>.**

If **say** is called with an argument of **$v2**, only method 1 is applicable. Note that **$v2** is not an instance of either of the limited-collection types we defined, even though **$v2** is a vector that contains three integers. (For example, we could store objects other than integers in **$v2**.)

9.4 Summary

In this chapter, we discussed types that are not classes:

- A **singleton type** is a type whose only member is one particular instance. An example of creating a singleton type is:

  ```
  singleton(#f);
  ```

- A **union type** is a type whose members include all the members of one or more base types. An example of creating a union type is:

  ```
  type-union(singleton(#f), <integer>);
  ```

- A **limited type** is a type that is a more restricted version of its base type. For example, a limited-integer type is based on **<integer>**, but has a given minimum or maximum value:

  ```
  limited(<integer>, min: 0);
  ```

  Another example of a limited type is a limited-collection type, which is a collection type that specifies the type of elements, and/or the size of the collection:

  ```
  limited(<vector>, of: <integer>, size: 3);
  ```

10

Slots

In this chapter, we show how to call getters and setters with the function-call syntax, and how to define methods for getters and setters. We show techniques for initializing slots, including slot options and **`initialize`** methods. We describe the different allocations that slots can have. We find a need for symbols, so we describe and use symbols as well.

10.1 Dot-syntax abbreviation for simple function calls

The dot syntax that we have shown for getters in Section 4.4, page 42, is an abbreviation for a function call. The first expression is an abbreviation for the second expression:

```
object.function-name
```

```
function-name(object)
```

The dot syntax used with the assignment operator also is an abbreviation for a function call. The first two expressions are abbreviations for the third expression:

```
object.name := new-value;
```

```
name(object) := new-value;
```

```
name-setter(new-value, object);
```

You can use the dot syntax as an abbreviation for any function call that takes a single argument and returns a single value. For example, in Section 5.1.3, page 54, we defined the following method:

```
define method past? (time :: <time-offset>) => (past? :: <boolean>)
  time.total-seconds < 0;
end method past?;
```

The following two calls are equivalent:

```
past?(*my-time-offset*);

*my-time-offset*.past?;
```

In the remainder of this book, we use the dot syntax for function calls that return a property of an object (such as the **past?** property of a **<time-offset>** instance), and that take a single argument and return a single value.

10.2 Getters and setters for slots

As shown in Section 4.4, page 42, when you define a class, Dylan automatically defines a getter method to return the value of a slot, and defines a setter method to change the value of a slot.

> **Performance note:** For slot accesses, given accurate type declarations, the compiler can typically optimize away not only the method dispatch, but also the function call, making the executed code just as efficient as it would be in a language such as C, where structure or record slots are accessed directly. See Chapter 19, *Performance and Flexibility*.

The name of the getter is always the name of the slot. Thus, the getter for the **total-seconds** slot is **total-seconds**. Let's look at an example of calling a getter. The first expression is an abbreviation for the second expression:

```
*my-time-of-day*.total-seconds;

total-seconds(*my-time-of-day*);
```

The preceding expressions are calls to the getter function named **total-seconds**. The choice of which syntax to use is purely a matter of personal style. The first syntax is provided for those people who prefer the slightly more concise dot syntax. The second syntax is provided for those people who prefer slot accesses to look like function calls. In this book, we use the dot syntax.

By default, the name of the setter is the slot's name followed by **-setter**. Thus, the setter for the **total-seconds** slot is **total-seconds-setter**. You can use the **:setter** slot option to specify a different name for the setter.

The dot-syntax abbreviation for assignment enables you to invoke the setter by using assignment with the name of the getter. For example, the first two expressions are abbreviations for the third expression:

```
*my-time-of-day*.total-seconds := 180;

total-seconds(*my-time-of-day*) := 180;

total-seconds-setter(180, *my-time-of-day*);
```

Each of these expressions stores the value **180** in the slot named **total-seconds** of the object that is the value of the ***my-time-of-day*** variable.

Most Dylan programmers do not use the syntax of the third expression to call a setter, because it is more verbose than the first and second expressions. However, it is important to know the name of the setter, so that you can define setter methods. For example, to define a method on the setter for the **total-seconds** slot, you define it on **total-seconds-setter**. For an example of a setter method, see Section 10.2.2.

If you do not want Dylan to define a setter method for a slot, you can define the slot to be constant, using the **constant** slot adjective, or you can give the **:setter #f** slot option.

For more information about accessing slots, see Section 12.1.2, page 163, and Section 12.1.6, page 166.

10.2.1 Advantages of accessing slots via generic functions

A slot is conceptually like a variable, in that it has a value. But the only way to access a slot's value is to call a generic function. Using generic functions and methods to gain access to slot values has three important advantages:

- Generic functions provide a public interface to the private implementation of a slot. By making the representation of the slot visible to only the methods of the generic functions, you can change the representation without changing any of the users of the information — the callers of the generic functions. In most cases, a compiler can optimize slot references to reduce or eliminate the cost of hiding the implementation.

- A subclass can specialize, or filter, references to superclass slots. For example, the classes **<latitude>** and **<longitude>** inherit the **direction** slot from their superclass **<directed-angle>**. In Section 10.6, we show how to provide a setter method for the direction slot of **<latitude>** that ensures that the value is north or south, and a setter method for the direction slot of **<longitude>** that ensures that the value is east or west.
- A slot access can involve arbitrary computation. For example, a slot can be **virtual**. See Section 10.6.

10.2.2 Setter methods

In most cases, the getter and setter methods that Dylan defines for each slot are perfectly adequate. In certain cases, however, you might want to change the way a getter or setter works.

For example, we can define a setter method to solve a problem in our time library. The class **<time-of-day>** inherits the **total-seconds** slot from the class **<sixty-unit>**. The type of the slot is **<integer>**. However, the semantics of **<time-of-day>** state that the **total-seconds** should not be less than 0. We can define a setter method for **<time-of-day>** to ensure that the new value for the total-seconds slot is 0 or greater.

In our setter method, we will use the type defined in Section 9.2, page 110, and repeated here:

```
// Define nonnegative integers as integers that are >= zero
define constant <nonnegative-integer> = limited(<integer>, min: 0);
```

The setter method is as follows:

```
define method total-seconds-setter
    (total-seconds :: <integer>, time :: <time-of-day>)
 => (total-seconds :: <nonnegative-integer>)
  if (total-seconds >= 0)
    next-method();
  else
    error("%d is invalid. total-seconds cannot be negative.", total-seconds);
  end if;
end method total-seconds-setter;
```

When the setter for the **total-seconds** slot is called with an instance of **<time-of-day>**, the preceding method will be invoked, because it is more specific than the method that Dylan generated on the **<sixty-unit>** class. If the new value for the **total-seconds** slot is valid (that is, is greater than or equal to 0), then this method calls **next-method**, which invokes the setter method on **<sixty-unit>**. If the new value is less than 0, an error is signaled.

The following example show what happens when you call **total-seconds-setter** with a negative value for **total-seconds**:

```
? begin
    let test-time-of-day = make(<time-of-day>);
    test-time-of-day.total-seconds := -15;
  end;
ERROR: -15 is invalid. total-seconds cannot be negative.
```

This setter method ensures that no one can assign an invalid value to the slot. For completeness, we must also ensure that no one can initialize the slot to an invalid value. The way to do that is to define an **initialize** method, as shown in Section 10.3.

10.2.3 Considerations for naming slots and other objects

A **binding** is an association between a name and an object. For example, there is a binding that associates the name of a constant and the value of the constant. The names of functions, module variables, local variables, and classes are also bindings. There is a potential problem that can occur if you use short names. If a client module uses other modules that also define and export bindings with short names, there is a significant chance that name clashes will occur, with different bindings with the same name being imported from different modules.

If you use the Dylan naming conventions, then a variable will not have the same name as a class, a function, or a constant. The naming conventions avoid name clashes between different kinds of objects.

A slot is identified by the name of its getter. The getter is visible to all client modules. There is no problem if two getters with the same name are defined by unrelated classes, because the appropriate getter is selected through method dispatch. There is a problem if a getter has the same name as a generic function with an incompatible parameter list or values declaration. (See Section 12.2.5, page 176.) When such a problem occurs, the only way to resolve it is to use options to **define module** to exclude or rename some of the problem bindings. This solution is undesirable, because it requires work on the part of the author of the client module, who must spot and resolve such clashes, and then use an interface that no longer matches its documentation.

Therefore, for getters that you intend to export, it makes sense prevent clashes by considering the name of the slot carefully. One technique is to prefix the name of the property with the name of the class. For example, you might define a **<person>** class with a slot **person-name**, instead of the shorter possibility, **name**. One drawback of this technique is that it might expose too much information about the implementation — that is, the name betrays the class that happens to implement the slot at a particular time, and you have to remember which superclass introduces a property if you are to access that property.

There is a compromise between using short names and using the class name as a prefix — you can choose a prefix for a whole group of classes beneath a given class. For example, you might use the prefix **person-** for slots of many classes that inherit from the **<person>** class, including **<employee>**, **<consultant>**, and so on.

```
define class <person> (<object>)
  slot person-name;
  slot person-age;
end class <person>;

define class <employee> (<person>)
  slot person-number;
  slot person-salary;
end class <employee>;

define class <consultant> (<employee>)
  slot person-perks;
  slot person-parking-lot;
end class <consultant>;
```

Now, in a method on **<consultant>**, all accesses are consistent, and we do not have to remember where the slots actually originate:

```
// Method 1
define method person-status (p :: <consultant>) => (status :: <integer>)
  (p.person-perks.evaluation + p.person-salary.evaluation)
    / p.person-age;
end method person-status;
```

If we had defined the classes differently, such that we prefixed each getter with the name of the class that defined it, the method would look like this:

```
// Method 2
define method person-status (p :: <consultant>) => (status :: <integer>)
  (p.consultant-perks.evaluation + p.employee-salary.evaluation)
    / p.person-age;
end method person-status;
```

Method 2 is more difficult to write and read than is Method 1, and is more fragile. If, at some point, all employees are allocated perks, then the use of the **consultant-perks** getter becomes a problem.

> **Comparison with C++:** In C++, the class is the namespace of its member functions. In Dylan, the module is the namespace of getters and setters. In general, the module is the namespace of all module bindings, including generic functions; getters and setters are generic functions.

10.3 Initialize methods

Every time you call **make** to create an instance of a class, **make** calls the **initialize** generic function. The purpose of the **initialize** generic function is to initialize the instance before it is returned by **make**. You can customize the initialization by defining a method on **initialize**. Methods for **initialize** receive the instance as the first argument, and receive all keyword arguments given in the call to **make**.

We define an **initialize** method:

```
define method initialize (time :: <time-of-day> #key)              // 1
  next-method();                                                    // 2
  if (time.total-seconds < 0)                                       // 3
    error("%d is invalid. total-seconds cannot be negative",        // 4
          time.total-seconds);                                      // 5
  end if;                                                           // 6
end method initialize;                                              // 7
```

On line 2, we call **next-method**. All methods for **initialize** should call **next-method** as their first action, to allow any less specific initializations (that is, **initialize** methods defined on superclasses) to execute first. If you call **next-method** as the first action, then, in the rest of the method, you can operate on an instance that has been properly initialized by any **initialize** methods of superclasses. If you forget to include the call to **next-method**, your **initialize** method will be operating on an improperly initialized instance.

Lines 3 through 6 contain the real action of this method. We check that the value is valid. If it is invalid, we signal an error.

The following example shows what happens when **total-seconds** is not valid when we are creating an instance:

```
? make(<time-of-day>, total-seconds: -15);
ERROR: -15 is invalid. total-seconds cannot be negative.
```

10.4 Slot options for initialization of slots

Unlike variables and constants, slots can be **uninitialized**; that is, you can create an instance without initializing all the slots. If you call a getter for a slot that has not been initialized, Dylan signals an error. In the following sections, we describe a variety of techniques for avoiding the problem of accessing an uninitialized slot. The most general technique is to define an **initialize** method for a slot, as shown in Section 10.3.

A slot can be uninitialized. Once a slot receives a value, however, it will always have a value: There is no way to return a slot to the uninitialized state. Sometimes it is useful to store in a slot a value that means none. To make that possible, you need to define a new type for that slot, as shown in Section 9.2, page 110. In Sections 10.4.1 through 10.4.4, we show techniques for initializing slots.

10.4.1 The init-value: slot option

We can use the **init-value:** slot option to give a default initial value to a slot:

```
define abstract class <sixty-unit> (<object>)
  slot total-seconds :: <integer>,
    init-keyword: total-seconds:, init-value: 0;
end class <sixty-unit>;
```

When we use **make** to create any subclass of **<sixty-unit>** (such as **<time-of-day>**), and we do not supply the **total-seconds:** keyword to **make**, the **total-seconds** slot is initialized to 0.

The **init-value:** slot option specifies an expression that is evaluated once, before the first instance of the class is made, to yield a value. Every time that an instance is made and the slot needs a default value, this same value is used as the default.

In general, a slot receives its default initial value when no init keyword is defined or when the caller does not supply the init-keyword argument to **make**.

10.4.2 The `required-init-keyword:` slot option

Instead of giving the slot a default initial value, we can require the caller of **make** to supply an init keyword for the slot. The **required-init-keyword:** slot option defines a required init keyword. If the caller of **make** does not supply the required init keyword, then an error is signaled.

```
define abstract class <sixty-unit> (<object>)
  slot total-seconds :: <integer>, required-init-keyword: total-seconds:;
end class <sixty-unit>;
```

The **total-seconds** slot is defined in the **<sixty-unit>** class. By making **total-seconds:** a required init keyword in this class, we make it required for every class that inherits from it, including **<time>**, **<angle>**, and all their subclasses.

10.4.3 Slot options for an inherited slot

You can define a slot in only one particular class in a set of classes related by inheritance. You can use the **inherited slot** specification to override the default initial value of an inherited slot, or the **init function** of an inherited slot. See Section 10.4.4.

In this example, assume that the **<sixty-unit>** class defines the **total-seconds** slot and the init keyword **total-seconds:**, and provides the default initial value of 0 for that slot, as shown:

```
define abstract class <sixty-unit> (<object>)
  slot total-seconds :: <integer>,
    init-keyword: total-seconds:, init-value: 0;
end class <sixty-unit>;

define abstract class <time> (<sixty-unit>)
end class <time>;
```

The **<time-offset>** class provides a different default initial value for the inherited slot **total-seconds**:

```
define class <time-offset> (<time>)
  inherited slot total-seconds, init-value: encode-total-seconds(1, 0, 0);
end class <time-offset>;
```

By using the **inherited slot** specification, we are not defining the slot, but rather are stating that this slot is defined by a superclass. We can then provide either a default initial value or an init function for the inherited slot.

10.4.4 The init-function: slot option

We can use the **init-function:** slot option to provide a function of no arguments to be called to return a default initial value for the slot. These functions are called **init functions**. They allow the initial value of a slot to be an arbitrary computation.

```
define class <time-of-day> (<time>)
  inherited slot total-seconds, init-function: get-current-time;
end class <time-of-day>;
```

Every time that we make an instance of the **<time-of-day>** class and we need a default value for the **total-seconds** slot, the **get-current-time** function is called to provide an initial value. Here, we assume that **get-current-time** is available as a library function; it is not part of the core Dylan language.

The **init-function:** slot option specifies an expression that is evaluated once, before the first instance of the class is made, to yield a function. The function must have no required arguments and must return at least one value. Every time that an instance is made and the slot needs a default value, this function is called with no arguments, and the value that it returns is used as the default. An init function is called during instance creation when no keyword argument is defined or when an optional keyword argument is not passed to **make**.

10.4.5 Init expressions

An **init expression** is another way of providing a default slot value. Here is an example:

```
define class <time-of-day> (<time>)
  inherited slot total-seconds = get-current-time();
end class <time-of-day>;
```

Every time that we make an instance of the **<time-of-day>** class and we need a default value for the **total-seconds** slot, the expression **get-current-time();** is evaluated to provide an initial value.

An init expression specifies an expression. Every time that an instance is made and the slot needs a default value, this expression is evaluated and its value is used as the default.

Notice the similarity between the **init-function:** slot option and an init expression. In fact, the following slot specifications are equivalent:

```
inherited slot total-seconds, init-function: get-current-time;
inherited slot total-seconds = get-current-time();
```

That substitution works for functions that have no required arguments. More generally, the following slot specifications are equivalent:

```
slot slot = expression;
slot slot, init-function: method () expression end method;
```

The expression can be a call to a function that requires arguments. Here, we use **method** to define a method with no name.

The **init-value:** slot option, **init-function:** slot option, and init expression are mutually exclusive. A given slot specification can have only one of these.

10.5 Allocation of slots

Each slot has a particular kind of **allocation**. The allocation of a slot determines where the storage for the slot's value is allocated, and it determines which instances share the value of the slot. There are four kinds of allocation:

Instance — Each instance allocates storage for the slot, and each instance of the class that defines the slot has its own value for the slot. Changing a slot in one instance does not affect the value of the same slot in a different instance. Instance allocation is the default, and is the most commonly used kind of allocation.

Virtual — No storage is allocated for the slot. You must provide a getter method that computes the value of the virtual slot. See Section 10.6.

Class — The class that defines the slot allocates storage for the slot. Instances of the class that defines the slot and instances of all that class's subclasses see the same value for the slot.

That is, all general instances of the class share the value for the slot.

Each-subclass — The class that defines the slot and each of its subclasses allocate storage for the slot. Thus, if the class that defines the slot has four subclasses, the slot is allocated in five places. All the direct instances of each class share a value for the slot.

We can give an example of an each-subclass slot by defining a **<vehicle>** class:

```
define class <vehicle> (<physical-object>)
  // Every vehicle has a unique identification code
  slot vehicle-id :: <string>, required-init-keyword: id:;
  // The normal operating speed of this class of vehicle
  each-subclass slot cruising-speed :: <integer>;
end class <vehicle>;
```

The slot **cruising-speed** is defined with the **each-subclass** slot allocation. We use **each-subclass** allocation to express that, for example, all instances of Boeing 747 aircraft share a particular cruising speed, and all instances of McDonnell Douglas MD-80 aircraft share a particular cruising speed, but the cruising speed of 747s does not need to be the same as the cruising speeds of MD-80s.

10.6 Virtual slots

Virtual slots are useful when there is information conceptually associated with an object that is better computed than stored in an ordinary slot. By using a virtual slot instead of writing a method, you make the information appear like a slot to the callers of the getter. The information appears like a slot because the caller cannot distinguish the getter of a virtual slot from a getter of an ordinary slot. In both cases, the getter takes a single required argument — the instance — and returns a single value.

A virtual slot does not occupy storage; instead, its value is computed. When you define a virtual slot, Dylan defines a generic function for the getter and setter. You must define a getter method to return the value of the virtual slot. Unlike those of other slots, the value of a virtual slot can change without a setter being called, because that value is computed, rather than stored. You can optionally define a setter method. If you want to initialize a virtual slot when you create an instance, you can define an **initialize** method.

We can use virtual slots to control the access to a slot. For example, we want to ensure that the value of the **direction** slot is north or south for **<latitude>**, and is east or west for **<longitude>**. (An alternative technique is to use enumeration types, as shown in Section 19.5, page 318.) To enforce this restriction, we must

- Check the value when the setter method is invoked. In this section, we show how to do this check using a virtual slot. We also show how to use symbols, instead of strings, to represent north, south, east, and west.
- Check the value of the **direction** slot when an instance is created and initialized. We do that checking in Section 10.6.3.

We redefine the **<directed-angle>** class to include a virtual slot and an ordinary slot:

```
define abstract class <directed-angle> (<angle>)
  virtual slot direction :: <symbol>;
  slot internal-direction :: <symbol>;
end class <directed-angle>;
```

We define the slot **direction** with the **virtual slot allocation**. Notice that the slot's allocation appears before the name of the slot (as contrasted with slot options, which appear after the name of the slot).

In the **<directed-angle>** class, we use the slot **internal-direction** to store the direction. We shall provide a setter method for the virtual slot **direction** that checks the validity of the value of the direction before storing the value in the **internal-direction** slot.

10.6.1 Symbols

Symbols are much like strings. A **symbol** is an instance of the built-in class **<symbol>**. The key difference between strings and symbols lies in the way similarity (as tested by **=**) and identity (as tested by **==**) are defined for each of them. Two string operands can be similar but not identical. However, two symbol operands that are similar are always identical — that is, they always refer to the same object.

There are two reasons to use symbols in certain cases where you might consider using strings. First, symbol comparison is not case sensitive. Second, comparison of two symbols is much faster than is comparison of two strings, because symbols are compared by identity, and strings are usually compared element by element.

In the **<directed-angle>** class, we define the type of the two slots as **<symbol>**, instead of **<string>**, which we used in previous versions of this class. If we use strings, then when we checked whether the direction slot of a latitude was **"north"** or **"south"**, we would have to worry about uppercase versus lowercase. For example, we would have to decide whether each of these were valid values: **"north"**, **"NORTH"**, **"North"**, **"NOrth"**, and so on. We simplify that decision by using the **<symbol>** type instead of **<string>**.

There are two equivalent syntaxes for specifying symbols:

- Examples of use of the keyword syntax are: **north:** and **south:**.
- Examples of use of the hash syntax are: **#"north"** and **#"south"**.

Here, we show that symbol comparison is not case sensitive:

```
? #"NORTH" == #"North";
#t
```

Here, we show that the two syntaxes are equivalent:

```
? north: == #"norTH";
#t
```

It is our convention in this book to reserve the keyword syntax for keyword parameters, and otherwise to use the hash syntax. For example, we would give the call:

```
make(<latitude>, direction: #"north")
```

instead of the call:

```
make(<latitude>, direction: north:)
```

10.6.2 Getter and setter methods for a virtual slot

Here is the getter method for the virtual slot **direction**:

```
// Method 1
define method direction (angle :: <directed-angle>) => (dir :: <symbol>)
  angle.internal-direction;
end method direction;
```

Here are the setter methods for the virtual slot **direction**:

```
// Method 2
define method direction-setter
    (dir :: <symbol>, angle :: <directed-angle>) => (new-dir :: <symbol>)
  angle.internal-direction := dir;
end method direction-setter;

// Method 3
define method direction-setter
    (dir :: <symbol>, latitude :: <latitude>) => (new-dir :: <symbol>)
  if (dir == #"north" | dir == #"south")
    next-method();
  else
    error("%= is not north or south", dir);
  end if;
end method direction-setter;

// Method 4
define method direction-setter
    (dir :: <symbol>, longitude :: <longitude>) => (new-dir :: <symbol>)
  if (dir == #"east" | dir == #"west")
    next-method();
  else
    error("%= is not east or west", dir);
  end if;
end method direction-setter;
```

The preceding methods work as follows:

- When you call **direction** on an instance of **<directed-angle>** or any of its subclasses, method 1 is invoked. Method 1 calls the getter **internal-direction**, and returns the value of the **internal-direction** slot.
- When you call **direction-setter** on a direct instance of **<latitude>**, method 3 is invoked. Method 3 checks that the direction is valid for latitude; if it finds that the direction is valid, it calls **next-method**, which invokes method 2. Method 2 stores the direction in the **internal-direction** slot.
- When you call **direction-setter** on a direct instance of **<longitude>**, method 4 is called. Method 4 checks that the direction is valid for longitude; if it finds that the direction is valid, it calls **next-method**, which invokes method 2. Method 2 stores the direction in the **internal-direction** slot.
- When you call **direction-setter** on a direct instance of **<directed-angle>**, method 2 is invoked. Method 2 stores the direction in the **internal-direction** slot.

In these methods, we use **dir**, rather than **direction**, as the name of the parameter that represents direction. Recall that **direction** is the name of a getter. Although we technically could use **direction** as the parameter name in these methods (because we do not call the **direction** getter in the bodies), **direction** as a parameter name might be confusing to other people reading the code.

The **error** function signals an error. For more information about signaling and handling errors, see Chapter 20, *Exceptions*.

The **direction-setter** methods check the direction when the setter is called. In Section 10.6.3, we check the direction when an instance is made.

10.6.3 Initialize method for a virtual slot

We define the **initialize** method:

```
define method initialize (angle :: <directed-angle>, #key direction: dir) //1
  next-method();                                                          //2
  angle.direction := dir;                                                 //3
end method initialize;                                                    //4
```

For keyword parameters, the name of the keyword that you supply to **make** is normally the same name as the parameter that is initialized within the body. In this case, we want to avoid confusion between the getter **direction** and the keyword parameter **direction:**, so we use **dir** as the name of the keyword parameter for the **initialize** method. When you call **make**, you use the **direction:** keyword. However, within this method, the parameter is named **dir**.

Line 3 calls the setter for the **direction** slot. We defined the methods for **direction-setter** in Section 10.6.2. If the argument is a latitude, then method 3 is invoked to check the value. If the argument is a longitude, then method 4 is invoked to check the value.

We can create a new instance of **<absolute-position>**.

```
? define variable *my-absolute-position* =
    make(<absolute-position>,
         latitude:
           make(<latitude>,
                total-seconds: encode-total-seconds(42, 19, 34),
                direction: #"north"),
         longitude:
           make(<longitude>,
                total-seconds: encode-total-seconds(70, 56, 26),
                direction: #"west"));
```

The preceding example works, because the values for direction are appropriate for latitude and longitude. The following example shows what happens when the direction is not valid when an instance is created:

```
? make(<latitude>, direction: #"nooth");
ERROR: nooth is not north or south
```

The following example shows what happens when the direction is not valid when the **direction** setter is used:

```
? begin
    let my-longitude = make(<longitude>, direction: #"east");
    my-longitude.direction := #"north";
  end;
ERROR: north is not east or west
```

10.7 Summary

In this chapter, we covered the following:

- We described techniques for initializing slots; see Table 10.1.
- We discussed the syntax of calling getters and setters; see Table 10.2.
- We showed how to define methods for getters and setters.
- We showed how and why you can use symbols instead of strings.
- We described the different kinds of slot allocation; see Table 10.3.

Technique	Summary
initialize method	You can define a method for **initialize** for a class to perform any actions to initialize the instance. The **make** function calls the **initialize** generic function after **make** creates an instance and supplies those initial slot values that it can. If you need to do any complex computation to determine and set the value of a slot, you can do it in an **initialize** method.

Table 10.1 Summary of slot-initialization techniques.

Technique	Summary
Init keyword	You can use the **`init-keyword:`** slot option to declare an optional keyword argument, or the **`required-init-keyword:`** slot option to declare a required keyword argument for **`make`** when you create an instance of the class. The value of the keyword argument becomes the value of the slot.
Init value	You can use the **`init-value:`** slot option to give a default initial value for the slot. This option specifies an expression that is evaluated once, before the first instance of the class is made, to yield a value. Every time an instance is made and the slot needs a default value, this same value is used as the default. The slot receives its default initial value when no init keyword is defined, or when the caller does not supply the init-keyword argument to **`make`**.
Init function	You can use the **`init-function:`** slot option to provide a function that returns a default value. This option specifies an expression that is evaluated once, before the first instance of the class is made, to yield a function. The function must have no required arguments and must return at least one value. Every time that an instance is made and the slot needs a default value, this function is called with no arguments, and the value that it returns is used as the default. The slot receives its default initial value when no init keyword is defined or when the caller does not supply the init-keyword argument to **`make`**.
Init expression	You can use an init expression to provide an expression that yields a default value. Every time that an instance is made and the slot needs a default value, this expression is evaluated, and its value is used as the default. The slot receives its default initial value when no init keyword is defined, or when the caller does not supply the init-keyword argument to **`make`**.

Table 10.1 Summary of slot-initialization techniques. *(continued)*

Call	Translation
object`.`*function-name*	*function-name*`(`*object*`)`
`*my-time-of-day*.total-seconds;`	`total-seconds(*my-time-of-day*);`
object`.`*name* `:=` *new-value*`;`	*name*`-setter(`*new-value*`,` *object*`);`
name`(`*object*`)` := *new-value*;	*name*`-setter(`*new-value*`,` *object*`);`
`*my-time-of-day*.total-seconds := 0;`	`total-seconds-setter (0, *my-time-of-day*);`
`total-seconds(*my-time-of-day*) := 0;`	`total-seconds-setter(0, *my-time-of-day*);`

Table 10.2 Syntax of calling getters and setters.

Allocation	Summary
Instance	Each instance allocates storage for the slot, and each instance of the class that defines the slot has its own value of the slot. Instance allocation is the default.
Virtual	No storage is allocated for the slot. You must provide a getter method that computes the value of the virtual slot.
Class	The class that defines the slot allocates storage for the slot. All general instances of the class share the value of the slot.
Each-subclass	The class that defines the slot and each of its subclasses allocate storage for the slot. All the direct instances of each class share the value of the slot.

Table 10.3 Summary of slot allocations.

11

Collections and Control Flow

A **collection** is a kind of container that can hold zero or more objects. In this chapter, we illustrate several useful built-in collections including strings, lists, vectors, arrays, and tables.

In Dylan, a collection is an instance of the built-in class **`<collection>`**. Dylan provides a rich set of collection classes, and a rich set of generic functions to iterate over and to manipulate instances of those classes. In addition to using the built-in collection classes, you can define new collection classes. We present an example of defining a new collection class in Chapter 16, *Definition of a New Collection*.

Control-flow functions enable you to alter the default (sequential) order of statement execution, including performing iteration. Dylan provides several ways of branching to different code depending on the value of one or more tests, as well as iterating over ranges of numbers and elements of collections.

In this chapter, we present collections and control flow together, because often Dylan control-flow constructs are used to operate on collections.

11.1 Built-in collection classes

Figure 11.1 shows the most common Dylan collection classes.

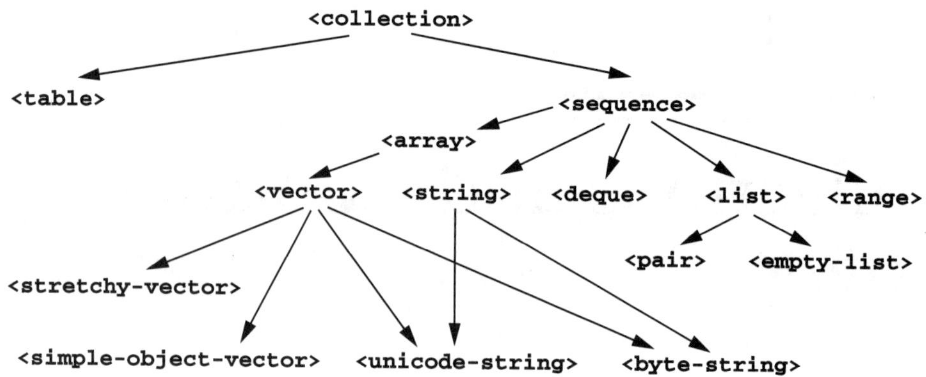

Figure 11.1 Built-in collection classes.

A collection holds a group of objects, called **elements**. Each element is associated with a key. Each class of collection can have different restrictions on keys or elements.

Sequences are an important subclass of collections. Sequences restrict their keys to be nonnegative integers starting at 0, and increasing by one for each additional value in the collection. Arrays, vectors, strings, and lists are sequences. Instances of **<string>** are sequences that can hold only characters. You can access instances of **<array>** using several subscripts. Instances of **<vector>** are one-dimensional arrays. Instances of **<simple-object-vector>** can hold any kind of Dylan object. Instances of most subclasses of **<vector>** cannot change size; the exception is instances of **<stretchy-vector>**.

11.2 Basic use of collections

In Sections 11.2.1 through 11.2.3, we show how to create collections, and how to access the elements of a collection.

11.2.1 Creation of strings and access to elements

First, we define a variable, initializing it with a string:

```
? define variable *greeting* = "Hello, world.";

? *greeting*;
"Hello, world."
```

We can access elements of the string:

```
? *greeting*[0];
'H'

? *greeting*[1];
'e'
```

The syntax **`*greeting*[n]`** refers to the *n*th element of the string in **`*greeting*`**. You can use this syntax to access any element of any collection. In Dylan, double quotes are used to enclose literal strings, and single quotes are used to enclose characters.

We can use the assignment operator to change an element of a string:

```
? *greeting* := copy-sequence(*greeting*);
"Hello, world."

? *greeting*[0] := 'j';
'j'

? *greeting*;
"jello, world."
```

We copied the greeting before modifying it, because modifying a literal constant is an error. A **literal constant** is an object whose contents are known completely at compile time. Dylan has a special syntax for each class of literal constant, so that they can be identified easily. The literal constant **`"Hello, world."`**, which is used to initialize the **`*greeting*`** variable, is part of the program executable, and is allocated when you compile the program.

The **`copy-sequence`** generic function returns a new collection with the same elements as its argument. The **`copy-sequence`** function creates the copy at run time, so modification of its results is permitted, because such changes do not alter the program itself. Note that, although the listener presents all objects in literal-constant syntax, not everything displayed by the listener is a literal constant.

The square-bracket syntax is an abbreviation for calling the generic function **`element`**. The following examples are equivalent:

```
? *greeting*[0];
'j'

? element(*greeting*, 0);
'j'
```

You can use either the square-bracket syntax or the **element** generic function on any collection. You must be careful if you use **element** as a local variable, however, because doing so will interfere with its use as a generic function, including the use of the square-bracket abbreviation.

11.2.2 Creation of vectors and access to elements

There are several ways to create collections. One way is to create a collection by using **make**. For example, here we create a vector that contains two elements:

```
? define variable *my-vector* = make(<vector>, size: 2);
```

We can change the first and second elements:

```
? *my-vector*[0] := 5;
5

? *my-vector*[1] := 3;
3

? *my-vector*;
#[5, 3]
```

If you want to create a sequence of a certain size, with every element having the same value, you can specify a **fill** keyword argument to **make**. The default value for the **fill** keyword parameter is **#f**. Thus, if you had read an element of ***my-vector*** before you wrote numbers into it, you would have received **#f**.

We can create and initialize a vector to different values all at once by using a built-in constructor. A **constructor** is a function that creates an instance; using it is a shorthand for calling **make**. Here, we use the **vector** constructor function to create a vector and to initialize it with data.

```
? define variable *my-vector* = vector(5, 3);

? *my-vector*;
#[5, 3]
```

As we saw in Section 11.2.1, certain collections have a literal syntax that enables you to specify a particular data structure as part of the program:

```
? define variable *my-vector* = #[5, 3];

? *my-vector*;
#[5, 3]
```

Figure 11.2 shows how you can picture the vector that we just created.

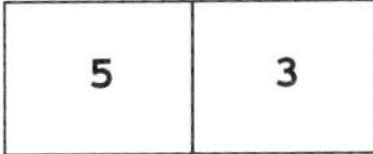

Figure 11.2 Diagram of the vector `#[5, 3]`.

You might think that `*my-vector*` is a direct instance of `<vector>`, but it is not: The `<vector>` class is abstract, but instantiable. When you use the `vector` function, or use `make` with `<vector>`, the result is a general instance of `<simple-object-vector>`. You specify the size of a `<simple-object-vector>` when you create one, and you cannot change that size later. If you need a vector that can change size, use the `<stretchy-vector>` class. See Section 16.1.1, page 246, for an example that uses stretchy vectors.

11.2.3 Creation of lists and access to elements

Lists are similar in purpose to vectors: Each one can store an ordered sequence of objects. Lists differ from vectors in that it is easy to add and remove elements from lists, especially at the front. In general, if the number of elements in a sequence will remain constant, lists are less efficient than vectors are.

Each element of a list is stored in a **pair**. A pair has two parts — a head and a tail. Typically, the head of a pair refers to an element, and the tail refers to the pair that holds the next element of the list. Normally, the final tail of the list is the empty list, represented by `#()`. Elements of lists can be any kind of object, including, of course, lists.

The `list` constructor function creates a list whose elements are the arguments provided:

```
? list(4, 5, 6);
#(4, 5, 6)
```

Figure 11.3 is a diagram of the list that we just created.

We can create a similar list by using the `pair` function, which creates one pair of the list at a time:

```
? pair(4, pair(5, pair(6, #())));
#(4, 5, 6)
```

As you can see, using `list` instead of `pair`, in this case, is much clearer. Note that Dylan provides functions called `head` and `tail`, which operate on lists:

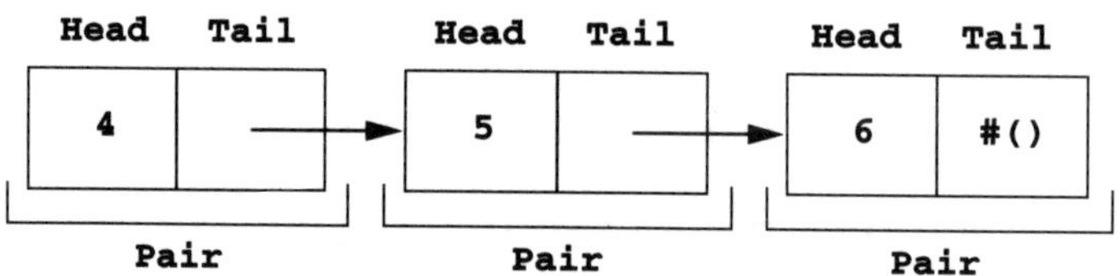

Figure 11.3 Diagram of the list `#(4, 5, 6)`.

```
? head(#(4, 5, 6));
4

? tail(#(4, 5, 6));
#(5, 6)

? tail(tail(#(4, 5, 6)));
#(6)
```

A reference to the first pair of a list is exactly the same as a reference to the entire list.

We use **`head`** and **`tail`** when we define a method for copying lists in Section 11.3.3. We use **`pair`** in a method that copies lists recursively in Section 11.3.6.

11.3 Iteration over a sequence

In the examples in Sections 11.3.1 through 11.3.9, we show how to process each element of a sequence using different techniques.

11.3.1 Building our own `copy-sequence`

How would we write our own **`copy-sequence`** function, if Dylan did not already provide one? There are many possible approaches. One way would be to use a **`while`** loop. A **`while`** loop has a **test expression** (surrounded by parentheses) and a **body**. As long as the value of the test expression is true, the body will be executed repeatedly.

```
define method my-copy-sequence
    (old-sequence :: <sequence>) => (new-sequence :: <sequence>)
  let seq-size = old-sequence.size;
  let new-sequence = make(type-for-copy(old-sequence), size: seq-size);
  let index = 0;
  while (index < seq-size)
    new-sequence[index] := old-sequence[index];
    index := index + 1;
  end while;
  new-sequence;
end method my-copy-sequence;
```

The method **my-copy-sequence** makes a new sequence of the same size as its argument, then iterates over all the elements of the argument, storing each element of the sequence into the appropriate element of the new sequence. The **size** generic function returns the number of elements in a collection. In this example, the **while** loop terminates when **index** reaches the size of the sequence.

The **type-for-copy** generic function returns an appropriate class for **make**, given an object that you wish to copy. For most collections, **type-for-copy** just returns the class of the collection provided.

11.3.2 Iteration with for

We can use the **for** to express concisely ia loop that increments a variable until a limit is reached.

```
define method my-copy-sequence
    (old-sequence :: <sequence>) => (new-sequence :: <sequence>)
  let new-sequence
    = make(type-for-copy(old-sequence), size: old-sequence.size);
  for (index from 0 below old-sequence.size)          // Iteration clause
    new-sequence[index] := old-sequence[index];       // Body
  end for;                                            // End of body
  new-sequence;
end method my-copy-sequence;
```

In the preceding example, the body is executed **old-sequence.size** times, with **index** bound to zero first, then rebound to one more than the previous value of **index** each time through the loop. The variable **index** is defined only within the body of the **for** iteration construct. The body of the **for** iteration construct begins after the iteration clause(s), and finishes with the matching **end**. For the **while** iteration construct shown in Section 11.3.1, the body starts after the predicate and finishes with the matching **end**.

The **`for`** loop can have many different kinds of iteration clauses. In this section, we have shown a simple iteration over a series of numbers. In Section 11.3.3, we use clauses that bind variables to initial values for the first time through a loop, and use expressions to rebind the variables for the second and subsequent times through the loop. We also demonstrate a clause that permits iteration to continue until an expression is true, both in Section 11.3.3 and Section 16.1.3, page 248.

The **`for`** loop has a simple type of iteration clause that we can use to iterate over any Dylan collection. The airport example in Section 17.2.2, page 257, demonstrates iteration over vectors using this kind of iteration clause.

11.3.3 Lists and efficiency

The **`my-copy-sequence`** method in Section 11.3.2 works efficiently for vectors. It does so because Dylan can store and retrieve arbitrary elements of vectors, and can determine the size of vectors in constant time.

Lists are quite a different data structure from vectors. Accessing elements and determining the size of a list takes linear time. Thus, you can access the thousandth element of a vector or string in the same amount of time as you can access the first element of a vector or string; when you uses lists, however, it takes about 1000 times longer to access the thousandth element than to access the first element. The difference in access times occurs because Dylan must walk over almost 1000 pairs to get to the thousandth pair, and thus get to the thousandth element of the list. Although the method defined in Section 11.3.2 can copy lists, it will be excessively slow, especially for long lists.

We would like to provide a special method for copying lists that uses a more efficient algorithm. In particular, we want to walk over the provided list element by element, without having to retrace over elements of the list that we have already copied.

```
// Assumes that old-list is a proper list (that is, it ends with #())
// and is not circular
define method my-copy-sequence (old-list :: <list>) => (new-list :: <list>)
  let new-list = make(<list>, size: old-list.size);
  for (old = old-list then old.tail,
       new = new-list then new.tail,
       until: empty?(old))
    new.head := old.head;
  end for;
  new-list;
end method my-copy-sequence;
```

First, **my-copy-sequence** makes a new list that is the same length as the old one. Next, the **for** iterator is used to bind the variables **old** and **new** to **old-list** and **new-list**, respectively. Then, the **for** iterator executes the **until:** expression to determine whether it is time to terminate the loop. If the **until:** expression returns true, then the **for** loop terminates, and the newly created list is returned from **my-copy-sequence**. Otherwise, the body of the **for** loop is executed — the body stores the head of the first pair in **old** into the head of the first pair in **new**. The result of that action is that the first element of **new** is indentical to the first element of **old**. For this iteration, that action causes the first element of **new-list** to be identical to the first element of **old-list**. In subsequent iterations, the body will access elements 1 closer to the end of the list. It will do so because, after the body is executed, the **for** iterator loops back to the iterator clauses, where the **then** clauses bind **old** to all but the first pair of **old**, and bind **new** to all but the first pair of **new**. The termination check occurs again, with the same consequences, depending on the value of the **until:** expression. Iteration then continues just like the second time through the loop until the end of **old** is reached.

In this method, we never have to search for the current spot of the old list that we are copying, or to search for the end of the new list that we are building. The variables **old** and **new** track exactly which pairs in the iteration to access, and that tracking saves a considerable amount of time for large lists. When the iteration is finished, **my-copy-sequence** returns the new list.

11.3.4 Polymorphism

An important advantage of programming in Dylan is that we can provide a general method for copying a sequence (as shown in Section 11.3.2), and also can provide special copying methods for particular subclasses of sequences (as shown in Section 11.3.3). Method dispatch takes care of picking the best method for the argument. Callers of **my-copy-sequence** do not need to worry about any performance optimizations that we have installed for lists. They simply use **my-copy-sequence** for lists, just as they would for any other sequence. This polymorphism can be useful for keeping interfaces between components of a program simple and extensible.

11.3.5 Mapping functions

Iterating over all the elements of a collection is a common idiom, and Dylan provides several different mapping functions that accomplish these kinds of iterations in different ways. In the following example, we redefine the **my-copy-sequence** method originally defined in Section 11.3.3. Here, we use the **do** iteration construct, instead of a **for** loop.

```
// Assumes that old-list is a proper list (that is, it ends with #())
// and is not circular
define method my-copy-sequence (old-list :: <list>) => (new-list :: <list>)
  let new-list = make(<list>, size: old-list.size);
  // Remember the pair of the copy that we are initializing
  let current-pair = new-list;
    // Iterate over all the elements of the existing list, making new pairs,
    // and splicing them into the end of the copy that we are building
  do(method (old-element)
       current-pair.head := old-element;
       current-pair := current-pair.tail;
     end method,
     old-list);
  new-list;
end method my-copy-sequence;
```

The **do** mapping function takes a function and one or more collections, and calls the function on each element of each collection. The function should take one argument if you provide **do** with one collection, two arguments if you provide two collections, and so on. The result of calling the function is ignored, and **do** itself returns no meaningful value. The **do** function is useful only if the method that you provide accomplishes a valuable side effect. In the preceding example, the supplied method stores an element of the old list into the head of the current pair of the new list, and moves to the next pair of the new list. Note that this method is actually a closure, which closes over the **current-pair** local variable. See Section 12.3.6, page 183, for more information about closures.

11.3.6 A recursive list copier

In many situations, the most concise way to manipulate lists (and other treelike structures) is to use recursion. In **recursion**, a function calls itself, directly or indirectly. In the following example, we redefine the `my-copy-sequence` method for lists to use recursion instead of iteration.

```
define method my-copy-sequence (old-list :: <list>) => (new-list :: <list>)
  if (empty?(old-list))
    #();
  else
    pair(old-list.head, my-copy-sequence(old-list.tail));
  end if;
end method my-copy-sequence;
```

Note that recursion can be just as efficient as iteration. For example, consider the function `my-reverse`, which creates a new list with elements in the reverse order from the list you supply.

```
define method my-reverse (old-list :: <list>) => (reversed-list :: <list>)
  local method rev (old :: <list>, results :: <list>)
    if (empty?(old)) results else rev(old.tail, pair(old.head, results)) end;
  end method;
  rev(old-list, #());
end method my-reverse;
```

The `local method` declaration inside the `my-reverse` method defines a function that is bound to the name `rev` only within a scope of the body of `my-reverse`. This declaration is different from `define method`, which creates module bindings that can be accessed outside the lexical scope of where they are defined.

The local method `rev` calls itself as the last expression in its body. Thus, the `rev` method can be optimized by the Dylan compiler into code that is exactly as efficient as if it was written with iteration.

Alternative ways of defining the `my-reverse` function are discussed in Section 11.4.1.

11.3.7 Using `map` and `curry`

Perhaps the easiest way to implement our simple sequence copier is to use the `map` function. The `map` function takes the same arguments as does `do`. However, instead of ignoring the return value of the function that you provide, `map` gathers into a new collection all the results of calling the provided function. The new collection will be an instance of the **type-for-copy** of the first collection argument to **map**.

```
define method my-copy-sequence
    (old-sequence :: <sequence>) => (new-sequence :: <sequence>)
  map(identity, old-sequence);
end method my-copy-sequence;
```

The **identity** function simply returns its argument without making any changes. A more interesting example is to define a method that multiplies a number by each element of a vector, yielding a new vector with the products. Here is a sample call to **scalar-multiply**, which we define next:

```
? scalar-multiply(3, #[4, 5, 6]);
#[12, 15, 18]
```

Here is our definition of **scalar-multiply**, using **map**:

```
define method scalar-multiply
    (scalar :: <number>, old-vector :: <vector>) => (result :: <vector>)
  map(method (vector-element) scalar * vector-element end,
      old-vector);
end method scalar-multiply;
```

We use the **method** statement to create a kind of function (a closure) that multiplies **scalar** by an element of the vector provided by **map**. The **map** iterator then calls that function on each element of **old-vector**, collecting the results in a new sequence. A variant of **map**, called **map-into**, replaces elements in an existing collection, rather than creating a new collection for the results. See Section 16.1.2, page 247, for an example of the use of **map-into**.

We can define this method more succinctly using **curry**, which is a function that generates a function:

```
define method scalar-multiply
    (scalar :: <number>, old-vector :: <vector>) => (result :: <vector>)
  map(curry(\*, scalar), old-vector);
end method scalar-multiply;
```

The **curry** function in this example creates exactly the same method as the one that we created in the previous definition of **scalar-multiply**. That is, **curry(*, scalar)** builds a function that multiplies its argument by **scalar**. This generated function is then used by **map** to compute the value of each element of the new sequence.

Mapping functions such as **do** and **map** work well when you want to operate over the entire collection. The **map** function works well only if there is a one-to-one correspondence between input-collection sizes and output-collection size. However, the other techniques that we have presented, such as using **for** and **while**, can work better when you want to operate on only part of a sequence. In Section 11.3.8, we take another look at how a **for** loop can help us to solve the problem of iterating over only part of a collection.

11.3.8 A sequence copier that can copy a portion of a sequence

The **copy-sequence** generic function provided by Dylan actually takes keyword arguments that allow only a portion of the sequence to be copied. Here is an example:

```
? copy-sequence("airport", start: 3);
"port"

? copy-sequence("snow", start: 1, end: 3);
"no"
```

In the following, we use a **for** loop with two iteration clauses to implement the more flexible version of the general purpose **my-copy-sequence**:

```
define method my-copy-sequence
    (old-sequence :: <sequence>,
     #key start = 0, end: limit = old-sequence.size)
 => (new-sequence :: <sequence>)
  let new-sequence = make(type-for-copy(old-sequence), size: limit - start);
  for (source-index from start below limit,
       destination-index from 0)
    new-sequence[destination-index] := old-sequence[source-index];
  end for;
  new-sequence;
end method my-copy-sequence;
```

In the preceding example, we force the keyword parameter **end:** to bind the variable **limit**, rather than binding **end**. It is illegal to use **end** as a variable name, because **end** is one of a few reserved words in Dylan. In the body of the **for** loop, **source-index** will range from **start** to 1 less than **limit**, and **destination-index** will range from 0 to 1 less then **limit** minus **start**, which is the length of the new sequence being created.

11.3.9 Changes to a generic function's signature

Note that the **my-copy-sequence** method defined in Section 11.3.8 has a parameter list that is not congruent with the parameter list of the generic function. That is, that method accepts the **start:** and **end:** keyword arguments, when previously only required arguments were allowed for that generic function. We did not explicitly define the **my-copy-sequence** generic function; Dylan created the generic function implicitly, when we defined the first method for it, in Section 11.3.1. The generic function accepts two required parameters, and no keyword parameters.

When you need to change the signature of a generic function, you must change all the methods for that generic function to have a compatible signature. In our example, we would have to fix the **my-copy-sequence** method for lists to accept the **start:** and **end:** keyword arguments, and would have to change the methods to operate on only a portion of the list provided. For more information about the congruence rules for methods of a generic function, see Section 12.2.5, page 176.

11.4 Manipulation of collections

Dylan provides an extensive library of functions that manipulate collections. In this section, we explore how to build complex collection functions from simpler ones, using the control-flow functions already shown in this chapter.

11.4.1 Reversal of sequences

Dylan provides two generic functions for reversing sequences: **reverse**, and **reverse!**. They both achieve the same objective, but **reverse!** is allowed to modify its argument, whereas **reverse** never modifies its argument.

```
? reverse("lever");
"revel"

? define variable *switch* = vector("switch", "on");

? reverse(*switch*);
#["on", "switch"]

? *switch*;
#["switch", "on"]
```

```
? reverse!(*switch*);
#["on", "switch"]
```

After the call to **reverse!**, the value of ***switch*** is not defined. Only the return value from **reverse!** will be meaningful. If we want ***switch*** to contain the reversed sequence, we must instead write

```
? *switch* := reverse!(*switch*);
#["on", "switch"]

? *switch*;
#["on", "switch"]
```

Note that **reverse!** cannot change the object to which ***switch*** refers; however, **reverse!** is allowed to alter the contents of that object. Also note that **reverse!** may not return the same object as that you provide as its argument. Consider the case of using **reverse!** on a list to see how this behavior can be useful.

> **Convention:** Dylan has a convention of putting an exclamation point at the ends of the names of functions that can destructively modify their arguments. For example, **reverse!** takes a sequence, and returns a sequence that has the same elements but in reverse order. The **reverse!** generic function may change the sequence that is its argument. In contrast, the **reverse** generic function performs a similar operation, but does not destructively modify its argument. Setters are an exception to this convention: They modify their argument, but do not typically end with **!**.

How can we write our own version of **reverse** using the iteration techniques presented so far?

```
define method my-reverse (seq :: <sequence>) => (reversed-seq :: <sequence>)
  let reversed-seq = make(type-for-copy(seq), size: seq.size);
  for (destination-index from seq.size - 1 to 0 by -1,
       source-index from 0)
    reversed-seq[destination-index] := seq[source-index];
  end for;
  reversed-seq;
end method my-reverse;
```

Once again, this algorithm is fine for vectors and strings, but has poor performance for lists. Here is a special **my-reverse** method for lists:

```
define method my-reverse (old-list :: <list>) => (reversed-list :: <list>)
  let reversed-list = #();
  for (old-element in old-list)
    reversed-list := pair(old-element, reversed-list);
  end for;
  reversed-list;
end method my-reverse;
```

It is easy to build up a list from its end to its start, and that is exactly what we do in the preceding method. We start with the empty list, and add pairs to the reversed list whose heads are the elements of the argument. We follow the old list from its start to its end, while we build the new list from its end to its start, thus reversing the list.

It is important to remember that, even though we created a new sequence to contain the elements of the old sequence, we still share those old elements with the new sequence. If two elements of a collection refer to the same object, then modifying the element of one of the collections affects the value of the element of the other collection. We illustrate this behavior in Section 11.4.2.

11.4.2 Destructive operations and shared structure

Consider the following example, and Figures 11.4 and 11.5.

```
// Firste we construct a vector of two vectors
? define variable *switch-states*
    = vector(vector("switch", "on"), vector("switch", "off"));

? *switch-states*;
#[#["switch", "on"], #["switch", "off"]]

// Now, we reverse the vector, holding on to the result
? define variable *rev-switch-states* = my-reverse(*switch-states*);
```

At this point, the states of the variables and vectors correspond to Figure 11.4.

We examine the two sequences:

```
? *rev-switch-states*;
#[#["switch", "off"], #["switch", "on"]]

// Although *switch-states* and *rev-switch-states* are different vectors,
// they share elements
? *switch-states* == *rev-switch-states*;
#f
```

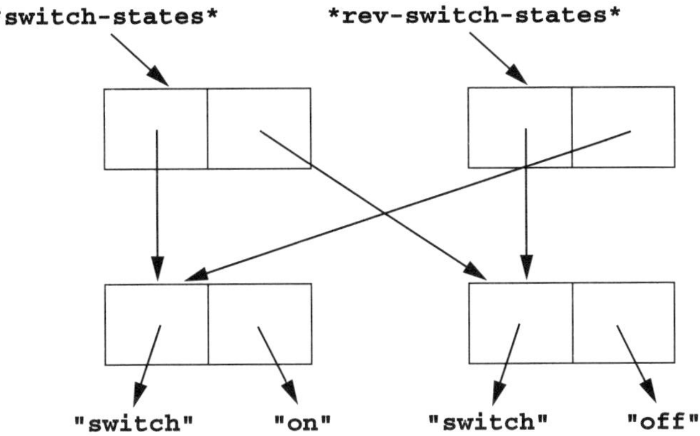

Figure 11.4 State before the element is changed.

Now, we change an element:

```
? *switch-states*[0] == *rev-switch-states*[1];
#t

// So, when we change an element in one, the same change occurs in the other
? (*switch-states*[0])[0] := "master switch";
"master switch"
```

At this point, the states of the variables and vectors correspond to Figure 11.5.

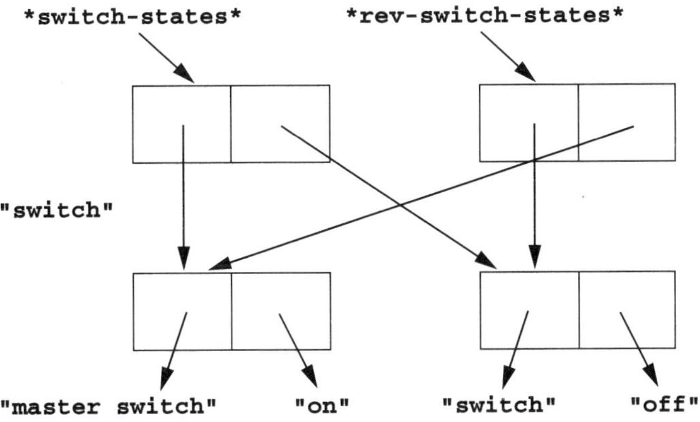

Figure 11.5 State after the element is changed.

We can look at the values of the variables:

```
? *switch-states*;
#[#["master switch", "on"], #["switch", "off"]]

? *rev-switch-states*;
#[#["switch", "off"], #["master switch", "on"]]
```

Each object pictured in Figures 11.4 and 11.5 is a vector. The strings in the figures are vectors, although we did not draw them as such, to keep the diagrams relatively simple. Variables are not objects in Dylan, but they are shown referring to objects. In Figure 11.5, the string **"switch"** is not referenced by any other object and is therefore garbage; eventually, it will be reclaimed by a garbage collector.

Changing an element of one collection can affect another collection if the two collections share elements. Two collections share an element if there is a value in one collection that is == (that is, identical) to a value in the other collection. Functions such as **copy-sequence** and **reverse** do only a **shallow copy** of their arguments: only the top level of the copy is new. Every other part is shared with the old sequence. Thus, it is important to take care when you modify objects that might be shared with other parts of your application. Using well-defined module boundaries that specify whether data structures can be modified by clients of the module can help you to keep application data consistent.

11.5 Conditional execution

In Sections 11.5.1 through 11.5.6, we consider ways to execute different code depending on the results of one or more tests.

11.5.1 if, else, and elseif

We showed the simplest use of **if** in Section 5.1.3, page 54. Consider the case where there is more than one test involved. Suppose that we want to write a method that describes a vote. Here are sample calls to **interpret-votes**:

```
? interpret-votes(yes: 4, no: 0);
"unanimously approved"

? interpret-votes(yes: 3, no: 1);
"approved"

? interpret-votes(yes: 2, no: 2);
"tie"
```

```
? interpret-votes(yes: 1, no: 3);
"not approved"
```

We can define the **interpret-votes** method using the **if** control structure and the **else** clause:

```
define method interpret-votes
    (#key yes :: <nonnegative-integer> = 0, no :: <nonnegative-integer> = 0)
 => (interpretation :: <string>)
  if (yes > 0 & no = 0)
    "unanimously approved";
  else if (yes > no)
    "approved";
  else if (yes = no)
    "tie";
  else
    "not approved";
  end if;
  end if;
  end if;
end method interpret-votes;
```

We defined the **<nonnegative-integer>** type in Section 9.2, page 110, using **limited**. Only positive integers and the integer 0 are instances of **<nonnegative-integer>**. We use this type in the **interpret-votes** method parameter list to ensure that no negative vote counts are accepted.

> **Quick summary of & infix operator**: *arg1* **&** *arg2*
>
> The infix operator **&** does the AND logical operation. If either or both of the arguments to the **&** operator are false, then **&** returns false.
>
> Note that the **&** operator is actually a control-flow operator. If the first argument to the **&** operator is false, then the value of the second argument is never computed, and false is returned. If the value of the first argument is true, then the value of the second argument is computed and returned.
>
> The | operator (logical OR) behaves in a similar manner, except that its second argument is computed and returned only if the first argument is false.

The syntax for the **if** control structure allows **elseif** clauses, which makes this style of conditionalization slightly more compact:

```
define method interpret-votes
    (#key yes :: <nonnegative-integer> = 0, no :: <nonnegative-integer> = 0)
 => (interpretation :: <string>)
  if (yes > 0 & no = 0)
    "unanimously approved";
  elseif (yes > no)
    "approved";
  elseif (yes = no)
    "tie";
  else
    "not approved";
  end if;
end method interpret-votes;
```

11.5.2 Branching with case

Dylan also provides the **case** control structure to give you an alternative way to express the branching style shown in Section 11.5.1:

```
define method interpret-votes
    (#key yes :: <nonnegative-integer> = 0, no :: <nonnegative-integer> = 0)
 => (interpretation :: <string>)
  case (yes > 0 & no = 0) => "unanimously approved";
       (yes > no)         => "approved";
       (yes = no)         => "tie";
       otherwise          => "not approved";
  end case;
end method interpret-votes;
```

The decision of whether to use **if** with **elseif** and **else**, as opposed to using **case**, is largely a matter of personal style.

11.5.3 Branching with select

In certain situations, you are working with a particular two-argument predicate (such as == or <). The value of the first argument to the predicate will always be the same, and you would like to perform different actions based on the second value. You can use both **if** and **case** to handle this situation, but the **select** control structure is more concise. The following example interprets traffic-light colors:

```
define method color-action
    (color :: <symbol>) => (action :: <symbol>)
  select (color)
    #"red"    => #"stop";
    #"yellow" => #"slow";
    #"green"  => #"go";
  end select;
end method color-action;
```

The **select** control structure uses **==** for the default predicate. For example, in the preceding **select** statement, the symbol **#"stop"** will be returned if **color == #"red"**. If you require a different predicate, use the **by** clause, as shown in the following example, which interprets age from a number representing years:

```
define method interpret-age
    (age :: <nonnegative-integer>) => (description :: <string>)
  select (age by \<)
    13        => "youngster";
    20        => "teenager";
    60        => "adult";
    otherwise => "senior";
  end select;
end method interpret-age;
```

The preceding method returns the string **"youngster"** when provided an age less then 13; returns **"teenager"** when the age is between 13 and 20; and returns **"adult"** when the age is between 20 and 60. In all other cases, it returns **"senior"**.

11.5.4 Tables: Dynamic associations

In Section 11.5.3, we saw how the **color-action** method associated traffic-light colors with actions by using **select**. These associations are *static*. They are determined at compile time, and you cannot change them without recompiling the **color-action** method. Sometimes, it is useful to associate one object with another *dynamically*, while the program is running. Collections are good data structures for this purpose. How could we rewrite **color-action** so that it uses a collection to associate colors with actions?

```
define variable *color-action-table* = make(<table>, size: 3);

*color-action-table*[#"red"]    := #"stop";
*color-action-table*[#"yellow"] := #"slow";
*color-action-table*[#"green"]  := #"go";
```

```
define method color-action (color :: <symbol>) => (action :: <symbol>)
  *color-action-table*[color];
end method color-action;
```

The tables provided by Dylan use **==** to compare keys.

During the execution of the program, we could add new associations to ***color-action-table***, or could change or remove existing associations. Tables grow as necessary to accommodate new associations that are added.

11.5.5 Search of arrays with `for` and `block`

Suppose that you wanted to search a two-dimensional array, and to return the first number greater than a given value.

```
define method find-larger-than
    (2d-array :: <array>, value :: <integer>)
 => (result :: type-union(singleton(#f), <integer>))
  let first-dimension = dimension(2d-array, 0);
  let second-dimension = dimension(2d-array, 1);
  block (return)
    for (i from 0 below first-dimension)
      for (j from 0 below second-dimension)
        if (2d-array[i, j] > value)
          return(2d-array[i, j]);
        end if;
      end for;
    end for;
    #f;
  end block;
end method find-larger-than;
```

In the preceding example, the **block** statement binds the variable **return** to a **nonlocal exit procedure**. If this exit procedure is called while the **block** is in effect, it will return immediately from the **block** statement, using any provided arguments as return values. Thus, if an element of **2d-array** is greater than **value**, then this element will be returned immediately from the **block**, and thus from the method. Array elements can be accessed with the square-bracket syntax, or with the function **aref**. (For more information about referencing elements of an array, see Section 12.1.3, page 164.) If the entire array is searched, and no element is found that is greater than **value**, then the **for** loops exit normally and the **block** statement returns the last value in the **block** body, which in this case is false. We use the **type-union** type-generating function to create a type that permits either false or an integer to be returned from this method.

11.5.6 Search of arrays with `find-key`

In Dylan, we can access multidimensional arrays as though they are linearized one-dimensional vectors by using the **`element`** generic function. Dylan provides a **`find-key`** generic function that uses **`element`** to find the index (or key) that corresponds to a desired value in a collection. Here, we rewrite **`find-larger-than`** to use **`find-key`**:

```
define method find-larger-than
    (array :: <array>, value :: <integer>)
 => (result :: type-union(singleton(#f), <integer>))
  let index
    = find-key(array, method (array-element) array-element > value end);
  index & array[index];
end method find-larger-than;
```

The **`find-key`** generic function searches an array, calling the function that we provided on each element. If our function ever returns true, **`find-key`** returns the linearized index of the array element containing the value. For a two-dimensional array, the linearized index is the index that would be the appropriate key of a one-dimensional array that we could construct by placing the rows of the two-dimensional array one after the other. Rows in a two-dimensional array are numbered with the first subscript, and the column within those rows is numbered by the second subscript.

If our function never returns true for any element, **`find-key`** returns false. In this example **`&`** is truly used as a control structure. If **`index`** is false, then **`&`** will return false without executing the array access. If **`index`** is true, then the array access occurs, and that is the value of the **`&`** expression, and thus the value returned from the method.

11.6 Summary

In this chapter, we covered the following:

- We showed a selection of built-in collection classes, including strings, lists, vectors, tables, and arrays.
- We showed various iteration facilities and control structures, including **`for`**, **`do`**, **`map`**, **`while`**, **`if`**, **`case`**, **`select`**, **`block`**, **`&`**, and **`|`**.
- We showed a simple example of recursion.

- We showed some basic collection functions: **`element`**, **`size`**, and **`find-key`**.
- We showed some basic sequence functions: **`copy-sequence`**, and **`reverse`**.
- We showed additional collection functions: **`head`**, **`tail`**, **`pair`**, **`list`**, and **`vector`**.
- We explored basic sequence algorithms, and found that, although the various sequence classes are related, algorithms that are efficient for one class of sequence may not be appropriate for a different class of sequence.
- We discussed destructive versus nondestructive functions.
- We demonstrated the **`curry`** function, which generates functions.
- We showed several examples of the use of closures as arguments to iterators.

12

Functions

Functions are ubiquitous in Dylan. Generic functions and methods — the two kinds of function — are the primary means of specialization. Many common operations, such as slot references and arithmetic operations, are accomplished through function calls. In Dylan, unlike in many languages, functions are first-class objects. They can be the values of variables or slots, arguments to other functions, or values returned by functions. Dylan has functions that build new functions out of existing functions. Much of the power of Dylan arises through its sophisticated treatment of functions.

This chapter discusses general aspects of the operation of functions in Dylan. It does not describe all aspects of functions. In particular, we discuss the process of method dispatch within generic functions elsewhere (see Sections 5.5, 6.2, 9.3, and 18.4). This chapter covers three main topics:

1. The syntax of function calls, including abbreviations for function calls
2. The function-calling protocol, and particularly the interaction between a function and its caller
3. The uses of functions as objects, including ways of creating and operating on functions

12.1 Function-calling syntax

This section describes the syntax of Dylan function calls. An explicit function call consists of the operand followed by the arguments enclosed in parentheses and separated by commas. Several other syntactic structures in Dylan are also abbreviations for function calls, including the following:

- Slot references
- References to elements of collections
- Most unary and binary operator calls
- Certain assignment operations

The remainder of this section describes these syntactic forms and the equivalent function calls. Unless otherwise noted, all expressions that make up any of these function calls are evaluated from left to right. (A notable exception is an expression containing the assignment operator, discussed in Section 12.1.6.) The common left-to-right rule makes it easy to understand the order of execution of Dylan code. But it also means that certain syntactic forms that we call *equivalent* — that is, syntactic forms that generally result in calls to the same function with the same arguments — differ in the order of evaluation of their components. The components can appear in different orders in otherwise equivalent syntactic forms. Usually, the order of evaluation makes no difference, and you can use whichever of the equivalent syntactic forms you find most convenient.

12.1.1 Explicit function calls

The Dylan syntax for an explicit function call has two parts:

1. The function to be called — This is an **operand** that is evaluated to yield the function itself. Usually, the operand is a reference to a variable or constant that names the function, although it can be any expression (except an operator call) whose value is a function. (For information on operator calls, see Sections 12.1.4 and 12.1.5.)
2. The arguments to which the function is applied — The arguments are represented by a series of expressions, enclosed in parentheses and separated by commas. Each expression is evaluated, and its value is passed to the function as an argument.

In the following function call, the function is the value of the variable **truncate/**; the two arguments are the value of the variable **n** and the number **3**:

```
truncate/(n, 3);
```

A function can be obtained in other ways: for example, it might be an element of an array, the value of a slot of an instance, or the value returned by a call to another function. The following example calls the function that is the element of an **operations** array designated by the constant **$trunc**:

```
operations[$trunc](n, 3);
```

12.1.2 Slot references

A slot reference is a reference to the value of a slot of an instance. The syntax for a slot reference has two parts, separated by a period:

- An operand whose value is the instance
- The name of the slot's getter generic function

In the following slot reference, the function **get-employee-named** returns an instance, which has a slot whose getter is named **employee-number**:

```
get-employee-named("Jane").employee-number;
```

Note that the operand that yields the instance can itself be a slot reference, so slot references can be chained:

```
plant.manager.employee-number;
```

Every slot value in Dylan is obtained by a call to the slot's getter generic function (although the compiler can often optimize this generic function call to a direct slot access). A slot reference is just an abbreviation for a function call. With one exception, the following examples are equivalent:

```
plant.manager;
manager(plant);
```

The one difference between these examples is that, in the first, **plant** is evaluated first, whereas in the second, **manager** is evaluated first.

In fact, you can use the slot-reference syntax for more than slot references. The object that is the value of the left side can be any object, and the function named by the right side can be any function that can take the object as an argument. The function named by the right side is always called with the object that is the value of the left side as its only argument. Thus, using the **plant.manager** syntax is just another way of calling the function named by **manager** with the object that is the value of **plant** as the only argument. The **plant** object does not have to have a **manager** slot.

In this book, we use slot-reference syntax for

- A call to a getter generic function for a slot
- A call to a function that takes one argument and returns one value that represents a property of an object

12.1.3 Element references

Collections in Dylan include such data structures as arrays, strings, lists, and tables. Each collection has a mapping from **keys** to **elements**. Dylan's syntax for referring to an element of a collection has two parts:

1. An operand whose value is the collection
2. An expression, in square brackets, whose value is the key that maps to the desired element of the collection

If the collection is a multidimensional array, the key expression in square brackets can be a series of expressions, separated by commas. Each expression yields the index for one dimension of the array. (Dylan array indices are zero based.)

The following example returns the first element of the array named by **my-array**:

```
my-array[0];
```

An element reference, like a slot reference, is an abbreviation for a function call. The generic function **element** takes a collection and a key as arguments, and returns the element of the collection that is associated with the given key. Except for the order of evaluation, the following examples are equivalent:

```
my-array[0];
element(my-array, 0);
```

For arrays of more than one dimension, the key expression in brackets is instead a comma-separated series of expressions. In this case, the element reference is an abbreviation for a call to the **aref** generic function. This function takes an array and any number of indices as arguments, and returns the element associated with the array indices. Except for the order of evaluation, the following examples are equivalent:

```
my-array[0, 2];
aref(my-array, 0, 2);
```

12.1.4 Unary operator calls

Dylan has two built-in unary operators, `-` and `~`. The syntax for a unary operator call has two parts:

1. The operator
2. An operand

The `-` operator performs the arithmetic negation of its operand, and the `~` operator performs the logical negation. Both operator calls are abbreviations for function calls. The following examples are equivalent:

```
- time-offset;
negative(time-offset);
```

The following examples also are equivalent:

```
~ test-condition(cond);
\~(test-condition(cond));
```

In the preceding example, we must escape `~` with `\` so that Dylan interprets `~` as a variable name, instead of as an operator. This syntax indicates an explicit call to the function that is the value of the variable named `~`.

12.1.5 Binary-operator calls

Dylan has 16 built-in binary operators, of the following kinds:

- Arithmetic operations: `+`, `-`, `*`, `/`, and `^`
- Comparisons: `=`, `==`, `<`, `>`, `<=`, `>=`, `~=`, and `~==`
- Logical operations: `&` and `|`
- Assignment: `:=`

The syntax for a binary-operator call has three parts:

1. An expression that serves as the first operand

2. The operator
3. An expression that serves as the second operand

All binary-operator calls, except those to the logical and assignment operators, are abbreviations for calls to functions that have the same names as do the operators. Except for the order of evaluation, the following examples are equivalent:

```
a + b;
\+(a, b);
```

The `&` and | operators are implemented as **macros**. (For information on macros, see Chapter 21, *Macros*.) In an expression that includes the `&` operator, if the first operand has a false value, the second operand is not evaluated. In an expression that includes the | operator, if the first operand has a true value, the second operand is not evaluated.

12.1.6 Assignment

The assignment binary operator, `:=`, also is implemented as a macro. An expression that includes this operator works in a special way.

The operand to the *right* of the operator is evaluated first. The result is the new value to be assigned.

The operand to the *left* of the operator determines the place to which the new value is assigned. This operand can have one of the following kinds of syntax:

Variable name — The variable name is not evaluated. Dylan assigns the new value to the variable.

Explicit function call — Dylan calls the function *name*-**`setter`**, where *name* is the name of the function in the function call. The first argument to *name*-**`setter`** is the new value, and the remaining arguments are the arguments to *name* in the original function call.

Slot reference — Dylan first converts the slot reference to the corresponding function call. Dylan then calls the function *name*-**`setter`** just as it would have if the slot reference had been an explicit function call.

Element reference — Dylan first converts the element reference to the corresponding function call, using **element** or **aref** as the name of the function, as appropriate. Dylan then calls the function **element-setter** or **aref-setter** just as it would have if the element reference had been an explicit function call.

Except for the order of evaluation and returned values, the following examples are equivalent:

```
*my-position*.distance := 3.0;
distance(*my-position*) := 3.0;
distance-setter(3.0, *my-position*);
```

The first two examples return **3.0**; the second returns whatever **distance-setter** returns. Usually, this value would be **3.0**. Note that, if **distance** is the name of a slot's getter, and if the slot is constant or has a setter with a name other than **distance-setter**, then the assignment operation results in an error.

Except for the order of evaluation and returned values, the following examples are equivalent:

```
vertices[2] := list(3.5, 4.5);
element(vertices, 2) := list(3.5, 4.5);
element-setter(list(3.5, 4.5), vertices, 2);
```

12.2 The function-calling protocol

We have seen that Dylan has two kinds of function: methods and generic functions. Both can be called; from the caller's point of view, the two are called in the same way. When a generic function is called, Dylan selects one of its methods to execute, in a process called method dispatch. This section discusses the interaction between a function and that function's caller, focusing on arguments, parameters, value declarations, and returned values. We discuss interactions between generic functions and their methods but do not describe the process of method dispatch. For information on method dispatch, see Section 5.5, page 63; Section 6.2, page 79; Section 9.3, page 111; and Section 18.4, page 300.

12.2.1 Parameters, arguments, and return values

In Dylan, a function is called with zero or more **arguments**. The function can perform computations, which may have side effects. It then **returns** zero or more **values** to its caller. Each argument and each returned value is an object.

A function has zero or more **parameters** that determine the number and types of arguments that the function takes. Following is a simplified description of what happens when a function is called (for a generic function, this description applies to the method that it invokes):

1. An implicit **body** is entered. A body establishes the scope for all local variables bound inside the body.
2. The parameters are matched with the arguments to the function.
3. A local variable is created with the name of each parameter.
4. Each parameter — that is, each local variable with the name of a parameter — is initialized, or bound, to one of the arguments. (In some cases, the parameter is bound to a list of arguments, or to a default value.)
5. The code that makes up the actual body of the function is executed.

A function can have a **value declaration** that determines the number and types of values the function returns. If there is no explicit declaration, a default declaration allows the function to return any number of values of any type. Following is a simplified description of what happens when a function returns (for a generic function, this description applies to the method that it invokes):

1. The values returned by the last expression in the function's implicit body are matched with the values declared in the value declaration.
2. The function's implicit body is exited, ending the scope of all local variables (including parameters) established in that body.
3. The values specified by the value declaration are returned to the caller of the function. (Depending on the value declaration, the number of values returned to the function's caller might be more or less than the number of values returned by the last expression in the function's body.)

Note these two important implications of the way that arguments are passed:

- All bindings of arguments to parameters are local to the body of the function called. Assignment to a parameter inside the called function's body does not affect any variables outside the body that have the same name.

  For example, consider these definitions:

```
define method calling-function ()
  let x = 1;
  let y = 2;
  format-out("In calling function, before call: x = %d, y = %d\n",
             x, y);
  called-function(x, y);
  format-out("In calling function, after call: x = %d, y = %d\n", x, y);
end method calling-function;

define method called-function (x, y)
  x := 3;
  y := 4;
  format-out("In called function, before return: x = %d, y = %d\n",
             x, y);
end method called-function;
```

  A call to **`calling-function`** produces the following output:

```
In calling function, before call: x = 1, y = 2
In called function, before return: x = 3, y = 4
In calling function, after call: x = 1, y = 2
```

- Although *parameters* are local to a function, all *arguments* and *return values* are shared between a function and its caller. If an argument or return value is a **mutable** object — one that can be changed — then any changes that a function makes to that object are visible to its caller.

  Consider the following definitions:

```
define class <test> (<object>)
  slot test-slot, required-init-keyword: test-slot:;
end class <test>;
```

```
define method calling-function ()
  let x = make(<test>, test-slot: "before");
  format-out("In calling function, before call: x.test-slot = %s\n",
             x.test-slot);
  called-function(x);
  format-out("In calling function, after call: x.test-slot = %s\n",
             x.test-slot);
end method calling-function;

define method called-function (x :: <test>)
  x.test-slot := "after";
  format-out("In called function, before return: x.test-slot = %s\n",
             x.test-slot);
end method called-function;
```

Note here that we have redefined the **calling-function** method, and have defined a new **called-function** method, which we first defined in the previous example. Our new **called-function** method has one parameter, whereas the previous method had two. The parameter list of this new method is not compatible with that of the previous method, and, if we actually tried to define the second **called-function** method, Dylan would signal an error. For more information on compatibility of parameter lists for generic functions and methods, see Section 12.2.5.

A call to **calling-function** now produces the following output:

```
In calling function, before call: x.test-slot = "before"
In called function, before return: x.test-slot = "after"
In calling function, after call: x.test-slot = "after"
```

In this case, **x** in the calling function and **x** in the called function are different variables. But the *values* of both variables are the same object: the instance of **<test>** that we make in the calling function. The change to the slot value of this object that we make in the called function is visible to the calling function.

It is equally proper to think of arguments that are **immutable**, like integers, as being shared between a function and its caller. By definition, however, a function cannot make any changes to such objects that are visible to the function's caller.

Comparison with C and C++: As in Dylan, the parameters of a C function are local to the body of the function, and assignment to a parameter does not affect the value of a variable that has the same name in the function's caller. But the relationship between **objects** and **values** is not the same in C and in Dylan. In C, a value can be an object (roughly meaning the contents of the object) or a **pointer** to an object (roughly meaning the location of the object in memory). The value of a parameter in C is always a copy of the corresponding argument. When a C structure is an argument to a function, the value of the corresponding parameter is a copy of the structure; it is not the structure itself. If the function changes the value of a member of this structure, the change is not visible to the caller, because the function is changing only its own copy of the structure. But if the argument is a pointer to a structure, the function can gain access to the caller's structure (by **dereferencing** the pointer). If the function changes the value of a member of such a structure by dereferencing the pointer, the change is visible to the caller.

In Dylan, a value is always an object, which has a unique identity. The value of a parameter is always the same object as the corresponding argument. When a function changes such an object (as by changing the value of a slot), the change is always visible to the caller. Dylan has no equivalent to C pointers.

In C++, a parameter declared using ordinary C syntax also receives a copy of a structure or an instance that is the corresponding argument. C++ has additional syntax for declaring that a parameter is a **reference** — essentially an implicit pointer — to the corresponding argument. In this case the argument is not copied, and if the function changes the object that the parameter refers to, the changes are visible to the caller. In some ways Dylan's argument-passing protocol is similar to C++ references.

In both C and C++, array arguments are always passed as pointers. In Dylan, arrays are instances of the `<array>` class, and array arguments are treated like all other arguments.

For more comparisons between Dylan and C objects, see Appendix B, *Dylan Object Model for C and C++ Programmers.*

12.2.2 Return and reception of multiple values

A Dylan function call — and, in general, a Dylan expression — can return any number of values, including none. The **values** function is the means of returning multiple values. This function takes zero or more arguments, and returns them as separate values.

Multiple values can be received as the initial values of local variables in a **let** declaration. If a **let** declaration contains multiple variables, they are matched with the values returned by the initialization expression, and each variable is bound to the corresponding value. The following example initializes **a** to **1** and **b** to **2**:

```
let (a, b) = values(1, 2);
```

The following example initializes **ans** to **2** and **rem** to **1** — the two values returned by this call to **truncate/**:

```
let (ans, rem) = truncate/(5, 2);
```

The variable list can also end with **#rest** followed by the name of a variable. In this case, the variable is initialized to a sequence. This sequence contains all the remaining values returned by the initialization expression. If there is no **#rest**, any excess values are discarded. If the number of variables in the **let** declaration is greater than the number of values returned, the remaining variables are initialized to **#f**. (But if the **let** declaration specifies a type for any of these variables, and if **#f** is not an instance of that type, then Dylan signals an error.)

Module variables and constants can also be initialized to multiple values. The variable list of a **define variable** or **define constant** definition can contain multiple variables, and can receive multiple values from its initialization expression in the same way as a **let** declaration.

12.2.3 Parameter lists

A function's parameter list is specified in the function definition. (If Dylan implicitly defines a function, such as the getter and setter functions for a slot, Dylan also defines the parameter list for that function.) In a function definition, the parameter list follows the function name and consists of zero or more parameter specifications, separated by commas and enclosed in parentheses. A parameter list can have three kinds of parameters:

1. **Required parameters** specify required arguments, or arguments that must be supplied when the function is called. All required parameters appear before other kinds of parameters in the parameter list.

2. A function can have at most one **rest parameter**, which allows the function to accept a variable number of arguments. The rest parameter is identified in the parameter list by `#rest` followed by the name of the parameter. When the function is called, all arguments that follow the required arguments are put into a sequence. This sequence is the initial value of the rest parameter in the function body.

3. **Keyword parameters** specify optional keyword arguments. In the parameter list, keyword parameters are identified by `#key` followed by the names of the parameters (and possibly by other information). Keyword parameters must follow all required parameters and the rest parameter (if any). When the function is called, the caller can supply any or none of the specified keyword arguments, in any order, after supplying all required arguments. The caller supplies each keyword argument as a symbol (usually in the form of the parameter name followed by a colon), followed by the argument value. This argument is the initial value of the corresponding keyword parameter in the function body.

The specification for each parameter in the parameter list includes the name of the parameter. In addition, a required parameter (or, for a method, a keyword parameter) can be **specialized** to correspond to an argument of a given type. The type specializer follows the parameter name and is identified by `::` followed by a type. When the function is called, the argument that corresponds to the parameter must be of the specified type, or Dylan signals an error. The default argument type is `<object>`.

The specification for a keyword parameter can have two additional pieces of information:

1. It may include a keyword for the caller to use in its argument list, if this keyword must be different from the parameter name. The keyword precedes the parameter name in the parameter list.

2. It may include a default value for the keyword argument, which is used if the caller does not supply that argument. The default expression appears at the end of the parameter specification, followed by `=`. If no default

expression is supplied and the caller does not supply the keyword argument, the argument's value is **#f**.

The following example shows how we could use a rest parameter to implement a function to sum an arbitrary number of values:

```
// Sum one or more values
define method sum (value, #rest more-values)
  for (next in more-values)
    value := value + next;
  end for;
  value;
end method sum;

? sum(3);
3

? sum(1, 2, 3, 4, 5);
15
```

In the preceding example, the **for** iteration statement performs the addition once for every element of **more-values**.

The following example shows how we could use keyword parameters in defining a method similar to **encode-total-seconds**:

```
// Convert days, hours, minutes, and seconds to seconds.
// Named (keyword) arguments are optional
define method convert-to-seconds
    (#key hours :: <integer> = 0, minutes :: <integer> = 0,
     seconds :: <integer> = 0) => (seconds :: <integer>)
  ((hours * 60) + minutes) * 60 + seconds;
end method convert-to-seconds;

? convert-to-seconds(minutes: 3, seconds: 9);
189

? convert-to-seconds(minutes: 1, hours: 2);
7260
```

Note from the preceding example that we can supply keyword arguments in any order. Note also that all keyword arguments are optional; however, if we try to call a function with a keyword argument that the function does not accept — such as **days:**, in this example — Dylan signals an error. For more information on function calls and keyword arguments, see Section 12.2.7, page 178.

Following are additional features and restrictions of keyword arguments:

- If a parameter list ends with **`#all-keys`** following **`#key`**, the function accepts (but ignores) any keyword argument. A parameter list can have specific keyword parameters and also end with **`#all-keys`**. In this case, the function accepts any keyword argument, and also has local variables whose values are the keyword-argument values (or their defaults) that correspond to the keyword parameters.
- If the parameter list of a method contains both **`#rest`** and **`#key`**, the sequence that is the value of the rest parameter contains alternating symbols and argument values representing the keyword arguments passed to the function. In this case, *all* optional arguments must be keyword arguments. A generic function's parameter list can have either **`#rest`** or **`#key`**, but cannot have both.
- Keyword parameters for a generic function cannot be specialized.

The restrictions on a generic function's parameter list have to do with parameter-list congruency and keyword-argument checking in generic function calls. For more information, see Sections 12.2.5 and 12.2.7.

12.2.4 Value declarations

A function definition's value declaration follows the parameter list and is preceded by **`=>`**. The syntax of a value declaration is similar to that of a parameter list. If the function returns no values, the value declaration is an empty set of parentheses. Otherwise, the declaration can contain separate declarations for all returned values, separated by commas. Each of these individual declarations consists of a name and, optionally, **`::`** followed by a type. The name does not specify a variable and has no use other than documentation. But the returned value that corresponds to the declaration must be of the declared type, or Dylan signals an error. The default return value type is **`<object>`**.

A value declaration can also end with **`#rest`** followed by a name and, optionally, **`::`** and a type. This declaration indicates that the function can return any number of additional arguments, each of which must be of the specified type.

If a function has no explicit value declaration, the default declaration is **`(#rest x :: <object>)`**. This declaration indicates that the function can return any number of arguments of any type.

The value declaration determines the number and types of values that the function returns, even if the last expression in the function's body returns a different number of values. If the function's body returns fewer values than are declared, the function defaults the remaining values to **`#f`** and returns them. (But if the value declaration specifies a type for any of these values, and if **`#f`** is not an instance of that type, Dylan signals an error.) If the function's body returns more values than are declared, the function returns the additional values if the declaration contains **`#rest`**; otherwise, the function discards the additional values.

12.2.5 Parameter-list congruence

A generic function and its methods must all have parameter lists that are compatible, or **congruent**. Following are the basic rules:

- A generic function and its methods must all have the same number of required arguments.
- The type of any given parameter in each method must be a subtype of the corresponding parameter in the generic function.
- If a generic function or any of its methods has only required arguments — that is, it has neither **`#rest`** nor **`#key`** in its parameter list — then the generic function and all its methods must have only required arguments.
- If a generic function or any of its methods accepts a variable number of arguments, but does not accept keyword arguments — that is, it has **`#rest`**, but does not have **`#key`**, in its parameter list — then the generic function and all its methods must accept a variable number of arguments, but must not accept keyword arguments.
- If a generic function or any of its methods accepts keyword arguments — that is, it has **`#key`** in its parameter list — then the generic function and all its methods must accept keyword arguments. For this rule, a generic function or method "accepts keyword arguments" even if its parameter list ends with just **`#key`**.
- If a generic function has any specific keyword parameters, then all its methods must have (at least) those specific keyword parameters. The appearance of **`#all-keys`** in a method's parameter list does not satisfy this requirement.

The following parameter lists are congruent, because both functions have only required arguments, they have the same number of required arguments, and the type of each method parameter is a subtype of the same parameter in the generic function:

```
define generic g (arg1 :: <complex>, arg2 :: <integer>);

define method g (arg1 :: <real>, arg2 :: <integer>)
  ...
end method g;
```

The following parameter lists are congruent, because both functions meet the tests for required arguments, both accept keyword arguments, and the generic function has no specific keyword parameters:

```
define generic g (arg1 :: <real>, #key);

define method g (arg1 :: <integer>, #key base :: <integer> = 10)
  ...
end method g;
```

The following parameter lists are not congruent, because the method's parameter list does not include the specific keyword **base** of the generic function, even though it does include **#all-keys**:

```
define generic g (arg1 :: <integer>, #key base);

define method g (arg1 :: <integer>, #key #all-keys)
  ...
end method g;
```

12.2.6 Return-value congruence

Like parameter lists, the value declarations of a generic function and that function's methods must be congruent. The rules depend on whether the generic function returns a fixed or a variable number of values:

- If the generic function returns a fixed number of values — that is, it does not have **#rest** in its value declaration — then its methods cannot have **#rest**, and must return the same number of required values as the generic function. For each method, the type of each returned value must be a subtype of the same returned value in the generic function.
- If the generic function returns a variable number of values — that is, it has **#rest** in its value declaration — then its methods can (but are not required to) have **#rest**, and must return at least as many required values as the generic function. For each method, the type of each returned value must be

a subtype of the same returned value in the generic function. If the method has more required returned values than the generic function, their types must all be subtypes of the generic function's **#rest** value.

The following value declarations are congruent, because the generic function implicitly returns any number of values of any type:

```
define generic g (arg1 :: <complex>, arg2 :: <integer>);

define method g
    (arg1 :: <real>, arg2 :: <integer>) => (result :: <real>)
  ...
end method g;
```

The following value declarations are not congruent, because the type of the method's returned value is not a subtype of the generic function's returned value:

```
define generic g
    (arg1 :: <complex>, arg2 :: <integer>) => (result :: <integer>);

define method g
    (arg1 :: <real>, arg2 :: <integer>) => (result :: <real>)
  ...
end method g;
```

12.2.7 Keyword-argument checking

When a function is called, Dylan determines which keyword arguments, if any, are permitted for that function call. The set of permitted keyword arguments depends on whether or not a generic function is being called:

- If a method is called directly, rather than through a generic function, the specific keywords in the method's parameter list are permitted. If the parameter list includes **#all-keys**, any keyword argument is permitted.
- If a generic function is called, all the specific keywords in the parameter lists of all **applicable** methods are permitted. If the parameter list of the generic function or of *any* applicable method includes **#all-keys**, any keyword argument is permitted.

When a generic function is called, one of its methods is **applicable** if every required argument is an instance of the type of the corresponding parameter of the method. For more information on applicable methods, see Section 5.5, page 63.

Consider the following definitions:

```
define generic g (arg1 :: <real>, #key);

// Method 1
define method g (arg1 :: <real>, #key real-key)
  ...
end method g;

// Method 2
define method g (arg1 :: <float>, #key float-key)
  ...
end method g;

// Method 3
define method g (arg1 :: <integer>, #key integer-key)
  ...
end method g;
```

Now, if we call the generic function **g** with an instance of **<float>**, we can supply the keyword arguments **real-key:** and **float-key:**, because the methods that have those keyword parameters are both applicable. If we call **g** with an instance of **<integer>**, we can supply the keyword arguments **real-key:** and **integer-key:**.

Suppose that, in this same example, we call the generic function **g** with an instance of **<float>**, and supply the keyword arguments **real-key:** and **float-key:**. Method 2 is most specific, and is called as a result of Dylan's method dispatch. But method 2 does not have a **real-key:** parameter. If we were calling this method directly, Dylan would signal an error. In this case, method 2 simply ignores the **real-key:** argument, because Dylan checks keyword arguments for a generic function call as a whole, rather than for a particular method chosen as a result of method dispatch.

There is an important subtlety of keyword-parameter specifications to note in this example. Because of the rules for parameter-list congruence, the generic function and all its methods must accept keyword arguments — that is, they must all have **#key** in their parameter lists. Notice that we terminated the generic function's parameter list with **#key**. This use indicates that the generic function permits — but does not require — individual methods to specify keyword parameters.

Suppose that we had instead terminated the generic function's parameter list with **#key, #all-keys**. This use also would have permitted, but would not have required, individual methods to specify keyword parameters. But it also would have allowed a caller of the generic function to supply *any* keyword argument. In the earlier example, only a small set of keyword arguments was permitted, and the members of the set varied with the applicable methods.

In general, when you define a generic function or a method that accepts keyword arguments, it is advisable not to specify **#all-keys** unnecessarily, because doing so defeats Dylan's keyword-argument checking. If a method needs to accept keyword arguments because of the rules of parameter-list congruence, but does not need to recognize any keywords itself, you should terminate its parameter list with **#key**.

12.3 Functions as objects

In Dylan, all functions are objects. A function can be the value of a variable, an argument to another function, or a value returned by a function. In fact, Dylan provides a number of operations on functions, including operations to compose new functions from existing functions.

12.3.1 Types of functions

All functions are instances of the class **<function>**. Dylan has two built-in instantiable subclasses of **<function>**: **<generic-function>** and **<method>**. Both methods and generic functions can be called in the same way. As we have seen, a generic function can contain zero or more methods. If a generic function is called, it must have at least one applicable method or Dylan signals an error.

12.3.2 Creation of generic functions

You can create a generic function in the following ways:

- You can create one explicitly by **define generic**.
- You can create one explicitly by calling **make** on the **<generic-function>** class. You rarely need to create a generic function this way.
- You can create one implicitly by **define method**. If the generic function named by this definition does not yet exist, Dylan creates it.
- You can create one implicitly by defining a slot in **define class**. If a getter generic function for the slot does not yet exist, Dylan creates it.

- You can create one implicitly by defining a slot (other than a constant slot) in **define class**. If a setter generic function for the slot does not yet exist, Dylan creates it.

Each of these procedures, except a call to **make**, defines a module constant whose value is the generic function created.

When Dylan creates a generic function implicitly, it creates a parameter list and a value declaration for the generic function that are designed to restrict the addition of subsequent methods to the generic function as little as possible. All required arguments to the generic function have type specializers of **<object>**, and the generic function can return any number of values of any type. The generic function's parameter list is congruent with that of the method being defined. If the generic function accepts keyword arguments, the parameter list ends with **#key**.

12.3.3 Creation of methods

You can create a method in the following ways:

- You can create one explicitly by **define method**. This definition also adds the method to a generic function, creating the generic function if the latter does not already exist.
- You can create one explicitly by a **method** statement. This statement does not add the method to a generic function.
- You can create one explicitly by a **local method** declaration. This declaration creates one or more methods, and assigns each to a local variable such that the binding is visible to all other methods defined in the same **local** declaration. This declaration does not add the method to a generic function.
- You can create one implicitly by defining a slot (other than a virtual slot) in **define class**. Dylan defines a getter method for the slot, and adds it to a generic function, creating the generic function if that function does not already exist.
- You can create one implicitly by defining a slot (other than a virtual or a constant slot) in **define class**. Dylan defines a setter method for the slot, and adds it to a generic function, creating the generic function if that function does not already exist.

Creating a method by using **method** is useful when the method does not need to be part of a generic function. For instance, various Dylan functions take as arguments other functions that act as predicates, or test functions. One of these is **choose**, which selects members of a sequence that satisfy a test function, and returns those members as a new sequence. We might pick all the strings out of a mixed sequence as follows:

```
define method choose-strings
    (sequence :: <sequence>) => (new-seq :: <sequence>)
  // choose takes two arguments: a function and a sequence
  choose(method (object) instance?(object, <string>) end method, sequence);
  end method choose-strings;
```

Creating a method by using **local method** is useful for a method that does not need to be part of a generic function, but does need to be given a name so that it can call itself recursively, or so that other code in the enclosing body can refer to it. For an example, see Section 11.3.6, page 147.

12.3.4 Application of a function to arguments

The Dylan function **apply** takes as arguments a function and one or more additional arguments, the final one of which must be a sequence. The **apply** function calls its first argument — the function — and passes that function the remaining arguments to **apply**. But instead of passing its final argument as a sequence, it passes each element of the sequence as an individual argument.

The **apply** function is perhaps most useful in the body of a function that receives a variable number of arguments and must pass those arguments to another function that also takes a variable number of arguments. For example, we can use **apply** to write a recursive version of the **sum** function that we defined iteratively in Section 12.2.3, page 172:

```
// Sum one or more values
define method sum (value, #rest more-values)
  // If only one value, that is the answer
  if (empty?(more-values))
    value;
  // Otherwise, add the first value to the sum of the rest
  else
    value + apply(sum, more-values);
  end if;
end method sum;
```

12.3.5 Operations on functions

Dylan has several functions that take functions as arguments, and return new functions that are transformations of those arguments. These operations permit many kinds of composition of functions and other objects to generate new functions.

Three of these functions take predicates as arguments, and return the complement, disjunction, or conjunction of the predicates. For example, **`complement`** takes a predicate and returns the latter's complement — a function that returns **`#t`** when the original predicate would have returned **`#f`**, and otherwise returns **`#f`**.

The **`curry`** function takes a function and any number of additional arguments. It returns a new function that applies the original function, first to the additional arguments to **`curry`**, then to the arguments to the new function. In Section 11.3.7, page 147, we call **`curry`** with **`\*`** and a number to return a function that multiplies that function's argument by the given number. We then map this new function over the elements of a vector to perform a scalar multiplication of the vector.

In fact, Dylan has a set of functions that map other functions over the elements of collections in different ways. We used one of these, **`choose`**, in Section 12.3.3, page 181. Some of these functions return new collections; others return single values. For more examples, see Section 11.3, page 142.

12.3.6 Closures

This section describes closures — an advanced concept. If you do not understand or wish to study this section, you can safely skip it.

Consider the following example:

```
define method call-and-show (function :: <function>, #rest arguments)
  format-out("The result is %=.\n", apply(function, arguments));
end method call-and-show;

define method show-next (x :: <integer>)
  call-and-show(method () x + 1 end method);
end method show-next;
```

When we execute this code, we get the expected result:

```
? show-next(41);
The result is 42.
```

But why did we get that result? We created an anonymous method in **show-next**, and passed that anonymous method into a completely separate method (**call-and-show**), where **x** is not bound to anything. And yet, when the **call-and-show** method executed the anonymous method that we made, somehow the anonymous method could still access the **x** binding. We got this reasonable result because the **method** statement can create a special kind of method called a closure.

Recall that Dylan has two kinds of variable: module variables and local variables. A local variable is defined explicitly by a **let** or **local** declaration, and implicitly by a function call, when a method's parameters are initialized to that method's arguments. Local variables are defined within a limited **lexical scope** — that is, they **bind** a name to a value only within a particular textual portion of the program. This portion of the program is that part of the innermost body that follows the definition of the local variable.

A **method** statement or a **local** declaration can define a method in a portion of a program where local variables are in effect. In the preceding example, we use a **method** statement to define a method inside the body of the **show-next** method, where the local variable **x** (the parameter for the **show-next** method) is bound to the argument to **show-next**. The method that we define inside **show-next** refers to that local variable **x**.

In general, when a program exits a body, the local variables defined inside that body cease to be defined, and it is an error for the program to refer to those variables. But there is an exception. If we use **method** or **local** to define a method, and if we then execute that method outside the body in which we define it, the method can still refer to the local variables that were in effect when the method was defined. Such a method is called a closure.

A **closure** is a method that **closes over** or captures local variables that are in effect when the method is defined and that are referred to in the body of the method. The closure created by the **method** statement in our example captures the local variable **x**. So, even though the local variable **x** is not defined in the lexical scope of the **call-and-show** method, the closure called by **call-and-show** can access the captured binding of **x**.

For examples of closures as iteration or mapping functions for collections, see Section 11.3.5, page 146, and Section 11.3.7, page 147.

12.4 Summary

In this chapter, we covered the following:

- We described the syntax of Dylan function calls, including syntactic structures that are abbreviations for function calls. These syntactic structures include slot references, element references, and most operator calls.
- We described how a function and its caller interact. In particular, we discussed the relations among arguments, parameters, value declarations, and returned values.
- We discussed the kinds of parameters that a function can have (required, rest, and keyword). We then outlined the rules for congruent parameter lists and value declarations of a generic function and its methods.
- We discussed ways of creating generic functions and methods, and of applying a function to arguments.
- We outlined Dylan's operations on functions.
- We introduced the concept of closures.

13

Libraries and Modules

As you create a program, you will often discover subsets of your code that are candidates for sharing, reuse, or resale. Alternatively, you may be working on a large program that has been divided into pieces that can be implemented separately, either to allow parallel development, or to make the programming task more manageable. For either of these reasons, you can package your code into a **reusable software component** so that

- Other programmers can easily add your component to their programs (which are called **client programs** of your component).
- You can develop your component independently from any clients.
- Clients can use your code without knowing or depending on the internal implementation of your component.
- You can sell your component to clients without revealing your source code.

Two important principles of software engineering apply here: information hiding and protocols. The principle of **information hiding** says that you should try to minimize the information that is passed between components in a system, thus minimizing the interdependencies of components. A **protocol** is the interface definition of a software component. The purpose of establishing protocols is to define a uniform interface that clients can use, even if the implementation of a component is enhanced or modified. Dylan supports software components, information hiding, and protocols in terms of **libraries** and **modules**.

Many Dylan environments support simple or exploratory programming with a **`dylan-user`** module that includes both the standard Dylan language facilities and a common subset of Dylan libraries. Because all but the simplest programs usually grow into projects or are reused in new projects, it is good practice to create a unique library and module for each program or component. If you are writing a simple, stand-alone program or a simple component, you can use the simple library and module structure illustrated in Section 2.5, page 20. You may want to skim this chapter, however, so you have an idea of the options available for more complex situations.

In this chapter, we start by describing the basic concepts of libraries (Section 13.1), modules and namespaces (Section 13.2), and programs and source records (Section 13.3). In the remainder of the chapter, we illustrate the concepts of libraries and modules by considering the classes and methods for times that we defined in Chapter 8, *A Simple Library*, and showing how they might be packaged into a reusable software component or library. We also show how the **`sixty-unit`** classes and methods could be a component substrate that the **`time`** library uses and shares with an **`angle`** library. Finally, we illustrate how to implement a **`say`** protocol that works with either or both of the **`time`** and **`angle`** libraries by creating a separate library that defines the shared protocol.

13.1 Libraries

A Dylan library defines a software component — a separately compilable unit that can be either a stand-alone program or a component (library) of some larger program. The elements of the core Dylan language are in a library called **`dylan`**. The simplest Dylan program consists of at least two libraries: the original program source in the program library, and the **`dylan`** library, which supplies the predefined Dylan language elements used by the program library. A simple Dylan component may consist of only a single library — the component library. The component library will be used by other libraries. The component library will use definitions from the **`dylan`** library (and possibly other components). Hence, when combined with other components into a complete program, the program will consist of several libraries.

In each Dylan implementation, a library is associated with implementation-specific export information that is automatically maintained by the compiler. The library export information completely describes whatever implementation-specific information is needed for other software components to use the library. Thus, you can use libraries to deliver components in compiled form, keeping the implementation of the library confidential.

> **Comparison with C++ and Modula:** Dylan libraries are similar to C++ libraries in that they both are potentially shared components of many programs. Unlike C++ libraries, Dylan libraries include all the information needed to be used by another Dylan library — there is no companion header file that must be kept up to date.
>
> Dylan libraries are analogous to Modula packages — all the information necessary to use a library is contained in the library.

13.2 Modules

A library is made up of modules, which hold the definitions of the library. Each module specifies an independent **namespace** for Dylan constants and variables. Each module can use definitions from other modules in the same library or in other libraries, and each module can provide definitions to other modules in the same or in other libraries. Each module controls the visibility of the names within a module from outside the module. You can use modules both to do information hiding and to prevent name clashes between constants and variables.

13.2.1 Namespaces

We mentioned in Section 2.3, page 14, that Dylan has module variables and module constants. Every module contains its own set of module variables and constants. Two independent modules **`a`** and **`b`** might both have variables named **`*x*`**. These are two different variables with possibly different values. Within module **`a`**, a reference to module variable **`*x*`** is a reference to **`a`**'s variable **`*x*`**. Within module **`b`**, a reference to module variable **`*x*`** is a reference to **`b`**'s variable **`*x*`**. In this sense, a module defines its own namespace.

13.2.2 Definitions

A module variable or module constant is declared and initialized by a **definition**. We have already seen that **`define variable`** is a definition that establishes a module variable, and `define constant` is a definition that establishes a module constant. Dylan also uses module constants to refer to classes, generic functions, and macros. The definition for a class, `define class`, establishes a module constant whose name is the class name and whose value is the class object. Similarly, the definitions for a generic function and a macro establish module constants. When we say that a module contains definitions, we mean that the classes, generic functions, macros, and other objects defined in that module are the values of variables and constants in that module.

13.2.3 Export and import of names by modules

Within each module, every name refers either to a definition owned by that module, or possibly to a definition owned by another module. Modules make the names of their definitions available to other modules by **exporting** those names. A module can refer to the names of another module by **using** the other module. Note that no module can access a definition in another module that is not exported; hence, modules provide a form of access control.

When a module exports its names and a second module uses the first module, importing the names of the first module, then the definitions of the second module can use the names of the first module, just as they can use any other name in their own module.

When one module uses a second module, it can use all the names exported from the second module, or it can specify a subset of those exports to **import**. In addition, imported names can be **renamed** — they can be given different names when imported. You can use renaming to document which definitions are from another module, by giving them all a uniform prefix; you can use renaming to resolve name conflicts; or you can use renaming to give nicknames or shorthand names for imported names.

> **Comparison with C:** Exported variables in Dylan are like external variables and functions in C. (By *external*, we do not mean the `extern` storage declaration, but rather the concept of an external variable — one that is available for linking to.)
>
> Unexported variables in Dylan are like `static` variables and functions in C.

> **Comparison with C++:** Dylan modules are similar to C++ namespaces in that they eliminate the problem of global namespace pollution or clashes between names used in individual libraries. Unlike C++ namespaces, Dylan modules also define a level of access control: Each module decides what names are externally visible, and no module can create or access names in another module, unless that other module explicitly exports those names. In contrast, the C++ `using` declaration allows the client of a namespace to access any name in that namespace.

13.2.4 Export and import of modules by libraries

Just as a module specifies a namespace for definitions, each library specifies an independent namespace of modules and controls the visibility of its modules. Within each library, every module refers either to a module owned by that library, or to a module owned by another library. Libraries make their modules available to other libraries by **exporting** those modules. A library can refer to the modules of another library by **using** the other library. No library can refer to the modules of another library that are not exported.

When a library exports a module and a second library uses the first library, importing its modules, then the modules of the second library can use the modules of the first library, just as they can use any other modules in their own library.

When one library uses another library, it can use all the modules exported from the second library, or it can specify a subset of those exports to **import**. Imported modules can be **renamed** as they are imported, just as imported module names can be removed.

You can see that libraries and modules together provide a two-level structure of naming, information hiding, and access control. The designers of Dylan believed that only a single level would not give sufficient flexibility, but that more than two levels was unnecessary. In essence, modules give a fine level of control that lets you organize within a single component, and libraries give a higher level of control that lets you organize components into a program. Also, libraries are the Dylan **compilation unit** — they are the level at which components can be exchanged without source code being exchanged. A software publisher would typically sell its wares as Dylan libraries.

13.2.5 Simple example of libraries and modules

To illustrate these concepts, we repeat the definition of the **library.dylan** file, first shown in Chapter 2, *Quick Start*. Here, we have used a more verbose, but also more precise, format.

The library file: **library.dylan**.

```
module: dylan-user

define library hello
  use dylan, import: { dylan };
  use format-out, import: { format-out };
end library hello;

define module hello
  use dylan, import: all;
  use format-out, import: all;
end module hello;
```

The first line of **library.dylan** states that the expressions and definitions in this file are in the **dylan-user** module. In this predefined module, you define the modules and library that make up your component or program. Every library has a unique **dylan-user** module. In the file **library.dylan**, we define a library named **hello** and a module named **hello**.

The module definition names the other modules whose names the **hello** module will use. In this case, the **hello** module uses the **dylan** and **format-out** modules. Here, we have explicitly stated that we are importing all the names from the modules that we use — using the **import: all** clause is not strictly necessary, because it is the default that is used if we do not specify what to import. By using another module, we import the names exported from that module, making them available in our namespace. For example, **format-out** is exported from the **format-out** module, so the **use format-out** clause enables our program to call the **format-out** function. The **use dylan** clause in the module definition makes available all the built-in Dylan language elements exported from the **dylan** module. When we define a module, it must **use** all the modules that export the definitions used by the definitions in our module.

The library definition tells the compiler which other libraries our program uses. Here, we have explicitly stated that we are interested in only the **dylan** and **format-out** modules from these other libraries. This clause is not strictly necessary, since the module definition tells the compiler which modules it uses; but it is good practice to document our intent. For example, the **`format-out`** module is in the **`format-out`** library. Therefore, our **`hello`** library must use the **`format-out`** library, and must import the **`format-out`** module for the **`hello`** module to use the **`format-out`** module. Similarly, the **`dylan`** module is in the **`dylan`** library, and therefore our **`hello`** library must use the **`dylan`** library and import the **`dylan`** module in order for the **`hello`** module to use the **`dylan`** module. When we define a library, it must **`use`** all the libraries that export the modules used by the modules in our library.

The module definition also specifies which variables and constants are exported from the module for use by other modules. The library definition specifies which modules are exported from the library for use by other libraries. In our simple example, the **`hello`** module exports no variables or constants, and the **`hello`** library exports no modules.

Figure 13.1 illustrates the relationships between libraries and modules in our example program. In Figure 13.1, and in the other figures in this chapter, we draw libraries as heavy bold boxes and modules as light boxes. We have tried to illustrate how libraries and modules build on one another through their "use" relationships. A library that uses another library is shown above the library that it uses, so we show the **`hello`** library above the **`format-out`** and **`dylan`** libraries. An exported module is illustrated as being on top of (overlapping) the library that

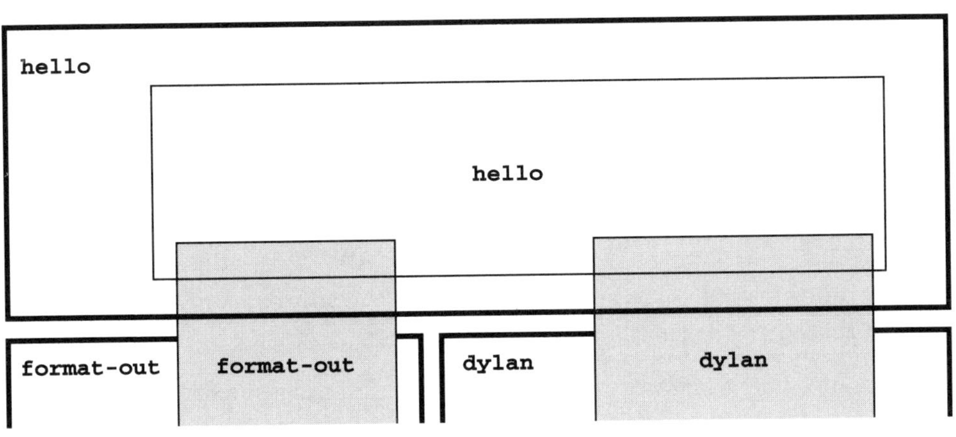

Figure 13.1 Libraries (heavy boxes) and modules (light boxes) in "Hello, world".

exports it (we have also shaded them, to illustrate this overlap). And a module that uses another module is illustrated as being on top of (overlapping) the used module. Try to envision the modules as semitransparent overlays, layered up from the surface of the paper. Thus, the **`hello`** module overlays the **`format-out`** and **`dylan`** modules that it uses.

Note that we intentionally do not show all the modules in the **`format-out`** and **`dylan`** libraries in Figure 13.1. The **`format-out`** and **`dylan`** libraries might well have other modules, but either those modules are not exported or our program does not use them.

13.3 Source code, modules, and libraries

How is Dylan source code associated with modules and libraries? In Sections 13.1 and 13.2, we looked at a Dylan program from the top down: A program contains libraries; a library contains modules; and a module contains variables and their definitions. We now look at a program from the bottom up, to see how source code is organized into modules, modules into libraries, and libraries into programs.

13.3.1 Source records and modules

All the Dylan source code for a program is organized into units called **source records**. How source records are stored is dependent on the implementation. Some implementations may store source records in a database, others may simply use **interchange format** files (see Section 13.6, page 203). No matter how they are stored, each source record is in a module; therefore,

- All the module's variables and constants, including those imported by using other modules, are visible to, and can be used by, the code in the source record.
- The module controls which definitions in the source record are exported, and therefore are visible, to other modules.
- Variables and constants in other modules that are not exported, or ones that are exported but are not imported by the source record's module, are not visible to the source record.

Dylan implementations can associate a source record with a module in different ways. The interchange format has a **header** at the front that specifies the module for its source records.

13.3.2 Modules and libraries

Every module is in a library; therefore,

- All the library's modules, including those imported by using other libraries, are visible to, and can be used by, the module.
- The library controls whether the module is exported, and therefore is visible, to other libraries.
- Modules in other libraries that are not exported, or ones that are exported but are not imported by the module's library, are not visible to the module.

Dylan implementations can associate a module with a library in different ways. The **library-interchange definition (LID)** format lists the interchange files that make up a library. The module definitions in those interchange files are thus in that library.

13.3.3 Libraries and programs

Every library is in a set of libraries that can be combined into a program; therefore,

- The library can import the exported modules of any other available library.
- The library's exported modules are visible to, and can be imported by, other available libraries.

The Dylan implementation determines what libraries are available; how they are combined into a program; and how they are compiled, linked, and run. Consult your implementation documentation for further information.

We have presented a simple hierarchical model: All Dylan code resides in source records; every source record resides in a module; every module resides in a library. Every module must be completely defined within its library, because the library is the Dylan unit of compilation. So that this restriction is enforced, every source record in a library must be in a module that is defined in the library; no source record can be in a module that is imported by the library. Within a library, it is possible for a name to be owned by one module and for that name's definition to be provided by another module. This flexibility helps us to structure code, as we shall see in Section 13.4.

13.4 Module definition

Enough theory. Let's see how modules and libraries can be used in practice by considering the classes and methods for representing and manipulating times that we defined in Chapter 8, *A Simple Library*, and showing how they might be packaged into a reusable software component.

First, let's examine what the external protocol of our time library might be. We have defined two kinds of time that can be created: **<time-of-day>** and **<time-offset>**. We have a generic function for printing times, **say**, and one, perhaps not so obvious, utility function for creating new times, **encode-total-seconds**.

We define a method, **\+**, for adding times, but a method is not a protocol. The protocol for the generic function **\+** is defined by the Dylan library, which already exports it, for any Dylan program. When we define our method for adding times, we are extending that protocol; we are not creating a new one.

The **decode-total-seconds** function, the **<sixty-unit>** class, and several other functions are used internally only, so they are not part of the external protocol.

Although **<time>** is used internally only within our library, it is good practice to make abstract superclasses such as **<time>** part of a library interface. When we do so, a client of the library that does not care which specific kind of time is being manipulated can simply use **<time>**.

Thus, five items (**<time>**, **<time-of-day>**, **<time-offset>**, **say**, and **encode-total-seconds**) define the external protocol of the time library.

13.4.1 Roles of modules

In our experience, we have found it useful to consider modules as having roles: interface, implementation, or client. These roles lead to a simple, low-maintenance structure. An **interface module** creates names that are to be visible to other modules and at a library interface. An **implementation module** contains the definitions that make up the library (including those visible through an interface module). A **client module** is a module that depends on other modules' definitions.

It is possible for a module to play more than one role — for example, a client module may also implement a higher-level interface. We recommend thinking of modules as having these roles, and in this chapter we use that design convention. When illustrating the roles of modules, we use the conventions shown in Figure 13.2. In Figure 13.2, we show a library with three modules: an interface module (with its interface sticking out of the top of the library), an implementation module (overlapping the interface, because it implements the interface by giving definitions to the names the interface exports), and a client module overlapping another library's interface module (using its exported interface module to import definitions from another library). As we noted, the implementation and client are often the same module, and the interface of one library is used by the clients of other libraries. Dylan modules and libraries are not allowed to have mutual dependencies, so we can use the convention of drawing at the top the interfaces that a library exports, and of drawing at the bottom the interfaces that a library uses. It is difficult simultaneously to illustrate the module "use" relationships in only two dimensions — the overlapping of one module by another is intended to depict usage.

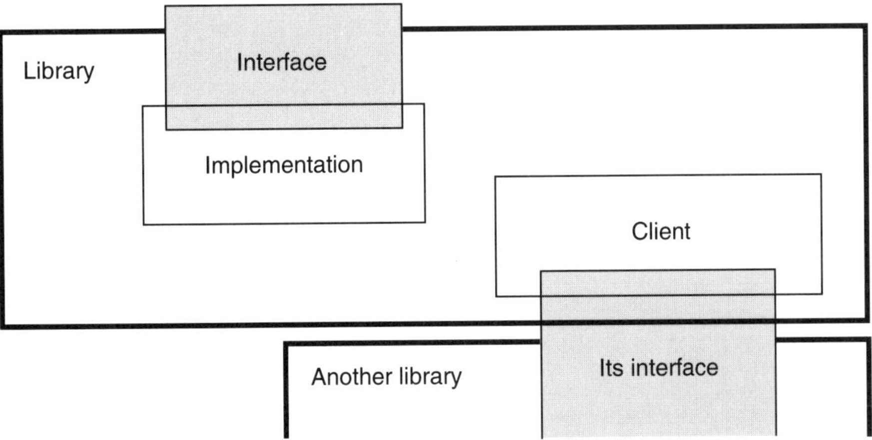

Figure 13.2 The roles of modules: interface, implementation, and client.

13.4.2 The interface module

We can now write a first draft of the interface module for our library:

```
define module time
  // Classes
  create <time>, <time-of-day>, <time-offset>;
  // Generics
  create say, encode-total-seconds;
end module time;
```

In the preceding definition, the **time** interface module creates and exports (makes visible) three classes and two functions. We use the **create** clause, because we do not intend to define any implementations in the time-library interface module itself — that will be done in an implementation module, which will use the time-library module as its interface. The **create** clause causes the names to be reserved in the **time** interface module, with the requisite that definitions be provided by some other module in the same library.

> **Comparison with C:** The Dylan **create** clause is roughly analogous to the C **extern** declaration.

13.4.3 The implementation module

Our **time** interface module specifies the names that are visible to clients of our library. It also serves to specify the names that must be defined in our implementation. To prepare to define those names, we create a separate implementation module:

```
define module time-implementation
  // Interface module
  use time;
  // Substrate modules
  use format-out;
  use dylan;
end module time-implementation;
```

In the preceding definition, the implementation module uses the **time** interface module so that it can give definitions to the names that the interface created. The implementation module is also a client module: It is a client of the **dylan** module, because its definitions use definitions such as **define class**, **<integer>**, and * (which are defined by the **dylan** module of the **dylan** library); it is also a client of the **format-out** module, because the **say** methods are implemented using the **format-out** function (which is defined in the **format-out** module of the **format-out** library).

We can start to envision the **time** library as shown in Figure 13.3. In a library more complicated than the time library, we might decompose the construction of the library into several implementation modules. For example, we might want to assign the implementation of the **<sixty-unit>** substrate to another programmer, and to create an interface between that substrate and the rest of the implementation so that work on either side of the interface can proceed in parallel. In that case, we might use the following module definitions:

```
define module sixty-unit
  // External interface
  use time;
  // Internal interface
  export <sixty-unit>, total-seconds, decode-total-seconds;
  // Substrate module
  use dylan;
end module sixty-unit;
```

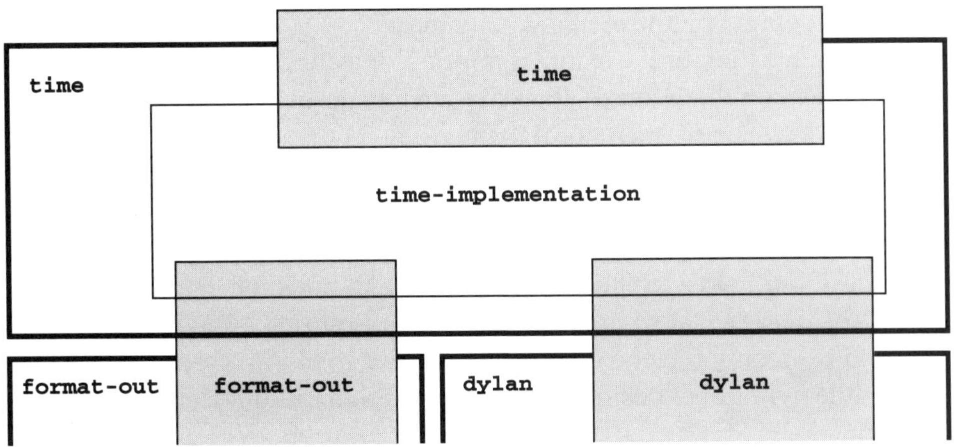

Figure 13.3 Initial **time** library.

```
define module time-implementation
  // External interface
  use time;
  // Substrate modules
  use sixty-unit;
  use format-out;
  use dylan;
end module time-implementation;
```

Here, because the **sixty-unit** module is an internal interface, we forgo the formality of creating a separate implementation module; we simply **export** the definitions that we expect to be used by other modules within the library. This approach is perhaps a short-sighted one. If later we want the **sixty-unit** functionality to be available to another library, we will be faced with reorganizing its module definitions (as we shall see in Section 13.8, page 209). Even within a library, it is good practice to organize modules as interface and implementation.

Notice the distinction between the way that we handled the external **time** interface, and the shortcut we took with **sixty-unit**. Although the **sixty-unit** module will *define* **encode-total-seconds**, which is part of the **time** interface, it does not *export* **encode-total-seconds**; rather, it *uses* the **time** interface module, which *created* **encode-total-seconds** (without defining that function). Because **sixty-unit** uses **time**, the name **encode-total-seconds** is the same object in both modules. Effectively, **encode-total-seconds** is owned by the **time** module, although it is defined by the **sixty-unit** module.

This organization of the external interface may appear odd at first, but it reduces duplication that would otherwise have to occur: If **sixty-unit** exported **encode-total-seconds**, then, for it to be visible at the interface of the library, either the **sixty-unit** module would have to be exported from the library as an interface (which export is undesirable, because the **sixty-unit** module has other exports that are not intended to be visible outside the library), or the **time** interface module would have to use **sixty-unit** and to re-export **encode-total-seconds**. The **create** clause provides the cleaner solution of allowing a name to be exported from only the one interface module, defined in a separate implementation module (without exposing the implementation module), and used by many client modules.

Dylan requires that all the variables exported via the **create** clause be defined by some module in the same library; however, they can be defined in any module, and the interface definitions can be spread over several implementation modules. The compiler will verify that the interface is implemented completely, even if its implementation is spread over several modules, by checking when the library is compiled that each created name has a definition.

The **sixty-unit** module exports the class **<sixty-unit>**, because **time-implementation** will subclass that class. The **sixty-unit** module also exports the generic functions **total-seconds**, and **decode-total-seconds**. The export of **total-seconds** might seem surprising at first, because, in many object-oriented languages, access to a class includes access to all the slots of a class. In Dylan, slots are simply methods on generic functions and names in the module namespace; hence, the functions must be exported if slot access from outside the module is to be allowed. Note that exporting **total-seconds** allows other modules only to get the current value of the **total-seconds** slot. To allow other modules also to set the slot value, we would have to export **total-seconds-setter**. It is not necessary to export the init keyword **total-seconds:**, which allows the initial value of the slot to be set when objects are created. Keywords, or symbols, all exist in a single global namespace that is separate from module variables.

> **Comparison with C++:** Dylan modules provide access control similar to that provided by the **private:** and **public:** keywords in C++ classes, but Dylan access control is done at the module, rather than at the class, level. Dylan has no equivalent to **protected:** access control, in that a class that subclasses a class from another module does *not* have access to slots or other generic functions on its superclass from the other module, unless they are explicitly exported from that module.
>
> Dylan does support multiple interfaces, however; different levels of access can be provided by having more than one interface module, each supplying the access needed for the particular interface.
>
> One way to think of Dylan access control in C++ terms is that all definitions in a module are **friend**s of all classes in the module, and the exported definitions of the module are **public**.

Breaking out the **sixty-unit** substrate to a separate module creates a slightly more complicated structure to our diagram, as shown in Figure 13.4.

In Figure 13.4, we show the definitions of **sixty-unit** in a separate module. The **sixty-unit** module is a client of **dylan**, an interface and implementation of

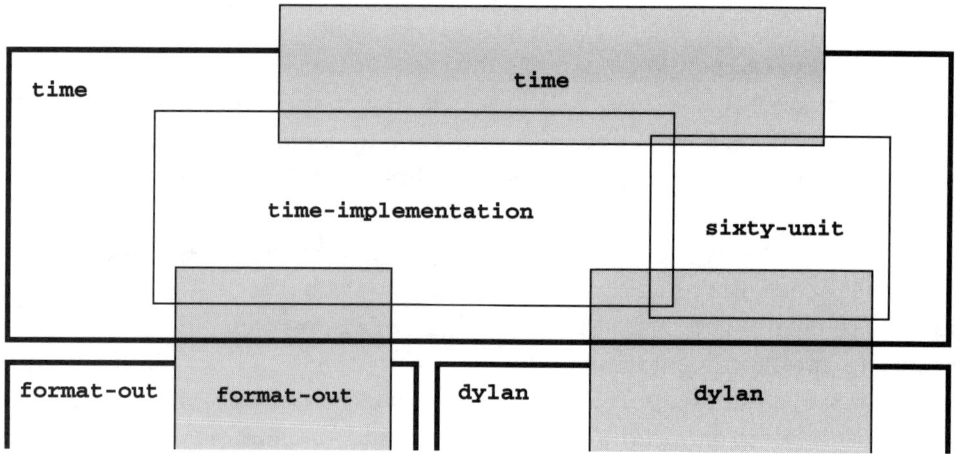

Figure 13.4 Internal modules of **time** library.

definitions used by **time-implementation** (that is, **time-implementation** is a client of **sixty-unit**), and an implementation of part of the interface created by **time**.

13.5 Library definition

We can now give the definition of the library:

```
define library time
  // Interface module
  export time;
  // Substrate libraries
  use format-out;
  use dylan;
end library time;
```

In the preceding definition, we declare that the interface to our library is defined by the **time** interface module. By exporting that module, we make all the exported names from that module accessible to clients of this library. We also declare that the **time** library relies on the **format-out** and **dylan** libraries (that is, that those libraries have interface modules of which our modules will be clients). Notice that no mention is made of the **time-implementation**, or **sixty-unit** modules, because they are completely internal to our library and are not visible to any clients of our library.

Recall that constant and variable names, module names, and library names are distinct, so it is possible to have a library, module, and constant all of the same name. A common convention in a library with only one interface module is to give them the same name, as we have done here.

To build our library, we would need to define the library, define all the modules, specify where and how the definitions or source records that implement our library are to be found, specify where the object code that results from compiling the source records are to be stored, and provide any particular instructions to the compiler regarding how to build the library. The details of how to provide this information vary from one Dylan implementation to the next.

To use our library, we would need to specify where to find the object code and the implementation-dependent export information that allows another library to use our library without access to our source records. The details of this information also depend on the Dylan implementation that we are using.

> **Comparison with C++:** The library definition, which names the modules exported and libraries used by a library, is similar to C++ header files and includes. The main difference is that the Dylan development environment extracts the information that it needs about exported and imported variables directly, rather than requiring exports to be duplicated in a set of header files, and requiring those header files to be included in every source file that uses the imports.

13.6 Interchange files

Source records in Dylan do not have to be stored in files. Certain environments use a database for storing source records, and a hypertextlike mechanism for exploring them. Dylan does, however, specify a portable interchange format, based on files, for exchanging Dylan source records among Dylan implementations.

A file in **interchange format** has a header and a body. The header consists of consecutive lines of keywords and values. The body consists of Dylan source records, and is separated from the header by at least one blank line. The only required keyword is one to specify to what module the source records in the file belong. Each file contains source records of a single module, although the source records of each module can be stored in any number of files. Standard keywords are also defined for author, copyright, and version, although an implementation may ignore them, or may define additional keywords.

So, for instance, if we wanted to publish our library source records, we might create the files shown in the following sections.

13.7 The `time-library` file

The **`time-library`** file: **`time-library.dylan`**.

```
Module: dylan-user

// Library definition
define library time
  // Interface module
  export time;
  // Substrate libraries
  use format-out;
  use dylan;
end library time;

// Interface module
define module time
  // Classes
  create <time>, <time-of-day>, <time-offset>;
  // Generics
  create say, encode-total-seconds;
end module time;

// Internal substrate module
define module sixty-unit
  // External interface
  use time;
  // Internal interface
  export <sixty-unit>, total-seconds, decode-total-seconds;
  // Substrate module
  use dylan;
end module sixty-unit;
```

The **time-library** file: **time-library.dylan**. *(continued)*

```
// Implementation module
define module time-implementation
  // External interface
  use time;
  // Substrate modules
  use sixty-unit;
  use format-out;
  use dylan;
end module time-implementation;
```

Because every file has to name the module to which its source records belong, you might wonder where to start. Every library implicitly defines a **dylan-user** module for this purpose. The **dylan-user** module imports all of the **dylan** module, so any Dylan definition can be used. You can think of **dylan-user** as being a scratch version of **dylan**. Each library has a private copy of **dylan-user**, so there is no concern that definitions in one library's **dylan-user** could be confused with those of another.

The purposes of the library file are to communicate to the Dylan compiler the structure of the module namespaces, to state which other libraries to search for the modules that are used in the implementation of this library, and to determine which modules implemented by this library are visible to other libraries (and programs) that use this library. The details of how these tasks are done depend on the implementation, but each environment will provide a mechanism for reading library and module definitions, either directly from an interchange file, or after conversion of the interchange file to an implementation-dependent format.

13.7.1 The sixty-unit implementation file

The **sixty-unit** implementation file: **sixty-unit.dylan**.

```
Module: sixty-unit

define abstract class <sixty-unit> (<object>)
  slot total-seconds :: <integer>,
    required-init-keyword: total-seconds:;
end class <sixty-unit>;
```

The **sixty-unit** implementation file: **sixty-unit.dylan**. *(continued)*

```
define method encode-total-seconds
    (max-unit :: <integer>, minutes :: <integer>, seconds :: <integer>)
 => (total-seconds :: <integer>)
  ((max-unit * 60) + minutes) * 60 + seconds;
end method encode-total-seconds;

define method decode-total-seconds
    (sixty-unit :: <sixty-unit>)
 => (max-unit :: <integer>, minutes :: <integer>, seconds :: <integer>)
  decode-total-seconds(sixty-unit.total-seconds);
end method decode-total-seconds;

define method decode-total-seconds
    (total-seconds :: <integer>)
 => (hours :: <integer>, minutes :: <integer>, seconds :: <integer>)
  let(total-minutes, seconds) = truncate/(abs(total-seconds), 60);
  let(hours, minutes) = truncate/(total-minutes, 60);
  values(hours, minutes, seconds);
end method decode-total-seconds;
```

The preceding implementation file is the first file in which we use one of our own modules. The header statement **Module: sixty-unit** tells the Dylan compiler where to look to resolve the names that we are using — it tells Dylan that, when we say **define class** or **<integer>** or *****, we mean the Dylan definitions of **define class**, **<integer>**, and *****, because **sixty-unit** uses the **dylan** module. When we define **encode-total-seconds**, we mean the **encode-total-seconds** created by the **time** module, because **sixty-unit** uses that module.

13.7.2 The time implementation file

The **time** implementation file: **time.dylan**.

```
Module: time-implementation

// Define nonnegative integers as integers that are >= zero
define constant <nonnegative-integer> = limited(<integer>, min: 0);

define abstract class <time> (<sixty-unit>)
end class <time>;
```

The **time** implementation file: **time.dylan**. *(continued)*

```
define method say (time :: <time>)
  let (hours, minutes) = decode-total-seconds(time);
  format-out("%d:%s%d",
             hours, if (minutes < 10) "0" else " " end, minutes);
end method say;

// A specific time of day from 00:00 (midnight) to before 24:00 (tomorrow)
define class <time-of-day> (<time>)
end class <time-of-day>;

define method total-seconds-setter
    (total-seconds :: <integer>, time :: <time-of-day>)
 => (total-seconds :: <nonnegative-integer>)
  if (total-seconds >= 0)
    next-method();
  else
    error("%d cannot be negative", total-seconds);
  end if;
end method total-seconds-setter;

define method initialize (time :: <time-of-day>, #key)
  next-method();
  if (time.total-seconds < 0)
    error("%d cannot be negative", time.total-seconds);
  end if;
end method initialize;

// A relative time between -24:00 and +24:00
define class <time-offset> (<time>)
end class <time-offset>;

define method past? (time :: <time-offset>) => (past? :: <boolean>)
  time.total-seconds < 0;
end method past?;

define method say (time :: <time-offset>) => ()
  format-out("%s ", if (time.past?) "minus" else "plus" end);
  next-method();
end method say;

define method \+
    (offset1 :: <time-offset>, offset2 :: <time-offset>)
 => (sum :: <time-offset>)
  let sum = offset1.total-seconds + offset2.total-seconds;
  make(<time-offset>, total-seconds: sum);
end method \+;
```

The `time` implementation file: `time.dylan`. *(continued)*

```
define method \+
    (offset :: <time-offset>, time-of-day :: <time-of-day>)
 => (sum :: <time-of-day>)
  make(<time-of-day>,
       total-seconds: offset.total-seconds + time-of-day.total-seconds);
end method \+;

define method \+ (time-of-day :: <time-of-day>, offset :: <time-offset>)
 => (sum :: <time-of-day>)
  offset + time-of-day;
end method \+;

define method \< (time1 :: <time-of-day>, time2 :: <time-of-day>)
  time1.total-seconds < time2.total-seconds;
end method \<;

define method \< (time1 :: <time-offset>, time2 :: <time-offset>)
  time1.total-seconds < time2.total-seconds;
end method \<;

define method \= (time1 :: <time-of-day>, time2 :: <time-of-day>)
  time1.total-seconds = time2.total-seconds;
end method \=;

define method \= (time1 :: <time-offset>, time2 :: <time-offset>)
  time1.total-seconds = time2.total-seconds;
end method \=;

// Two useful time constants
define constant $midnight
  = make(<time-of-day>, total-seconds: encode-total-seconds(0, 0, 0));

define constant $tomorrow
  = make(<time-of-day>,
         total-seconds: encode-total-seconds(24, 0, 0));
```

In the preceding implementation file, it is the **`time-implementation`** module that specifies what we mean when we write Dylan expressions, and in which module namespace our definitions will appear.

13.7.3 The library-interchange definition (LID)

As described in Section 2.5.1, page 21, most Dylan implementations also accept a LID file that enumerates the files of a library and the order in which those files will be initialized, if there are any top-level forms. The LID file for our **`time`** library would be as follows.

The LID file: **`time.lid`**.

```
library: time
files:   library
         sixty-unit
         time
```

In a LID file, only the base file name is given. Information about the folder or directory where the files are stored, and about the file extension (**`.dylan`** in our examples), is implementation dependent and must be supplied by the individual implementation.

13.8 Component library

In previous examples, we have shown how the **`<angle>`** class can use the **`<sixty-unit>`** class as a base class. We could have simply included the **`<angle>`** class in our time library (presumably calling it a time-and-angle library), but it seems plausible that clients might not want both classes all the time. Another organization would be to make an angle library that uses the time library, which would be burdensome only to clients who want angles without time. Clearly, the right solution is to make a separate **`sixty-unit`** library that is shared by the time and angle libraries.

Because we had already broken out **`sixty-unit`** into a separate module and file, we can create this new organization by

- Moving the **`sixty-unit`** module to its own library file
- Updating the **`time`** library file
- Opening the **`<sixty-unit>`** class

Note that no changes are required to the **`time`** implementation file, so we do not present it again.

13.8.1 The `sixty-unit-library` file

The **sixty-unit** library file: **sixty-unit-library.dylan**.

```
Module: dylan-user

// Library definition
define library sixty-unit
  // Interface module
  export sixty-unit;
  // Substrate library
  use dylan;
end library sixty-unit;

// Interface module
define module sixty-unit
  // External interface
  create <sixty-unit>;
  create total-seconds, encode-total-seconds, decode-total-seconds;
end module sixty-unit;

// Implementation module
define module sixty-unit-implementation
  // External interface
  use sixty-unit;
  // Substrate module
  use dylan;
end module sixty-unit;
```

Notice that we have taken this opportunity to reorganize the **sixty-unit** module into a separate interface and implementation. We also have to create **encode-total-seconds** in the **sixty-unit** module, rather than to create it in the **time** interface and to define it in **sixty-unit**. Recall that all created names must be defined in the library in which they are created; we cannot use the create–define structure across libraries. We still want **encode-total-seconds** to be part of the interface of the **time** library, so we will have to change the **time** interface module to import it and to re-export it from the time library, as shown in Section 13.8.2.

If we had followed our own recommendations in Section 13.4.3, page 198, we would probably have discovered that **encode-total-seconds** belonged in the **sixty-unit** interface, and we would have avoided most of this reorganization.

13.8.2 The updated `time-library` file

The **time-library** file: **time-library.dylan**.

```
Module: dylan-user

// Library definition
define library time
  // Interface module
  export time;
  // Substrate libraries
  use sixty-unit;
  use format-out;
  use dylan;
end library time;

// Interface module
define module time
  // Classes
  create <time>, <time-of-day>, <time-offset>;
  // Generics
  create say;
  // Shared protocol
  use sixty-unit, import: { encode-total-seconds }, export: all;
end module time;

// Implementation module
define module time-implementation
  // External interface
  use time;
  // Substrate modules
  use sixty-unit;
  use format-out;
  use dylan;
end module time-implementation;
```

Note that the **time** interface module imports only **encode-total-seconds** from **sixty-unit**. It then re-exports all the names that it has imported — in this case, just **encode-total-seconds**. In this way, the **time** interface is acting as a filter and is passing on only a subset of the **sixty-unit** interface to its clients.

At this point, we need to **open** the **<sixty-unit>** class. Because it is now in a separate library, it must be defined to be open to allow other libraries, such as **time** or **angle**, to subclass it. Opening a class simply amounts to changing the

define class to **define open class**. The exact implications of this declaration are discussed in Chapter 19, *Performance and Flexibility*.

13.8.3 The updated sixty-unit implementation file

The **sixty-unit** implementation file: **sixty-unit.dylan**.

```
Module: sixty-unit-implementation

define open abstract class <sixty-unit> (<object>)
  slot total-seconds :: <integer>,
    required-init-keyword: total-seconds:;
end class <sixty-unit>;

define method encode-total-seconds
    (max-unit :: <integer>, minutes :: <integer>, seconds :: <integer>)
 => (total-seconds :: <integer>)
  ((max-unit * 60) + minutes) * 60 + seconds;
end method encode-total-seconds;

define method decode-total-seconds
    (sixty-unit :: <sixty-unit>)
 => (max-unit :: <integer>, minutes :: <integer>, seconds :: <integer>)
  decode-total-seconds(sixty-unit.total-seconds);
end method decode-total-seconds;

define method decode-total-seconds
    (total-seconds :: <integer>)
 => (hours :: <integer>, minutes :: <integer>, seconds :: <integer>)
  let(total-minutes, seconds) = truncate/(abs(total-seconds), 60);
  let(hours, minutes) = truncate/(total-minutes, 60);
  values(hours, minutes, seconds);
end method decode-total-seconds;
```

Figure 13.5 shows the relationships among our libraries and modules at this point. Note that **sixty-unit** is now a separate library. It uses the **dylan** library and is used by the **time** library. We illustrate the **time** module importing and re-exporting part of the **sixty-unit** interface module (the method **encode-total-seconds**) by the darker grey area.

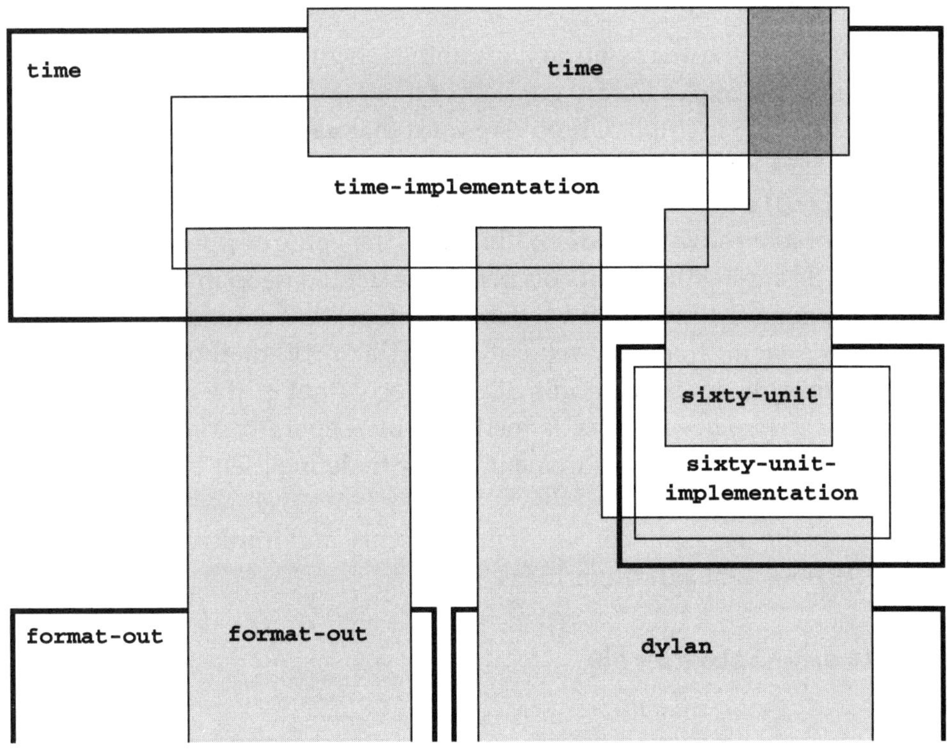

Figure 13.5 `sixty-unit` as a separate library.

13.8.4 Two LID files

Here, we show the LID files for each library.

The LID file: `sixty-unit.lid`.

```
library: sixty-unit
files:   sixty-unit-library
         sixty-unit
```

The LID file: `time.lid`.

```
library: time
files:   time-library
         time
```

13.9 Protocol design

We can now define the **`angle`** library as another client of the **`sixty-unit`** library. The interface of the **`angle`** library consists of the classes **`<angle>`** and **`<directed-angle>`**, and the **`say`** method. Uh-oh! We want that **`say`** method to be another method on the **`say`** generic function defined by the **`time`** library, so that a client of the **`time`** *and* **`angle`** libraries sees a single generic function, **`say`**, that applies to either times or angles. This situation illustrates the value of putting a lot of thought into designing our protocols before we get too deep into an implementation. The **`say`** generic function is a separate protocol that could apply to many classes in our system. To permit separate libraries to add methods to a Dylan generic function, the module defining the protocol (that is, the module defining the generic function) needs to be defined first, in a separate, common library. Other libraries then use this component library to define their particular implementation of the protocol.

To create the **`say`** protocol, we define a library and implementation file as shown in Sections 13.9.1 through 13.9.4.

13.9.1 The `say-library` file

The **`say-library`** file: **`say-library.dylan`**.

```
Module: dylan-user

// Library definition
define library say
  // Interface modules
  export say, say-implementor;
  // Substrate libraries
  use format-out;
  use dylan;
end library say;

// Protocol interface
define module say
  create say;
end module say;
```

The **say-library** file: **say-library.dylan**. *(continued)*

```
// Implementor interface
define module say-implementor
  use say, export: all;
  use format-out, export: all;
end module say-implementor;

// Implementation module
define module say-implementation
  use say;
  use dylan;
end module say-implementation;
```

13.9.2 The say implementation file

The **say** implementation file: **say.dylan**.

```
Module: say-implementation

define open generic say (object :: <object>) => ();
```

Here, we have created the recommended interface and implementation structure, having learned our lesson with the **sixty-unit** module. Even though it looks like overkill to have a separate implementation module for a single generic function definition, we have planned for future expansion.

The **say** protocol library is an example of the multiple-interface capability of Dylan libraries. The **say** library has two interfaces that it makes available: **say** defines the **say** protocol, and **say-implementor** provides the substrate for protocol implementors. This interface is cleaner than the one that we used for **sixty-unit**, where **encode-total-seconds** played more of an interface role, and **<sixty-unit>** and **decode-total-seconds** played more of a substrate role. The result is seen in the clients of the **sixty-unit** library, who must split out these roles for themselves.

Note that the **say-implementor** module is both a client and an interface module. It is the interface of the **say** protocol for clients who will implement **say** methods, and it is a client of the **format-out** module. Because most **say** methods use **`format-out`** in their implementations, it makes sense to re-export all of the **`format-out`** module for **`say-implementor`** clients.

The explicit definition of the **`say`** generic function is good protocol documentation. It is also required: All module variables must have a definition for a library to be complete. (An alternative would have been to define a default method for **`say`**, which would also create an implicit generic-function definition. However, implicit generic-function definitions are **sealed**, and, for a protocol, we need an **open** generic function, because we intend clients to add methods to it. The exact implications of this declaration are discussed in Chapter 19, *Performance and Flexibility*.) The designer of the **`say`** protocol still has to choose whether to require each type to define its own **`say`** method, or to provide a universal default. In this case, we choose not to provide a default, so that an error will be signaled if **`say`** is called on a type that does not either provide or inherit a **`say`** method.

> **Comparison with C++:** Dylan modules enforce a structured design of protocols. To create a shared protocol, to which methods can be added from independent libraries, we must ensure that the module defining the protocol (the module defining the generic function) is defined first, in a separate, common library. The common library defines the protocol in one place, easing documentation and maintenance.
>
> In C++ however, a **`using`** directive can create a local alias to overload a function in any other library, even if it is in another namespace.
>
> The library-use relationships of Dylan modules form a directed graph, centralizing shared functionality, whereas C++ namespaces can be interconnected arbitrarily, making documentation and maintenance of shared protocols difficult.

To complete our restructuring, we must reorganize the **`time`** library and module files to use the **`say`** protocol, so that the **`say`** protocol is shared with the **`angle`** library that we intend to build.

13.9.3 The updated `time-library` file

The **time-library** file: **time-library.dylan**.

```
Module: dylan-user

// Library definition
define library time
  // Interface module
  export time;
  // Substrate libraries
  use sixty-unit;
  use say;
  use dylan;
end library time;

// Interface module
define module time
  // Classes
  create <time>, <time-of-day>, <time-offset>;
  // Shared protocol
  use say, export: all;
  use sixty-unit, import: { encode-total-seconds }, export: all;
end module time;

// Implementation module
define module time-implementation
  // External interface
  use time;
  // Substrate modules
  use sixty-unit;
  use say-implementor;
  use dylan;
end module time-implementation;
```

The **time** module is modified to use **say**, which it exports to its clients. The implementation module is modified to use **say-implementor**, which includes **format-out**, so it would be superfluous to continue to include **format-out** in **time-implementation**. Similarly, the **time** library definition replaces its use of the **format-out** library with the **say** library.

Note that the compiler recursively finds all the libraries necessary for compilation. In this case, the **format-out** library will be included in the compilation of the **time** library, even though it is not directly named.

13.9.4 The `angle` library

At this point, we are ready to define the **`angle`** library, which will share the **`sixty-unit`** and **`say`** libraries with the **`time`** library. In Chapter 14, *Four Complete Libraries*, we present the consolidated changes to the **`sixty-unit`**, **`say`**, and **`time`** libraries that we have developed in this chapter, followed by the complete definition of the **`angle`** library.

13.10 Summary

In this chapter, we covered the following:

- We illustrated Dylan modules and libraries.
- We showed how to design modules using three roles: interface modules, implementation modules, and client modules.
- We described how a library might appear in Dylan interchange format.
- We showed how to create a component library.
- We illustrated the complexity of component and protocol design.
- We discussed how to create a protocol that can be extended by multiple client libraries.
- We discussed namespaces in Dylan, and their applicable scope; see Table 13.1.

Namespace	Scope
library	global
module	per library
constant or variable	per module
symbol or keyword	global

Table 13.1 Namespace scopes.

- We described the roles of modules and the definition clauses that modules use; see Table 13.2.

Role	Example clause
interface	*// Interface class* **create <time>;** *// Re-exported interface* **use say, export: all;**
client	*// Substrate module* **use dylan;**
implementation	*// Interface module* **use time;**
implementation and interface	*// Interface protocol* **export say;**

Table 13.2 Module roles.

14

Four Complete Libraries

In this chapter, we show all the files that the complete **`time`**, **`angle`**, **`sixty-unit`**, and **`say`** libraries comprise.

14.1 The `sixty-unit` library

The **`sixty-unit`** library is an example of a shared substrate library. Both the **`time`** and **`angle`** libraries use the **`sixty-unit`** library to create more specialized classes that build on a common substrate.

The **`sixty-unit`** library comprises two Dylan interchange-format files: a library file, containing the library and module definitions; and an implementation file, containing a single source record, defining the generic function that is the **`say`** protocol. For completeness, we also show the LID file that describes the library and its component files.

14.1.1 The `sixty-unit-library` file

The **sixty-unit-library** file: **sixty-unit-library.dylan**.

```
Module: dylan-user

// Library definition
define library sixty-unit
  // Interface module
  export sixty-unit;
  // Substrate library
  use dylan;
end library sixty-unit;

// Interface module
define module sixty-unit
  // Classes
  create <sixty-unit>;
  // Generics
  create total-seconds, encode-total-seconds, decode-total-seconds;
end module sixty-unit;

// Implementation module
define module sixty-unit-implementation
  // External interface
  use sixty-unit;
  // Substrate module
  use dylan;
end module sixty-unit;
```

14.1.2 The `sixty-unit` implementation file

The **sixty-unit** implementation file: **sixty-unit.dylan**.

```
Module: sixty-unit-implementation

define open abstract class <sixty-unit> (<object>)
  slot total-seconds :: <integer>, required-init-keyword: total-seconds:;
end class <sixty-unit>;
```

The **sixty-unit** implementation file: **sixty-unit.dylan**. *(continued)*

```
define method encode-total-seconds
    (max-unit :: <integer>, minutes :: <integer>, seconds :: <integer>)
 => (total-seconds :: <integer>)
  ((max-unit * 60) + minutes) * 60 + seconds;
end method encode-total-seconds;

define method decode-total-seconds
    (sixty-unit :: <sixty-unit>)
 => (max-unit :: <integer>, minutes :: <integer>, seconds :: <integer>)
  decode-total-seconds(sixty-unit.total-seconds);
end method decode-total-seconds;

define method decode-total-seconds
    (total-seconds :: <integer>)
 => (max-unit :: <integer>, minutes :: <integer>, seconds :: <integer>)
  let(total-minutes, seconds) = truncate/(abs(total-seconds), 60);
  let(max-unit, minutes) = truncate/(total-minutes, 60);
  values(max-unit, minutes, seconds);
end method decode-total-seconds;
```

14.1.3 The sixty-unit LID file

The LID file: **sixty-unit.lid**.

```
library: sixty-unit
files:   sixty-unit-library
         sixty-unit
```

14.2 The say library

The **say** library is an example of a library that defines a shared protocol. All our other libraries use the **say** library, so that they can add to the **say** generic function methods that appropriately display the objects of the classes that they define.

The **say** library comprises two Dylan interchange-format files: a library file, containing the library and module definitions; and an implementation file, containing a single source record, defining the generic function that is the **say** protocol. For completeness, we also show the LID file that describes the library and its component files.

14.2.1 The `say-library` file

The `say-library` file: `say-library.dylan`.

```
Module: dylan-user

// Library definition
define library say
  // Interface modules
  export say, say-implementor;
  // Substrate libraries
  use format-out;
  use dylan;
end library say;

// Protocol interface
define module say
  create say;
end module say;

// Implementor interface
define module say-implementor
  use say, export: all;
  use format-out, export: all;
end module say-implementor;

// Implementation module
define module say-implementation
  use say;
  use dylan;
end module say-implementation;
```

14.2.2 The `say` implementation file

The `say` implementation file: `say.dylan`.

```
Module: say-implementation

define open generic say (object :: <object>) => ();
```

14.2.3 The say LID file

The LID file: **say.lid**.

```
library: say
files:   say-library
         say
```

14.3 The time library

The **time** library is a client of the **sixty-unit** and **say** libraries, and it will serve as a substrate library for the rest of our application. Like the previous two libraries, it comprises a library file and an implementation file; we also show the corresponding LID file.

14.3.1 The time-library file

The **time-library** file: **time-library.dylan**.

```
Module: dylan-user

// Library definition
define library time
  // Interface module
  export time;
  // Substrate libraries
  use sixty-unit;
  use say;
  use dylan;
end library time;
```

The `time-library` file: `time-library.dylan`. *(continued)*

```
// Interface module
define module time
  // Classes
  create <time>, <time-of-day>, <time-offset>;
  // Types
  create <nonnegative-integer>;
  // Constants
  create $midnight, $tomorrow;
  // Shared protocol
  use say, export: all;
  use sixty-unit, import: { encode-total-seconds }, export: all;
end module time;

// Implementation module
define module time-implementation
  // External interface
  use time;
  // Substrate modules
  use sixty-unit;
  use say-implementor;
  use dylan;
end module time-implementation;
```

14.3.2 The `time` implementation file

The `time` implementation file: `time.dylan`.

```
Module: time-implementation

// Define nonnegative integers as integers that are >= zero
define constant <nonnegative-integer> = limited(<integer>, min: 0);

define abstract class <time> (<sixty-unit>)
end class <time>;

define method say (time :: <time>)
  let (hours, minutes) = decode-total-seconds(time);
  format-out("%d:%s%d",
             hours, if (minutes < 10) "0" else " " end, minutes);
end method say;
```

The **time** implementation file: **time.dylan**. *(continued)*

```
// A specific time of day from 00:00 (midnight) to before 24:00 (tomorrow)
define class <time-of-day> (<time>)
end class <time-of-day>;

define method total-seconds-setter
    (total-seconds :: <integer>, time :: <time-of-day>)
 => (total-seconds :: <nonnegative-integer>)
  if (total-seconds >= 0)
    next-method();
  else
    error("%d cannot be negative", total-seconds);
  end if;
end method total-seconds-setter;

define method initialize (time :: <time-of-day>, #key)
  next-method();
  if (time.total-seconds < 0)
    error("%d cannot be negative", time.total-seconds);
  end if;
end method initialize;

// A relative time between -24:00 and +24:00
define class <time-offset> (<time>)
end class <time-offset>;

define method past? (time :: <time-offset>) => (past? :: <boolean>)
  time.total-seconds < 0;
end method past?;

define method say (time :: <time-offset>) => ()
  format-out("%s ", if (time.past?) "minus" else "plus" end);
  next-method();
end method say;

define method \+
    (offset1 :: <time-offset>, offset2 :: <time-offset>)
 => (sum :: <time-offset>)
  let sum = offset1.total-seconds + offset2.total-seconds;
  make(<time-offset>, total-seconds: sum);
end method \+;
```

The `time` implementation file: `time.dylan`. *(continued)*

```
define method \+
    (offset :: <time-offset>, time-of-day :: <time-of-day>)
 => (sum :: <time-of-day>)
  make(<time-of-day>,
       total-seconds: offset.total-seconds + time-of-day.total-seconds);
end method \+;

define method \+ (time-of-day :: <time-of-day>, offset :: <time-offset>)
 => (sum :: <time-of-day>)
  offset + time-of-day;
end method \+;

define method \< (time1 :: <time-of-day>, time2 :: <time-of-day>)
  time1.total-seconds < time2.total-seconds;
end method \<;

define method \< (time1 :: <time-offset>, time2 :: <time-offset>)
  time1.total-seconds < time2.total-seconds;
end method \<;

define method \= (time1 :: <time-of-day>, time2 :: <time-of-day>)
  time1.total-seconds = time2.total-seconds;
end method \=;

define method \= (time1 :: <time-offset>, time2 :: <time-offset>)
  time1.total-seconds = time2.total-seconds;
end method \=;

// Two useful time constants
define constant $midnight
  = make(<time-of-day>, total-seconds: encode-total-seconds(0, 0, 0));

define constant $tomorrow
  = make(<time-of-day>,
         total-seconds: encode-total-seconds(24, 0, 0));
```

14.3.3 The `time` LID file

The LID file: `time.lid`.

```
library: time
files:   time-library
         time
```

14.4 The angle library

The **angle** library is the second client of the **sixty-unit** substrate. The **angle** library extends the **say** protocol to handle objects of the classes that it defines, such as **<latitude>**, **<longitude>**, and **<absolute-position>**. For the time being, we have included positions with angles, as we do not foresee any benefit to breaking them out into yet another library, at least for the current application. Nevertheless, we have defined separate interface and implementation modules for positions, and we have broken out the position source records into a separate interchange file.

Like with the **time** library, the **angle** library file does not have to specify the use of the **format-out** library. It will be transitively included because it is exported by the **say** library. Similarly, clients of the **angle** library do not need to know anything about the **say** and **sixty-unit** libraries, since those libraries are imported and re-exported to clients of **angle**.

Note that the **position-implementation** module uses the **angle** module — it is an internal client of the **angle** module. This structure means that we can easily break out positions as a separate library, should the need arise.

Also note that we have used the **angle** interface module to enforce access control on the **internal-direction** slot. It should be accessed only through the **direction** and **direction-setter** methods, which ensure that valid values are used for our **<latitude>** and **<longitude>** classes. Because only the approved generic functions are created in the interface module, only they will be accessible to clients of the **angle** library. The **internal-direction** slot is truly internal to the **angle** library — no client library can even determine its existence.

14.4.1 The `angle-library` file

The `angle-library` file: `angle-library.dylan`.

```
Module: dylan-user

// Library definition
define library angle
  // Interface module
  export angle, position;
  // Substrate libraries
  use sixty-unit;
  use say;
  use dylan;
end library angle;

// Interface module
define module angle
  // Classes
  create <angle>, <directed-angle>, <latitude>, <longitude>;
  // Generics
  create direction, direction-setter;
  // Shared protocol
  use say, export: all;
  use sixty-unit, import: { encode-total-seconds }, export: all;
end module angle;

// Interface module
define module position
  // Classes
  create <position>, <absolute-position>, <relative-position>;
  // Generics
  create distance, angle, latitude, longitude;
  // Shared protocol
  use say, export: all;
end module angle;

// Implementation module
define module angle-implementation
  // External interface
  use angle;
  // Substrate modules
  use sixty-unit;
  use say-implementor;
  use dylan;
end module angle-implementation;
```

The **angle-library** file: **angle-library.dylan**. *(continued)*

```
// Implementation module
define module position-implementation
  // External interface
  use position;
  // Substrate modules
  use angle;
  use say-implementor;
  use dylan;
end module angle-implementation;
```

14.4.2 The angle implementation file

The **angle** implementation file is simply a collection of the source records that we developed earlier for creating and saying angles, latitudes, and longitudes.

The **angle** implementation file: **angle.dylan**.

```
Module: angle-implementation

define abstract class <angle> (<sixty-unit>)
end class <angle>;

define method say (angle :: <angle>) => ()
  let(degrees, minutes, seconds) = decode-total-seconds(angle);
  format-out("%d degrees %d minutes %d seconds",
             degrees, minutes, seconds);
end method say;

define class <relative-angle> (<angle>)
end class <relative-angle>;

define method say (angle :: <relative-angle>) => ()
  format-out(" %d degrees", decode-total-seconds(angle));
end method say;

define abstract class <directed-angle> (<angle>)
  virtual slot direction :: <symbol>;
  slot internal-direction :: <symbol>;
  keyword direction:;
end class <directed-angle>;
```

The `angle` implementation file: `angle.dylan`. *(continued)*

```
define method initialize (angle :: <directed-angle>, #key direction: dir)
  next-method();
  angle.direction := dir;
end method initialize;

define method direction (angle :: <directed-angle>) => (dir :: <symbol>)
  angle.internal-direction;
end method direction;

define method direction-setter
    (dir :: <symbol>, angle :: <directed-angle>) => (new-dir :: <symbol>)
  angle.internal-direction := dir;
end method direction-setter;

define method say (angle :: <directed-angle>) => ()
  next-method();
  format-out(" %s", angle.direction);
end method say;

define class <latitude> (<directed-angle>)
end class <latitude>;

define method say (latitude :: <latitude>) => ()
  next-method();
  format-out(" latitude\n");
end method say;

define method direction-setter
    (dir :: <symbol>, latitude :: <latitude>) => (new-dir :: <symbol>)
  if (dir == #"north" | dir == #"south")
    next-method();
  else
    error("%= is not north or south", dir);
  end if;
end method direction-setter;

define class <longitude> (<directed-angle>)
end class <longitude>;

define method say (longitude :: <longitude>) => ()
  next-method();
  format-out(" longitude\n");
end method say;
```

The **angle** implementation file: **angle.dylan**. *(continued)*

```
define method direction-setter
    (dir :: <symbol>, longitude :: <longitude>) => (new-dir :: <symbol>)
  if (dir == #"east" | dir == #"west")
    next-method();
  else
    error("%= is not east or west", dir);
  end if;
end method direction-setter;
```

14.4.3 The `position` implementation file

The **position** implementation file is simply a collection of the source records that we developed earlier for creating and saying absolute and relative positions.

The **position** implementation file: **position.dylan**.

```
Module: position-implementation

define abstract class <position> (<object>)
end class <position>;

define class <absolute-position> (<position>)
  slot latitude :: <latitude>, required-init-keyword: latitude:;
  slot longitude :: <longitude>, required-init-keyword: longitude:;
end class <absolute-position>;

define method say (position :: <absolute-position>) => ()
  say(position.latitude);
  say(position.longitude);
end method say;

define class <relative-position> (<position>)
  // Distance is in miles
  slot distance :: <single-float>, required-init-keyword: distance:;
  // Angle is in degrees
  slot angle :: <angle>, required-init-keyword: angle:;
end class <relative-position>;

define method say (position :: <relative-position>) => ()
  format-out("%s miles away at heading ", position.distance);
  say(position.angle);
end method say;
```

14.4.4 The `angle` LID file

Because we have chosen to put the source records for positions in a separate interchange file, the LID file lists three Dylan files that make up the **`angle`** library.

The LID file: `angle.lid`.

```
library: angle
files:   angle-library
         angle
         position
```

14.5 Summary

The structure of protocol and substrate libraries that we have created is perhaps overly complex for the simple functionality that we have implemented here. However, the libraries illustrate the power of the Dylan module and library system to modularize large projects into easily manageable sub-projects, and to control the interfaces among those projects.

Part III. Sample Application

Chapter 15, *Design of the Airport Application*, describes the goals and overall design of the airport example.

Chapter 16, *Definition of a New Collection*, shows you how to build a new class of sequence, called a **sorted sequence**.

Chapter 17, *The Airport Application*, contains the complete, working code of the airport example. This chapter illustrates many techniques described in the previous chapters, including collections, control-flow operators, initialization of slots, and libraries and modules. The chapters in Part IV describe advanced techniques that you can use to improve the code presented in Part III.

15

Design of the Airport Application

In this chapter, we explore the design of an airport application that uses the **`time`**, **`angle`**, and **`say`** libraries.

15.1 Goals of the airport application

Throughout this book, we have been developing components for an airport application. This application deals with airports, aircraft, gates, and related objects. Figure 15.1 shows a diagram of a simple airport.

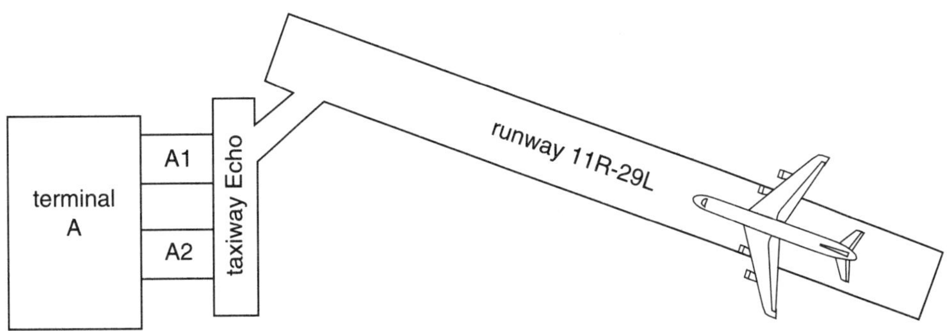

Figure 15.1 Objects in a simple airport.

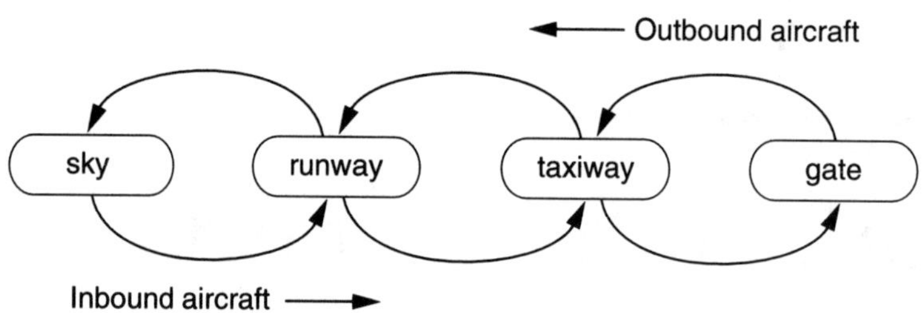

Figure 15.2 Transitions between sky and gate for outbound and inbound aircraft.

In Figure 15.1, we see a single **terminal**, A. It has two **gates**, A1 and A2, a **taxiway**, Echo, a **runway**, 11R-29L, and an **aircraft** approaching the runway.

When landing, an aircraft goes from the sky to a runway to a taxiway to a gate. Figure 15.2 is a state diagram showing these transitions for both inbound and outbound aircraft.

Our first goal for this application is as follows: given a set of incoming aircraft at various positions in the sky, we want to predict which gate each aircraft will use when it arrives, and to estimate the arrival time of the aircraft at the gate. This information is displayed on the Arrivals monitors in an airport.

Our second goal for the application is to provide additional information for the ground crew. We must state the entire path that an incoming aircraft will take, including the runway, the taxiway, and the gate. We must also state the time that an aircraft is expected to be at each point. For example, for an inbound aircraft, we want to display information like the following:

```
12:30: Aircraft Cardinal at Runway 11R-29L
12:43: Aircraft Cardinal at Taxiway Echo
12:47: Aircraft Cardinal at Gate A2
```

The application considers departing aircraft as well as arriving aircraft.

15.2 Objects that model an airport

We need to define classes that represent the objects in Figures 15.1 and 15.2. Note that the application displays information about the path of an aircraft from gate to sky and sky to gate; the aircraft stops at the gate and does not enter the terminal itself. Therefore, we do not need to define a terminal class. Our design includes these airport classes:

```
<airport>, <gate>, <taxiway>, <runway>, <sky>, <vehicle>, <aircraft>
```

A vehicle is any object that is self-propelled. Aircraft are vehicles that are capable of flying. In our design, the sky around the airport, the gates, the taxiways, and the runways each keep track of each aircraft as the latter moves from the sky to the gate and back to the sky again. One common attribute of the sky, gates, taxiways, and runways is that each of them can hold an aircraft, or more than one aircraft. Because these objects can hold vehicles, we can think of them as containers. Our design uses this class to represent all types of containers:

```
<vehicle-storage>
```

In our design, containers are connected to other containers. In the airport diagram in Figure 15.1, gate A1 is connected to taxiway Echo, which is connected to runway 11R-29L. We can use a slot in the `<vehicle-storage>` class to model these connections.

Since some containers can hold only one aircraft, whereas other containers have more complex behavior, our design includes two subclasses of `<vehicle-storage>`:

```
<single-storage>, <multiple-storage>
```

Instances of `<single-storage>` may hold a single aircraft regardless of the direction of travel. Instances of `<multiple-storage>` may hold more than one aircraft, and each direction is treated separately. For example, `<gate>` is a subclass of `<single-storage>`, and `<sky>` is a subclass of `<multiple-storage>`.

All subclasses of `<vehicle-storage>` must comply with the vehicle-storage protocol. In particular, designers of `<vehicle-storage>` subclasses must ensure that the subclasses either inherit or define methods for all the key vehicle-storage generic functions.

Certain classes — such as the time and position classes — represent intangible concepts. Other classes — such as airports, gates, runways, and aircraft — represent physical objects. It may be useful to make that distinction in our classes, so we define a class from which all physical objects inherit:

```
<physical-object>
```

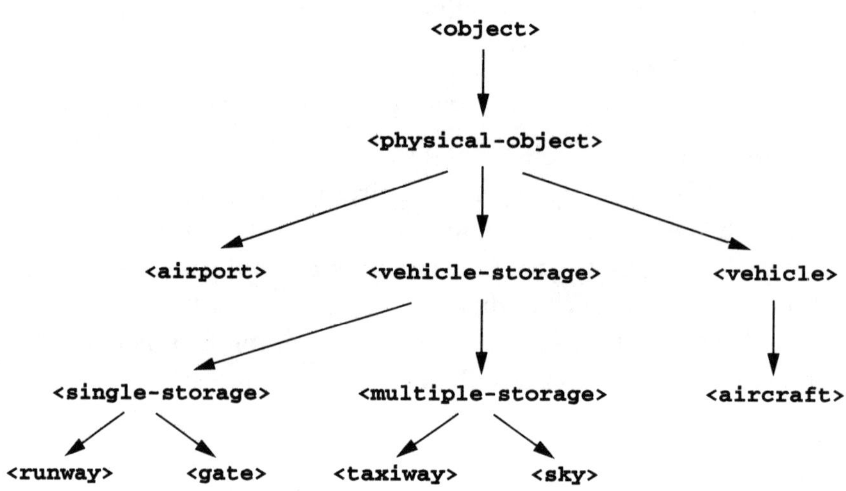

Figure 15.3 Inheritance relationships among classes that represent physical objects.

Figure 15.3 shows the inheritance relationships among the classes that represent physical objects.

15.3 Behaviors of the objects

The top-level function of our application is called **`process-aircraft`**. Given an airport that has been properly initialized, **`process-aircraft`** will simulate and document the movement of all inbound aircraft through all the containers of the airport, from landing through takeoff.

To predict how long it will take for an aircraft to arrive at the airport, we need to compute the distance between the position of the aircraft and the position of the airport. Then, we must divide the distance by the speed to determine how long it will take the aircraft to get from one position to the other. The **`flying-time`** method will implement that computation in our design.

Once an aircraft approaches the airport, it enters a series of containers. The generic functions that constitute the vehicle-storage protocol help us to generate and simulate the transitions of the aircraft from container to container.

We summarize some of the operations in our design here; we summarize the vehicle-storage protocol in Section 15.4.

process-aircraft *airport time* *Generic Function*

This generic function simulates and documents the movement of aircraft through the airport, including the time of each transition — for example,

```
12:30: Aircraft Cardinal at Runway 11R-29L
12:43: Aircraft Cardinal at Taxiway Echo
12:47: Aircraft Cardinal at Gate A2
```

The *airport* is an instance of **<airport>**. The *time* is an instance of **<time-of-day>**.

distance-3d *aircraft airport* *Generic Function*

This generic function returns the distance between its two arguments. The *aircraft* is an instance of **<aircraft>**, and the *airport* is an instance of **<airport>**.

flying-time *aircraft airport* *Generic Function*

This generic function returns the time that it would take for the *aircraft* to fly to the *airport*.

15.4 The vehicle-container protocol

Once the aircraft approaches the airport, it enters a set of connected containers on its way inbound to a particular gate. The aircraft eventually turns around and heads outbound toward the sky. The vehicle-container protocol manages the transition of aircraft from one container to another. The generic functions that make up this protocol are summarized next. For all the generic functions that follow, the value of the *vehicle* parameter must be an instance of **<vehicle>**, the value of the *container* parameter must be an instance of **<vehicle-storage>**, and the value of the *direction* parameter must be either the symbol **#"inbound"** or **#"outbound"**.

available? *vehicle container direction* *Generic Function*

This generic function returns true if there is space in *container* for *vehicle* to enter for traveling in *direction*.

`move-in-vehicle` *vehicle container direction* *Generic Function*

This generic function moves the *vehicle* into the *container* in the *direction* given.

`move-out-vehicle` *vehicle container direction* *Generic Function*

This generic function moves the *vehicle* out of the *container* in the *direction* given.

`next-out` *container direction* *Generic Function*

This generic function determines what vehicle, if any, could move to the next container. If there is such a vehicle, then **`next-out`** returns the vehicle, the next container in the direction of travel, and the time it would take to make that transition.

`next-landing-step` *container vehicle* *Generic Function*

This generic function returns two values. The first value is the class of the next container into which *vehicle* may move from *container*. The second value is how long it will take *vehicle* to move into the next container. This generic function is used by the **`next-out`** generic function to accomplish part of the latter's work.

15.5 Sorted sequences

Part of what **`process-aircraft`** will do in our example is to generate a collection of possible transition steps for aircraft in or around the airport. For example, if an aircraft is on the runway, then one possible transition step would be to move the aircraft to the taxiway. If there are many aircraft in the airport, there are many possible transitions that might take place at various time. The **`process-aircraft`** method needs to consider these transitions in order. That is, if an aircraft is ready to land on a runway in 5 minutes, but another one is ready to take off in 2 minutes, **`process-aircraft`** should attempt to complete the take-off transition before completing the landing transition. To keep these transitions in time order, we use a collection called a **sorted sequence**.

Dylan does not provide a sorted sequence class in its built-in collection library. However, Dylan does provide an extensible collection framework that permits us to define sorted sequences ourselves. In fact, Dylan already provides all the generic functions that we need to interact with sorted sequences: **`size`**,

shallow-copy, **element**, **add!**, **pop**, **remove!**, and **forward-iteration-protocol**. We just need to provide methods for each of these generic functions that implement these operations for sorted sequences. By defining a method for **forward-iteration-protocol**, we allow sorted sequences to work with the standard Dylan collection iterators discussed in Chapter 11, *Collections and Control Flow*. Because sorted sequences are generally useful, we define them in their own library, in the same manner as we did the time and angle components.

15.6 Testing

We include in the application a test library, which creates instances of the classes described in this chapter, initializes these instances to a reasonable state, and calls **process-aircraft**. Providing test cases (in a separate library) is a good way to check the design, interface, and implementation of an application library.

15.7 Summary

In this chapter, we covered the following:

- We discussed the goals of the airport application: to predict the arrival time and gate of an incoming aircraft, and to describe the entire path that an incoming aircraft will take, including the time it is expected to be at each point.
- We discussed the design of the airport application classes, and the operations to be performed on instances of the classes, including the vehicle-container protocol.
- We discussed how the time, angle, sorted sequence, and testing libraries interact with the main airport application library.

In Chapter 16, *Definition of a New Collection*, we implement sorted sequences. In Chapter 17, *The Airport Application*, we implement the airport application.

16

Definition of a New Collection

In this chapter, we implement a data structure called a **sorted sequence**. A sorted sequence is a sequence that automatically keeps the elements of the sequence in a particular order, based on some value computed from each element. Elements are added and removed from sorted sequences; however, the sorted sequence determines the key associated with the element. Thus, it does not make sense to store an element in a sorted sequence at a specific key, because the sorted sequence will determine the correct key to satisfy the automatic-ordering constraint.

We use Dylan's **forward-iteration protocol** to implement the connection between our new collection class and Dylan's standard collection generic functions. Dylan's forward-iteration protocol is a well-defined interface that collection implementors and collection-iterator implementors can use to enable iterators to operate over new collections, and to enable collections to work with new iterators. Once the forward iteration protocol is defined on `<sorted-sequence>`, many of the standard Dylan collection generic functions that we covered in Chapter 11, *Collections and Control Flow*, will work with instances of the new sequence.

The airport application uses a sorted sequence to keep track of aircraft transition in time order. See Chapter 17, *The Airport Application*, for more details.

16.1 The `sorted-sequence.dylan` file

The **`sorted-sequence.dylan`** file contains the module constants, classes, and methods that build on Dylan's collection framework to define the structure and behavior of the new **`<sorted-sequence>`** collection.

16.1.1 A new collection class

The **`sorted-sequence.dylan`** file.

```
module: sorted-sequence

define class <sorted-sequence> (<sequence>)
  // The vector that stores the elements of the sorted sequence, in order
  slot data :: <stretchy-vector> = make(<stretchy-vector>, size: 0);
  // The function used to extract the comparison value from an element
  constant slot value-function :: <function> = identity,
    init-keyword: value-function:;
  // The function used to determine whether one comparison value is
  // smaller than another comparison value
  constant slot comparison-function :: <function> = \<,
    init-keyword: comparison-function:;
end class <sorted-sequence>;
```

Because is there is a well-defined ordering of the elements of sorted sequences, we choose **`<sequence>`** to be the superclass of **`<sorted-sequence>`**. We use the built-in collection class called **`<stretchy-vector>`** to store the elements of our sorted sequence, because we want to be able to have the sorted sequence grow to any size in a convenient way.

The slots **`comparison-function`** and **`value-function`** are constant slots, because we intend to have clients specify these functions only when they create the sorted sequence. If we had decided to let clients change the value of these slots, we would have made the slots virtual, so that we could reorder the data vector after either function had changed.

Now that we have covered the structure and initialization of the sorted sequence data structure, we can define basic collection methods.

16.1.2 Basic collection methods

The **sorted-sequence.dylan** file. *(continued)*

```
define method size (sorted-sequence :: <sorted-sequence>)
    => (sorted-sequence-size :: <integer>)
  sorted-sequence.data.size;
end method size;

define method shallow-copy (sorted-sequence :: <sorted-sequence>)
    => (copy :: <sorted-sequence>)
  let copy
    = make(<sorted-sequence>,
           value-function: sorted-sequence.value-function,
           comparison-function: sorted-sequence.comparison-function);
  // The map-into function replaces the elements of the copy's data array
  // to be the identical elements of the data array of sorted sequence
  copy.data.size := sorted-sequence.data.size;
  map-into(copy.data, identity, sorted-sequence.data);
  copy;
end method shallow-copy;

define constant $unsupplied = list(#f);

define method element
    (sorted-sequence :: <sorted-sequence>, key :: <integer>,
     #key default = $unsupplied)
 => (element :: <object>);
  if (key < sorted-sequence.data.size)
    sorted-sequence.data[key];
  elseif (default = $unsupplied)
    error("Attempt to access key %= which is outside of %=.", key,
          sorted-sequence);
  else default;
  end if;
end method element;
```

In the preceding code, we define methods for determining the number of elements in the sorted sequence, for copying the sorted sequence (but not the elements stored in the sorted sequence), and for accessing a particular item in the sorted sequence. Once we have defined the **element** method for sorted sequences, we can use the subscripting syntax to access particular items in the sorted sequence. Our **element** method implements the standard Dylan protocol, which allows the caller to specify a default value if the key is not contained within the collection. If the key is not part of the collection, and no default value is specified, then an error is signaled. Since we do not export **$unsupplied** from our library, we can be certain that no one can supply that value as the **default** keyword parameter for our **element** method.

Note that the **element-setter** method is not defined, because it does not make sense to store an element at a particular position within the sorted sequence. The sorted sequence itself determines the correct key for each item added to the sorted sequence, based on the item being added and on the value and comparison functions.

Next, we show methods for adding and removing elements from sorted sequences.

16.1.3 Adding and removing elements

The **sorted-sequence.dylan** file. *(continued)*

```
// Add an element to the sorted sequence
define method add!
    (sorted-sequence :: <sorted-sequence>, new-element :: <object>)
 => (sorted-sequence :: <sorted-sequence>)
  let element-value = sorted-sequence.value-function;
  let compare = sorted-sequence.comparison-function;
  add!(sorted-sequence.data, new-element);
  sorted-sequence.data
    := sort!(sorted-sequence.data,
             test: method (e1, e2)
                     compare(element-value(e1), element-value(e2))
                   end);
  sorted-sequence;
end method add!;

// Remove the item at the top of the sorted sequence
define method pop (sorted-sequence :: <sorted-sequence>)
    => (top-of-sorted-sequence :: <object>)
  let data-vector = sorted-sequence.data;
  let top-of-sorted-sequence = data-vector[0];
  let sorted-sequence-size = data-vector.size;
  if (empty?(sorted-sequence))
    error("Trying to pop empty sorted-sequence %=.", sorted-sequence);
```

The **sorted-sequence.dylan** file. *(continued)*

```
  else
    // Shuffle up existing data, removing the top element from the
    // sorted sequence
    for (i from 0 below sorted-sequence-size - 1)
      data-vector[i] := data-vector[i + 1];
    end for;
    // Decrease the size of the data vector, and return the top element
    data-vector.size := sorted-sequence-size - 1;
    top-of-sorted-sequence;
  end if;
end method pop;

// Remove a particular element from the sorted sequence
define method remove!
    (sorted-sequence :: <sorted-sequence>, value :: <object>,
     #key test = \==, count = #f)
 => (sorted-sequence :: <sorted-sequence>)
  let data-vector = sorted-sequence.data;
  let sorted-sequence-size = data-vector.size;
  for (deletion-point from 0,
        // If we have reached the end of the sequence, or we have reached
        // the user-specified limit, we are done
        // Note that specifying a bound in the preceding clause for
        //deletion-point does not work, because bounds are computed only
        // once, and we change sorted-sequence-size in the body
       until: (deletion-point >= sorted-sequence-size)
              | (count & count = 0))
    // Otherwise, if we found a matching element, remove it from the
    // sorted sequence.
    if (test(data-vector[deletion-point], value))
      for (i from deletion-point below sorted-sequence-size - 1)
        data-vector[i] := data-vector[i + 1]
      end for;
      sorted-sequence-size
         := (data-vector.size := sorted-sequence-size - 1);
      if (count) count := count - 1 end;
    end if;
  end for;
  sorted-sequence;
end method remove!;
```

The **remove!** method uses a form of the **for** loop that includes an **until:** clause, much like the **my-copy-sequence** method defined in Section 11.3.3, page 144. Note that all termination checks are tested prior to the execution of the body.

Although the **pop** method is not used in the airport application, it is included for completeness. We could make the **pop** method faster by storing the data elements in reverse order; however, that would lead to either odd behavior or odd implementation of the **element** function on sorted sequences.

16.1.4 The forward-iteration protocol

Dylan's forward-iteration protocol allows us to connect the usual collection iteration functions to our new collection class. Connecting to the forward-iteration protocol is as simple as defining an appropriate method for the **forward-iteration-protocol** generic function. This method must return two objects and six functions.

The **sorted-sequence.dylan** file. *(continued)*

```
// This method enables many standard and user-defined collection operations
define method forward-iteration-protocol
    (sorted-sequence :: <sorted-sequence>)
 => (initial-state :: <integer>, limit :: <integer>,
     next-state :: <function>, finished-state? :: <function>,
     current-key :: <function>, current-element :: <function>,
     current-element-setter :: <function>, copy-state :: <function>)
  values(
         // Initial state
         0,

         // Limit
         sorted-sequence.size,

          // Next state
         method (collection :: <sorted-sequence>, state :: <integer>)
           state + 1
         end,

         // Finished state?
         method (collection :: <sorted-sequence>, state :: <integer>,
                 limit :: <integer>)
           state = limit;
         end,

         // Current key
         method (collection :: <sorted-sequence>, state :: <integer>)
           state
         end,
```

The **sorted-sequence.dylan** file. *(continued)*

```
        // Current element
        element,

        // Current element setter
        method (value :: <object>, collection :: <sorted-sequence>,
                state :: <integer>)
          error("Setting an element of a sorted sequence
                is not allowed.");
        end,

        // Copy state
        identity);
end method forward-iteration-protocol;
```

If we are to iterate over any collection, we must maintain some state to help the iterator remember the current point of iteration. For the forward-iteration protocol, we maintain this state using any object suitable for a given collection. In this case, an integer is sufficient to maintain where we are in the iteration process. The first object returned by **forward-iteration-protocol** is a state object that is suitable for the start of an iteration. The second object returned is a state object that represents the ending state of the iteration. Since, in this case, the state object is just the current key of the sorted sequence, the integer 0 is the correct initial state, and the integer that represents the size of the collection is the correct ending state.

The third value returned is a function that takes the collection and the current iteration state, and returns a state that is the next step in the iteration. In this case, we can determine the next state simply by adding 1 to the current state.

The fourth value returned is a function that receives the collection, the current state, and the ending state, and that determines whether the iteration is complete. In this case, we need only to check whether the current state is equal to the ending state.

The fifth value returned is a function that generates the current key into the collection, given a collection and a state. In this case, the key is the state object.

The sixth value returned is a function that receives a collection and a state, and returns the current element of the collection. In this case, the **element** function is the obvious choice, since our state is just the key.

The seventh value returned is a function that receives a new value, a collection, and a state, and changes the current element to be the new value. In this case, such an operation is illegal, since the only rational way to add elements to sorted sequences is with **add!**. Because this operation is illegal, an error is signaled.

The eighth and final value returned is a function that receives a collection and a state, and returns a copy of the state. In this case, we just return the state, because it is an integer and thus has no slots that are modified during the iteration process. If we represented the state with an object that had one or more slots that did change during iteration, we would have to make a new state instance and to copy the significant information from the old state instance to the new state instance.

Once we have defined a **forward-iteration-protocol** method for sorted sequences, we can iterate over them using **for** loops, mapping functions, and other collections iterators described in Chapter 11, *Collections and Control Flow*. Also, if someone defines a new iterator that uses the forward-iteration protocol, then this new iterator will work with sorted sequences.

Dylan has several other related protocols for backward iteration and for tables. See the *The Dylan Reference Manual* for details.

16.2 The sorted-sequence-library.dylan file

The definitions for the sorted sequence library and module are simple. The only module variable that we need to export is for the sorted sequence class itself. All the generic functions that we want clients to use on sorted sequences are exported by the **dylan** module.

The **sorted-sequence-library.dylan** file.

```
module: dylan-user

define library sorted-sequence
  export sorted-sequence;
  use dylan;
  use definitions;
end library sorted-sequence;

define module sorted-sequence
  export <sorted-sequence>;
  use dylan;
  use definitions;
end module sorted-sequence;
```

The **definitions** library and module are defined in Chapter 17, *The Airport Application*.

16.3 The `sorted-sequence.lid` file

The LID file for sorted sequences is also straightforward. The entire library is contained within two files (in addition to the LID file itself). The library and module definitions are in the file **sorted-sequence-library.dylan**. The definitions of module constants, classes, and methods are in the implementation file, **sorted-sequence.dylan**.

The **sorted-sequence.lid** file.

```
library:  sorted-sequence
files:    sorted-sequence-library
           sorted-sequence
```

16.4 Summary

In this chapter, we covered the following:

- We explored how to define our own collection class.
- We showed how to integrate that class into Dylan's collection framework.
- We used several variations of the control structures presented in Chapter 11, *Collections and Control Flow*.

17

The Airport Application

In this chapter, we present the entire first draft of our airport example application. The code in this chapter is complete, and, given the libraries defined in Chapter 14, *Four Complete Libraries*, and Chapter 16, *Definition of a New Collection*, the code should run in a standard Dylan implementation. This example pulls together many of the techniques presented so far.

17.1 The `definitions.dylan` file

This file contains common definitions that are used throughout several libraries in the airport example.

The `definitions.dylan` file.

```
module: definitions

// This file contains constants and other definitions used in common with
// the other parts of the airport example

// The capital letters of the alphabet
define constant $letters = "ABCDEFGHIJKLMNOPQRSTUVWXYZ";

// This type represents positive integers
define constant <positive-integer> = limited(<integer>, min: 1);

define constant $hours-per-day = 24;
```

The **definitions.dylan** file. *(continued)*

```
define constant $minutes-per-hour = 60;

define constant $seconds-per-minute = 60;

define constant $seconds-per-hour
  = $minutes-per-hour * $seconds-per-minute;

// This method returns the union of the false type and a type you specify,
// as a simple shorthand
// This method may already be provided by your Dylan implementation
define method false-or (other-type :: <type>) => (combined-type :: <type>)
  type-union(singleton(#f), other-type);
end method false-or;
```

17.2 The `airport-classes.dylan` file

This file contains all the main classes specific to the airport example. Several methods that describe or initialize these objects are included as well.

17.2.1 Physical objects

The classes that follow describe fundamental attributes of tangible objects.

The **airport-classes.dylan** file.

```
module: airport

// PHYSICAL OBJECTS AND SIZE

// Used to keep track of object dimensions and object capacities
// All dimensions are in feet
define class <size> (<object>)
  slot length :: <positive-integer>, init-keyword: length:;
  slot width :: <positive-integer>, init-keyword: width:;
  slot height :: <positive-integer>, init-keyword: height:;
end class <size>;

define abstract class <physical-object> (<object>)
  slot current-position :: <position>, init-keyword: current-position:;
  slot physical-size :: <size>, init-keyword: physical-size:;
end class <physical-object>;
```

The **airport-classes.dylan** file.

```
define method say (physical-object :: <physical-object>) => ()
  format-out("object at ");
  say(physical-object.current-position);
end method say;
```

In the preceding portion of the **airport-classes.dylan** file, we define the class **<size>**, which allows us to specify the external dimensions and container volume of various objects. For example, we might want to specify that certain gate areas might be too small to hold the large aircraft. We also define the base class for all tangible objects, **<physical-object>**.

Next, we define the classes where aircraft are normally located.

17.2.2 Vehicle containers

The **airport-classes.dylan** file. *(continued)*

```
// VEHICLE STORAGE

// The default size for a vehicle container
define constant $default-capacity
  = make(<size>, length: 350, width: 200, height: 100);

// This class represents a location where an aircraft could be stored
define abstract class <vehicle-storage> (<physical-object>)
  slot storage-capacity :: <size> = $default-capacity,
    init-keyword: capacity:;
  each-subclass slot name-prefix :: <string> = "Storage", setter: #f;
  slot identifier :: <string>, required-init-keyword: id:;
  slot connected-to :: <simple-object-vector>;
end class <vehicle-storage>;

// By using the name-prefix each-subclass slot, we share one say method
// for all vehicle containers
define method say (storage :: <vehicle-storage>) => ()
  format-out("%s %s", storage.name-prefix, storage.identifier);
end method say;
```

The **airport-classes.dylan** file. *(continued)*

```
define method object-fits?
    (object :: <physical-object>, container :: <vehicle-storage>)
 => (fits? :: <boolean>)
  let object-size = object.physical-size;
  let container-capacity = container.storage-capacity;
  object-size.length < container-capacity.length
    & object-size.height < container-capacity.height
    & object-size.width < container-capacity.width;
end method object-fits?;

// Vehicle storage that can hold only one aircraft regardless of direction
// Direction in this context is either #"inbound" or #"outbound"
define abstract class <single-storage> (<vehicle-storage>)
  slot vehicle-currently-occupying :: false-or(<aircraft>) = #f;
end class <single-storage>;

// Vehicle storage that can hold multiple aircraft, with distinct queues
// for each direction
define abstract class <multiple-storage> (<vehicle-storage>)
  slot vehicles-by-direction :: <object-table> = make(<object-table>);
  slot maxima-by-direction :: <object-table> = make(<object-table>);
  keyword directions:;
  keyword maxima:;
end class <multiple-storage>;

// In a real airport, there would be many paths an aircraft could take
// For our simple airport example, we define only the #"inbound" and
// #"outbound" paths
// The directions parameter is a sequence of these aircraft path names
// Multiple storage containers can limit the number of aircraft that
// they can hold for each path; this is the maxima parameter
// This initialize method creates a queue to hold aircraft for each
// direction, and stores the queue in a table indexed by direction
// This method also stores the maximum number of aircaft for that
// direction in a different table
define method initialize
    (object :: <multiple-storage>, #key directions :: <sequence>,
     maxima :: <sequence>)
  next-method ();
  for (direction in directions,
       maximum in maxima)
    object.vehicles-by-direction[direction] := make(<deque>);
    object.maxima-by-direction[direction] := maximum;
  end for;
end method initialize;
```

The **airport-classes.dylan** file. *(continued)*

```
// From the preceding basic vehicle containers, we can build specific
// containers for each aircraft-transition location
define class <gate> (<single-storage>)
  inherited slot name-prefix, init-value: "Gate";
end class <gate>;

// Given a zero-based terminal number, and a one-based gate number, create
// an return a string with a gate letter and a terminal number in it
define method generate-gate-id
    (term :: <positive-integer>, gate :: <positive-integer>)
 => (gate-id :: <string>)
  format-to-string("%c%d", $letters[term], gate);
end method generate-gate-id;

// Gates-per-terminal is a vector; each element of the vector is the
// number of gates to create for the terminal at that index
// Returns a vector of all the gate instances
define method generate-gates
    (gates-per-terminal :: <vector>, default-gate-capacity :: <size>)
 => (gates :: <vector>)
  let result = make(<vector>, size: reduce1(\+, gates-per-terminal));
  let result-index = 0;
  for (term from 0 below gates-per-terminal.size)
    for (gate from 1 to gates-per-terminal[term])
      result[result-index]
        := make(<gate>, id: generate-gate-id(term, gate),
                capacity: default-gate-capacity);
      result-index := result-index + 1;
    end for;
  end for;
  result;
end method generate-gates;

// This class represents the part of the airspace over a given airport
define class <sky> (<multiple-storage>)
  // The airport over which this piece of sky is located
  slot airport-below :: <airport>, required-init-keyword: airport:;
  inherited slot name-prefix, init-value: "Sky";
  required keyword inbound-aircraft:;
end class <sky>;
```

The **airport-classes.dylan** file. *(continued)*

```
// When a sky instance is created, a sequence of inbound aircraft is
// provided
// This method initializes the direction slot of the aircraft to
// #"inbound", and places the aircraft in the inbound queue of the sky
// instance
define method initialize
    (sky :: <sky>, #key inbound-aircraft :: <sequence>)
  next-method(sky, directions: #[#"inbound", #"outbound"],
              maxima: vector(inbound-aircraft.size,
                             inbound-aircraft.size));
  let inbound-queue = sky.vehicles-by-direction [#"inbound"];
  for (vehicle in inbound-aircraft)
    vehicle.direction := #"inbound";
    push-last(inbound-queue, vehicle);
  end for;
  // Connect the airport to the sky
  sky.airport-below.sky-above := sky;
end method initialize;

// This class represents a strip of land where aircraft land and take off
define class <runway> (<single-storage>)
  inherited slot name-prefix, init-value: "Runway";
end class <runway>;

// Taxiways connect runways and gates
define class <taxiway> (<multiple-storage>)
  inherited slot name-prefix, init-value: "Taxiway";
end class <taxiway>;
```

In the preceding portion of the **airport-classes.dylan** file, we define the tangible objects that represent the various normal locations for aircraft in and around an airport. These locations are known as containers or vehicle storage. We can connect vehicle-storage instances to one another to form an airport. Instances of **<single-storage>** can hold only one aircraft at a time, whereas instances of **<multiple-storage>** can hold more than one aircraft at a time. Also, instances of **<multiple-storage>** treat inbound aircraft separately from outbound aircraft. We define the **object-fits?** method, which determines whether a physical object can fit into a container. We also define methods for creating, initializing, and describing various containers. Note the use of the **each-subclass** slot **name-prefix**, which permits one **say** method on the **<vehicle-storage>** class to cover all the vehicle-container classes. Each subclass of vehicle storage can override the inherited value of this slot, to ensure that the proper name of the vehicle storage is used in the description of instances of that subclass.

The **<vehicle-storage>**, **<multiple-storage>**, and **<single-storage>** classes are all abstract, because it is not sensible to instantiate them. They contain partial implementations that they contribute to their subclasses.

In the **generate-gates** method, the **gates-per-terminal** parameter is a vector that contains the count of gates for each terminal. By adding up all the elements of that vector with **reduce1**, we can compute the total number of gates at the airport, and thus the size of the vector that can hold all the gates.

Next, we examine the classes, initialization methods, and **say** methods for the vehicles in the application.

17.2.3 Vehicles

The **airport-classes.dylan** file. *(continued)*

```
// VEHICLES

// The class that represents all self-propelled devices
define abstract class <vehicle> (<physical-object>)
  // Every vehicle has a unique identification code
  slot vehicle-id :: <string>, required-init-keyword: id:;
  // The normal operating speed of this class of vehicle in miles per hour
  each-subclass slot cruising-speed :: <positive-integer>;
  // Allow individual differences in the size of particular aircraft,
  // while providing a suitable default for each class of aircraft
  each-subclass slot standard-size :: <size>;
end class <vehicle>;

define method initialize (vehicle :: <vehicle>, #key)
  next-method();
  unless (slot-initialized?(vehicle, physical-size))
    vehicle.physical-size := vehicle.standard-size;
  end unless;
end method initialize;

define method say (object :: <vehicle>) => ()
  format-out("Vehicle %s", object.vehicle-id);
end method say;
```

The **airport-classes.dylan** file. *(continued)*

```
// This class represents companies that fly commercial aircraft
define class <airline> (<object>)
  slot name :: <string>, required-init-keyword: name:;
  slot code :: <string>, required-init-keyword: code:;
end class <airline>;

define method say (object :: <airline>) => ()
  format-out("Airline %s", object.name);
end method say;

// This class represents a regularly scheduled trip for a commercial
// airline
define class <flight> (<object>)
  slot airline :: <airline>, required-init-keyword: airline:;
  slot number :: <nonnegative-integer>,
    required-init-keyword: number:;
end class <flight>;

define method say (object :: <flight>) => ()
  format-out("Flight %s %d", object.airline.code, object.number);
end method say;

// This class represents vehicles that normally fly for a portion of
// their trip
define abstract class <aircraft> (<vehicle>)
  slot altitude :: <integer>, init-keyword: altitude:;
  // Direction here is either #"inbound" or #"outbound"
  slot direction :: <symbol>;
  // The next step this aircraft might be able to make
  slot next-transition :: <aircraft-transition>,
    required-init-keyword: transition:, setter: #f;
end class <aircraft>;

define method initialize (vehicle :: <aircraft>, #key)
  next-method();
  // There is a one-to-one correspondance between aircraft instances and
  // transition instances
  // An aircraft can only make one transition at a time
  // Connect the aircraft to its transition
  vehicle.next-transition.transition-aircraft := vehicle;
end method initialize;
```

The **airport-classes.dylan** file. *(continued)*

```
// The next step an aircraft might be able to make
define class <aircraft-transition> (<object>)
  slot transition-aircraft :: <aircraft>, init-keyword: aircraft:;
  slot from-container :: <vehicle-storage>, init-keyword: from:;
  slot to-container :: <vehicle-storage>, init-keyword: to:;
  // The earliest possible time that the transition could take place
  slot earliest-arrival :: <time-of-day>, init-keyword: arrival:;
  // Has this transition already been entered in the sorted sequence?
  // This flag saves searching the sorted sequence
  slot pending? :: <boolean> = #f, init-keyword: pending?:;
end class <aircraft-transition>;

// Describes one step of an aircraft's movements
define method say (transition :: <aircraft-transition>) => ()
  say(transition.earliest-arrival);
  format-out(": ");
  say(transition.transition-aircraft);
  format-out(" at ");
  say(transition.to-container);
end method say;

// Commercial aircraft are aircraft that may have a flight
// assigned to them
define abstract class <commercial-aircraft> (<aircraft>)
  slot aircraft-flight :: false-or(<flight>) = #f, init-keyword: flight:;
end class <commercial-aircraft>;

define method say (object :: <commercial-aircraft>) => ()
  let flight = object.aircraft-flight;
  if (flight)
    say(flight);
  else
    format-out("Unscheduled Aircraft %s", object.vehicle-id);
  end if;
end method say;

// The class that represents all commericial Boeing 707 aircraft
define class <B707> (<commercial-aircraft>)
  inherited slot cruising-speed, init-value: 368;
  inherited slot standard-size,
    init-value: make(<size>, length: 153, width: 146, height: 42);
end class <B707>;
```

The **airport-classes.dylan** file. *(continued)*

```
define method say (aircraft :: <B707>) => ()
  if (aircraft.aircraft-flight)
    next-method();
  else
    format-out("Unscheduled B707 %s", aircraft.vehicle-id);
  end if;
end method say;
```

In the preceding code, we model everything from the most general class of vehicle down to the specific class that represents the Boeing 707. We also model the transition steps that an aircraft may take as it travels throughout the airport, and the airlines and flights associated with commercial aircraft.

17.2.4 Airports

Finally, we present the class that represents the entire airport and provide the method that briefly describes the airport.

The **airport-classes.dylan** file. *(continued)*

```
// AIRPORTS

// The class that represents all places where people and aircraft meet
define class <airport> (<physical-object>)
  // The name of the airport, such as "San Fransisco International Airport"
  slot name :: <string>, init-keyword: name:;
  // The three letter abbreviation, such as "SFO"
  slot code :: <string>, init-keyword: code:;
  // The airspace above the airport
  slot sky-above :: <sky>;
end class <airport>;

define method say (airport :: <airport>) => ()
  format-out("Airport %s", airport.code);
end method say;
```

17.3 The `vehicle-dynamics.dylan` file

The **`vehicle-dynamics.dylan`** file contains stubs for calculations that predict the behavior of the aircraft involved in the example. True aeronautical calculations are beyond the scope of this book.

The **`vehicle-dynamics.dylan`** file.

```
module: airport

// We do not need to type these constants strongly, because the Dylan
// compiler will figure them out for us

define constant $average-b707-brake-speed = 60.0; // Miles per hour

define constant $feet-per-mile = 5280.0;

define constant $average-b707-takeoff-speed = 60.0; // Miles per hour

define constant $takeoff-pause-time = 120; // Seconds

define constant $average-b707-taxi-speed = 10.0;

define constant $average-b707-gate-turnaround-time
  = 34 * $seconds-per-minute; // Seconds

// Computes how long it will take an aircraft to reach an airport
define method flying-time
    (aircraft :: <aircraft>, destination :: <airport>)
 => (duration :: <time-offset>)
  // A simplistic calculation that assumes that the aircraft will
  // average a particular cruising speed for the trip
  make(<time-offset>,
       total-seconds:
         ceiling/(distance-3d(aircraft, destination),
                  aircraft.cruising-speed
                    / as(<single-float>, $seconds-per-hour)));
end method flying-time;
```

The **vehicle-dynamics.dylan** file. *(continued)*

```
// Computes the distance between an aircraft and an airport,
// taking into account the altitude of the aircraft
// Assumes the altitude of the aircraft is the height
// above the ground level of the airport
define method distance-3d
    (aircraft :: <aircraft>, destination :: <airport>)
 => (distance :: <single-float>)  // Miles
  // Here, a squared plus b squared is equals to c squared, where c is the
  // hypotenuse, and a and b are the other sides of a right triangle
  sqrt((aircraft.altitude / $feet-per-mile) ^ 2
       + distance-2d(aircraft.current-position,
                     destination.current-position) ^ 2);
end method distance-3d;

// The distance between two positions, ignoring altitude
define method distance-2d
    (position1 :: <relative-position>, position2 :: <absolute-position>)
 => (distance :: <single-float>) // Miles
  // When we have a relative position for the first argument (the
  // aircraft), we assume the relative position is relative to the second
  // argument (the airport)
  position1.distance;
end method distance-2d;

// It would be sensible to provide a distance-2d method that computed
// the great-circle distance between two absolute positions
// Our example does not need this computation, which is
// beyond the scope of this book

// The time it takes to go from the point of touchdown to the entrance
// to the taxiway
define method brake-time
    (aircraft :: <b707>, runway :: <runway>)
 => (duration :: <time-offset>)
  make(<time-offset>,
       total-seconds:
         ceiling/(runway.physical-size.length / $feet-per-mile,
                  $average-b707-brake-speed / $seconds-per-hour));
end method brake-time;
```

The **vehicle-dynamics.dylan** file. *(continued)*

```
// The time it takes to go from the entrance of the taxiway to the point
// of takeoff
define method takeoff-time
    (aircraft :: <b707>, runway :: <runway>)
 => (duration :: <time-offset>)
  make(<time-offset>,
       total-seconds:
         ceiling/(runway.physical-size.length / $feet-per-mile,
                  $average-b707-takeoff-speed / $seconds-per-hour)
           + $takeoff-pause-time);
end method takeoff-time;

// The time it takes to taxi from the runway entrance across the taxiway
// to the gate
define method gate-time
    (aircraft :: <b707>, taxiway :: <taxiway>)
 => (duration :: <time-offset>)
  make(<time-offset>,
       total-seconds:
         ceiling/(taxiway.physical-size.length / $feet-per-mile,
                  $average-b707-taxi-speed / $seconds-per-hour));
end method gate-time;

// The time it takes to taxi from the gate across the taxiway to the
// entrance of the runway
define method runway-time
    (aircraft :: <b707>, taxiway :: <taxiway>)
 => (duration :: <time-offset>)
  gate-time(aircraft, taxiway);
end method runway-time;

// The time it takes to unload, service, and load an aircraft.
define method gate-turnaround
    (aircraft :: <b707>, gate :: <gate>) => (duration :: <time-offset>)
  make(<time-offset>, total-seconds: $average-b707-gate-turnaround-time);
end method gate-turnaround;
```

17.4 The `schedule.dylan` file

This file contains the key generic functions and methods that compute the schedule of aircraft transitions using the sorted sequence, time, and position libraries, as well as the classes and methods described so far in this chapter.

First, we present the five key generic functions that make up our container protocol, followed by an implementation of that protocol for the container classes defined in Section 17.2.2, page 257.

17.4.1 The container protocol and implementation

The **schedule.dylan** file.

```
module: airport

// The following generic functions constitute the essential protocol for
// interaction between containers and vehicles

// Returns true if container is available for aircraft in direction
define generic available? (vehicle, container, direction);

// Moves vehicle into container in the given direction
define generic move-in-vehicle (vehicle, container, direction);

// Moves vehicle out of container in the given direction
define generic move-out-vehicle (vehicle, container, direction);

// Returns the aircraft next in line to move out of container in direction
define generic next-out (container, direction);

// Returns the class of the next container to move vehicle into,
// and how long it will take to get there
define generic next-landing-step (container, vehicle);

// A single storage container is available if the aircraft fits into the
// the container, and there is not already a vehicle in the container
define method available?
    (vehicle :: <aircraft>, container :: <single-storage>,
     direction :: <symbol>)
 => (container-available? :: <boolean>)
  object-fits?(vehicle, container)
  & ~ (container.vehicle-currently-occupying);
end method available?;
```

The **schedule.dylan** file. *(continued)*

```
// A multiple storage container is available if the aircraft fits into
// the container, and there are not too many aircraft already queued in
// the container for the specified direction
define method available?
    (vehicle :: <aircraft>, container :: <multiple-storage>,
     direction :: <symbol>)
 => (container-available? :: <boolean>)
  object-fits?(vehicle, container)
  & size(container.vehicles-by-direction[direction])
    < container.maxima-by-direction[direction];
end method available?;

// Avoids jamming the runway with inbound traffic, which would prevent
// outbound aircraft from taking off
// The runway is clear to inbound traffic only if there is space in the
// next container inbound from the runway
define method available?
    (vehicle :: <aircraft>, container :: <runway>,
     direction :: <symbol>)
 => (container-available? :: <boolean>)
  next-method()
    & select (direction)
        #"outbound" => #t;
        #"inbound"
          => let (class) = next-landing-step(container, vehicle);
             if (class)
               find-available-connection(container, class, vehicle);
             end if;
      end select;
end method available?;

// A slot is used to keep track of which aircraft is in a single
// storage container
define method move-in-vehicle
    (vehicle :: <aircraft>, container :: <single-storage>,
     direction :: <symbol>)
 => ()
  container.vehicle-currently-occupying := vehicle;
  values();
end method move-in-vehicle;
```

The **schedule.dylan** file. *(continued)*

```
// A deque is used to keep track of which aircraft are traveling in a
// particular direction in a multiple storage container
define method move-in-vehicle
    (vehicle :: <aircraft>, container :: <multiple-storage>,
     direction :: <symbol>)
 => ()
  let vehicles = container.vehicles-by-direction[direction];
  push-last(vehicles, vehicle);
  values();
end method move-in-vehicle;

// When an aircraft reaches the gate, it begins its outbound journey
define method move-in-vehicle
    (vehicle :: <aircraft>, container :: <gate>,
     direction :: <symbol>)
 => ()
  next-method();
  vehicle.direction := #"outbound";
  values();
end method move-in-vehicle;

define method move-out-vehicle
    (vehicle :: <aircraft>, container :: <single-storage>,
     direction :: <symbol>)
 => ()
  container.vehicle-currently-occupying := #f;
  values();
end method move-out-vehicle;

define method move-out-vehicle
    (vehicle   :: <aircraft>,
     container :: <multiple-storage>, direction :: <symbol>)
 => ()
  let vehicles = container.vehicles-by-direction[direction];
  // Assumes that aircraft always exit container in order, and
  // that this aircraft is next
  pop(vehicles);
  values();
end method move-out-vehicle;
```

The **schedule.dylan** file. *(continued)*

```
// Determines what vehicle, if any, could move to the next container
// If there is such a vehicle, then this method returns the vehicle,
// the next container in the direction of travel,
// and the time that it would take to make that transition
define method next-out
    (container :: <vehicle-storage>, direction :: <symbol>)
 => (next-vehicle :: false-or(<vehicle>),
     next-storage :: false-or(<vehicle-storage>),
     time-to-execute :: false-or(<time-offset>));
  let next-vehicle = next-out-internal(container, direction);
  if (next-vehicle)
    let (class, time) = next-landing-step(container, next-vehicle);
    if (class)
      let next-container
        = find-available-connection(container, class, next-vehicle);
      if (next-container)
        values(next-vehicle, next-container, time);
      end if;
    end if;
  end if;
end method next-out;

// This method is just a helper method for the next-out method
// We need different methods based on the class of container
define method next-out-internal
    (container :: <single-storage>, desired-direction :: <symbol>)
 => (vehicle :: false-or(<aircraft>))
  let vehicle = container.vehicle-currently-occupying;
  if (vehicle & vehicle.direction == desired-direction) vehicle; end;
end method next-out-internal;

define method next-out-internal
    (container :: <multiple-storage>, desired-direction :: <symbol>)
 => (vehicle :: false-or(<aircraft>))
  let vehicle-queue = container.vehicles-by-direction[desired-direction];
  if (vehicle-queue.size > 0) vehicle-queue[0]; end;
end method next-out-internal;
```

The **schedule.dylan** file. *(continued)*

```
// The following methods return the class of the next container to which a
// vehicle can move from a particular container
// They also return an estimate of how long that transition will take
define method next-landing-step
    (storage :: <sky>, aircraft :: <aircraft>)
 => (next-class :: false-or(<class>), duration :: false-or(<time-offset>))
  if (aircraft.direction == #"inbound")
    values(<runway>, flying-time(aircraft, storage.airport-below));
  end if;
end method next-landing-step;

define method next-landing-step
    (storage :: <runway>, aircraft :: <aircraft>)
 => (next-class :: <class>, duration :: <time-offset>)
  select (aircraft.direction)
    #"inbound"  => values(<taxiway>, brake-time(aircraft, storage));
    #"outbound" => values(<sky>, takeoff-time(aircraft, storage));
  end select;
end method next-landing-step;

define method next-landing-step
    (storage :: <taxiway>, aircraft :: <aircraft>)
 => (next-class :: <class>, duration :: <time-offset>)
  select (aircraft.direction)
    #"inbound"  => values(<gate>, gate-time(aircraft, storage));
    #"outbound" => values(<runway>, runway-time(aircraft, storage));
  end select;
end method next-landing-step;

define method next-landing-step
    (storage :: <gate>, aircraft :: <aircraft>)
 => (next-class :: <class>, duration :: <time-offset>)
  values(<taxiway>, gate-turnaround(aircraft, storage));
end method next-landing-step;
```

17.4.2 The scheduling algorithm

The next methods form the core of the airport application.

The **schedule.dylan** file. *(continued)*

```
// Searches all of the vehicle storage of class class-of-next, which is
// connected to container and has room for aircraft
define method find-available-connection
    (storage :: <vehicle-storage>, class-of-next :: <class>,
     aircraft :: <aircraft>)
 => (next-container :: <vehicle-storage>)
  block (return)
    for (c in storage.connected-to)
      if (instance?(c, class-of-next)
          & available?(aircraft, c, aircraft.direction))
        return(c);
      end if;
    end for;
  end block;
end method find-available-connection;

// Generate new transitions to be considered for the next move
// The transitions will be placed in the sorted sequence, which will order
// them by earliest arrival time
define method generate-new-transitions
    (container :: <vehicle-storage>, active-transitions :: <sorted-
sequence>,
     containers-visited :: <object-table>)
 => ()
  unless(containers-visited[container])
    // Keep track of which containers we have searched for new possible
    // transitions
    // We avoid looping forever by checking each container just once
    containers-visited[container] := #t;

    local method consider-transition (direction)
      // See whether any vehicle is ready to transition out of a container
      let (vehicle, next-container, time)
        = next-out(container, direction);
      unless (vehicle == #f | vehicle.next-transition.pending?)
        // If there is a vehicle ready, and it is not already in the
        // sorted sequence of pending transitions, then prepare the
        // transition instance associated with the vehicle
        let transition = vehicle.next-transition;
        transition.from-container := container;
        transition.to-container := next-container;
```

The **schedule.dylan** file. *(continued)*

```
        // The vehicle may have been waiting
        // Take this situation into account when computing the earliest
        // arrival into the next container
        transition.earliest-arrival := transition.earliest-arrival + time;
        // Flag the vehicle as pending, to save searching through the
        // active-transitions sorted sequence later
        transition.pending? := #t;
        // Add the transition to the set to be considered
        add!(active-transitions, transition);
      end unless;
    end method consider-transition;

    // Consider both inbound and outbound traffic
    consider-transition(#"outbound");
    consider-transition(#"inbound");
    // Make sure that every container connected to this one is checked
    for (c in container.connected-to)
      generate-new-transitions(c, active-transitions, containers-visited);
    end for;
  end unless;
end method generate-new-transitions;

// Main loop of the program
// See what possible transitions exist, then execute the earliest
// transitions that can be completed
// Returns the time of the last transition
define method process-aircraft
    (airport :: <airport>, #key time = $midnight)
 => (time :: <time-of-day>)
  format-out("Detailed aircraft schedule for ");
  say(airport);
  format-out("\n\n");
  let sky = airport.sky-above;
  let containers-visited = make(<object-table>);
  let active-transitions = make(<sorted-sequence>,
                                value-function: earliest-arrival);
```

The **schedule.dylan** file. *(continued)*

```
// We do not have to use return as the name of the exit procedure
block (done)
  while (#t)
    // Each time through, start by considering every container
    fill!(containers-visited, #f);
    // For every container, see if any vehicles are ready to transition
    // If any are, add transition instances to the active-transitions
    // sorted sequence
    generate-new-transitions(sky, active-transitions,
                             containers-visited);

    // If there are no more transitions, we have completed our task
    if (empty?(active-transitions)) done(); end;
    // Find the earliest transition that can complete, because there is
    // still room available in the destination container
    let transition-index
      = find-key(active-transitions,
                 method (transition)
                   available?(transition.transition-aircraft,
                              transition.to-container,
                              transition.transition-aircraft.direction);
                 end);

    // If none can complete, there is a problem with the simulation
    // This situation should never occur, but is useful for debugging
    // incorrect container configurations
    if (transition-index == #f)
      error("Pending transitions but none can complete.");
    end if;

    // Otherwise, the earliest transition that can complete has been
    // found: Execute the transition
    let transition = active-transitions[transition-index];
    let vehicle = transition.transition-aircraft;
    let vehicle-direction = vehicle.direction;
    move-out-vehicle(vehicle, transition.from-container,
                     vehicle-direction);
    move-in-vehicle(vehicle, transition.to-container, vehicle-direction);
```

The `schedule.dylan` file. *(continued)*

```
      // This transition is complete; remove it from consideration
      transition.pending? := #f;
      remove!(active-transitions, transition);
      // Compute the actual time of arrival at the next container, and
      // display the message
      time := (transition.earliest-arrival
                 := max(time, transition.earliest-arrival));
      say(transition);
      format-out("\n");
    end while;
  end block;
  time;
end method process-aircraft;
```

The **`process-aircraft`** method uses components from the time, space and sorted sequence libraries, the container classes and protocols, and the vehicle classes and methods to schedule the aircraft arriving and departing from an airport. The **`generate-new-transitions`** method assists by examining the current state of all containers in the airport, and by noting any new steps that vehicles could take.

17.5 The `airport-test.dylan` file

The **`airport-test.dylan`** file contains test data, and the code that constructs a model of the simple airport described in Section 15.1, page 237. The final method is a top-level testing function that builds the airport model and executes the main aircraft scheduling function. After defining the test, we show the results of running it.

The `airport-test.dylan` file.

```
module: airport-test

// To keep the example relatively simple, we will use variables to hold
// test data for the flights and aircraft
// Ordinarily, this information would be read from a file or database

define variable *flight-numbers* = #[62, 7, 29, 12, 18, 44];
```

The **airport-test.dylan** file. *(continued)*

```
define variable *aircraft-distances*
  = #[3, 10, 175, 450, 475, 477];        // Miles

define variable *aircraft-headings*
  = #[82, 191, 49, 112, 27, 269];        // Degrees

define variable *aircraft-altitudes*
  = #[7000, 15000, 22000, 22500, 22000, 21000];     // Feet

define variable *aircraft-ids*
  = #["72914", "82290", "18317", "26630", "43651", "40819"];

define constant $default-runway-size
  = make(<size>, length: 10000, width: 200, height: 100);     // Feet

define constant $default-taxiway-size
  = make(<size>, length: 900, width: 200, height: 100);     // Feet

// Assumes that there is only one runway, and one taxiway
// The taxiway-count variable will determine how many aircraft can wait
// in line for each direction of the taxiway
define method build-simple-airport
    (#key gates-per-terminal :: <vector> = #[2],
     capacity :: <size> = $default-capacity,
     runway-size :: <size> = $default-runway-size,
     taxiway-size :: <size> = $default-taxiway-size,
     taxiway-count :: <positive-integer> = 5,
     position-report-time :: <time-of-day>
       = make(<time-of-day>,
           total-seconds: encode-total-seconds(6, 0, 0)))
 => (airport :: <airport>)

  let gates = generate-gates(gates-per-terminal, capacity);
  let taxiway
    = make(<taxiway>, id: "Echo", directions: #[#"inbound", #"outbound"],
           maxima: vector(taxiway-count, taxiway-count),
           capacity: capacity, physical-size: taxiway-size);
  let runway = make(<runway>, id: "11R-29L", capacity: capacity,
                    physical-size: runway-size);
  let keystone-air = make(<airline>, name: "Keystone Air", code: "KN");
  let flights
    = map(method (fn)
          make(<flight>, airline: keystone-air, number: fn) end,
          *flight-numbers*);
```

The **airport-test.dylan** file. *(continued)*

```
let aircraft
  = map(method (aircraft-flight, aircraft-distance, aircraft-heading,
                aircraft-altitude, aircraft-id)
          make(<b707>,
               flight: aircraft-flight,
               current-position:
                 make(<relative-position>,
                      distance: aircraft-distance,
                      angle:
                        make(<angle>,
                             total-seconds:
                               encode-total-seconds
                                 (aircraft-heading, 0, 0))),
               altitude: aircraft-altitude,
               id: aircraft-id,
               transition: make(<aircraft-transition>,
                                arrival: position-report-time));
        end,

        flights, *aircraft-distances*, *aircraft-headings*,
        *aircraft-altitudes*, *aircraft-ids*);

let airport
  = make(<airport>,
         name: "Belefonte Airport",
         code: "BLA",
         current-position:
           make(<absolute-position>,
                latitude:
                  make(<latitude>,
                       total-seconds: encode-total-seconds(40, 57, 43),
                       direction: #"north"),
                longitude:
                  make(<longitude>,
                       total-seconds: encode-total-seconds(77, 40, 24),
                       direction: #"west")));
```

The **airport-test.dylan** file. *(continued)*

```
  let sky = make(<sky>, inbound-aircraft: aircraft, airport: airport,
                 id: concatenate("over ", airport.code));
  airport.sky-above := sky;
  runway.connected-to := vector(taxiway, sky);
  let taxiway-vector = vector(taxiway);
  for (gate in gates)
    gate.connected-to := taxiway-vector;
  end for;
  let runway-vector = vector(runway);
  taxiway.connected-to := concatenate(runway-vector, gates);
  sky.connected-to := runway-vector;
  airport;
end method build-simple-airport;

define method test-airport () => (last-transition :: <time-of-day>)
  process-aircraft(build-simple-airport());
end method test-airport;
```

Now, we show the result of running **test-airport**:

```
? test-airport():
Detailed aircraft schedule for Airport BLA
6:00: Flight KN 62 at Runway 11R-29L
6:02: Flight KN 62 at Taxiway Echo
6:02: Flight KN 7 at Runway 11R-29L
6:03: Flight KN 62 at Gate A1
6:04: Flight KN 7 at Taxiway Echo
6:05: Flight KN 7 at Gate A2
6:28: Flight KN 29 at Runway 11R-29L
6:30: Flight KN 29 at Taxiway Echo
6:37: Flight KN 62 at Taxiway Echo
6:37: Flight KN 29 at Gate A1
6:38: Flight KN 62 at Runway 11R-29L
6:39: Flight KN 7 at Taxiway Echo
6:42: Flight KN 62 at Sky over BLA
6:42: Flight KN 7 at Runway 11R-29L
6:46: Flight KN 7 at Sky over BLA
7:11: Flight KN 29 at Taxiway Echo
7:12: Flight KN 29 at Runway 11R-29L
7:16: Flight KN 29 at Sky over BLA
7:16: Flight KN 12 at Runway 11R-29L
7:18: Flight KN 12 at Taxiway Echo
7:18: Flight KN 18 at Runway 11R-29L
```

```
7:19: Flight KN 12 at Gate A1
7:20: Flight KN 18 at Taxiway Echo
7:20: Flight KN 44 at Runway 11R-29L
7:21: Flight KN 18 at Gate A2
7:22: Flight KN 44 at Taxiway Echo
7:53: Flight KN 12 at Taxiway Echo
7:53: Flight KN 44 at Gate A1
7:54: Flight KN 12 at Runway 11R-29L
7:55: Flight KN 18 at Taxiway Echo
7:58: Flight KN 12 at Sky over BLA
7:58: Flight KN 18 at Runway 11R-29L
8:02: Flight KN 18 at Sky over BLA
8:27: Flight KN 44 at Taxiway Echo
8:28: Flight KN 44 at Runway 11R-29L
8:32: Flight KN 44 at Sky over BLA
{class <TIME-OF-DAY>}
```

17.6 The `definitions-library.dylan` file

The **definitions-library.dylan** file provides common definitions for all the libraries in the airport example.

Note that this library and module, and the other libraries and modules that follow, do not separate the library implementation module from the library interface module, as discussed in Section 13.4.1, page 196. Dylan allows several different approaches to library and module architecture. Here, we present an alternative organization.

The **definitions-library.dylan** file.

```
module: dylan-user

define library definitions
  export definitions;
  use dylan;
end library definitions;

define module definitions
  export $letters, <positive-integer>;
  export $hours-per-day, $minutes-per-hour;
  export $seconds-per-minute, $seconds-per-hour, false-or;
  use dylan;
end module definitions;
```

17.7 The definitions.lid file

The **definitions.lid** file.

```
library:  definitions
files:    definitions-library
          definitions
```

17.8 The airport-library.dylan file

The airport library implements the main scheduling system for the airport example. This library assumes that your Dylan implementation provides a **format-out** library, which supplies the **format-out** and **format-to-string** functions. This library also assumes that there is a **transcendentals** library, which supplies the **sqrt** (square root) function.

The **airport-library.dylan** file.

```
module: dylan-user

define library airport
  export airport;
  use dylan;

  use transcendentals;
  use say;
  use format-out;
  use definitions;
  use sorted-sequence;
  use angle;
  use time;
end library airport;
```

The **airport-library.dylan** file. *(continued)*

```
define module airport
  export <size>, length, height, width, current-position,
    current-position-setter;
  export physical-size, physical-size-setter, $default-capacity;
  export storage-capacity, storage-capacity-setter, indentifier;
  export connected-to, connected-to-setter;
  export <gate>, generate-gates, <sky>, <runway>, <taxiway>;
  export <airline>, name, name-setter, code, code-setter, <flight>;
  export flight, flight-setter, number, number-setter, altitude,
    altitude-setter;
  export <aircraft-transition>, <b707>, <airport>, sky-above,
    sky-above-setter;
  export process-aircraft;
  use dylan;
  use transcendentals, import: {sqrt};
  use say;
  use format-out, import: {format-out};
  use format, import: {format-to-string};
  use definitions;
  use sorted-sequence;
  use time;
  use angle, export: {direction, direction-setter};
  use position;
end module airport;
```

17.9 The airport.lid file

The **airport.lid** file.

```
library:  airport
files:    airport-library
          airport-classes
          vehicle-dynamics
           schedule
```

17.10 The airport-test-library.dylan file

The **airport-test** library implements a simple test case for the scheduling system defined in the **airport** library.

The `airport-test-library.dylan` file.

```
module: dylan-user

define library airport-test
  export airport-test;
  use dylan;
  use time;
  use angle;
  use airport;
end library airport-test;

define module airport-test
  export test-airport;
  use dylan;
  use time;
  use angle;
  use position;
  use airport;
end module airport-test;
```

17.11 The `airport-test.lid` file

The `airport-test.lid` file.

```
library:  airport-test
files:    airport-test-library
          airport-test
```

17.12 Summary

In this chapter, we presented a complete first draft of the airport application, based on the techniques presented in previous chapters. Although the example is complete and meets its stated design goals, we can still make a number of improvements. For example, we could take advantage of Dylan's multiple inheritance to eliminate certain repetitive slots. We could provide a container-implementor module interface, and open the classes and generic functions so that users could add their own classes of containers and extend the scope of the application. We could take advantage of Dylan's exception handling to better deal with unusual situations that might occur during the simulation. In the chapters that follow, we show the Dylan language features that enable such improvements.

Part IV. Advanced Topics

Chapter 18, *Multiple Inheritance,* describes how multiple inheritance works in Dylan. It describes how method dispatch is affected by multiple inheritance. It gives an example of using the mix-in style of designing classes with multiple inheritance.

Chapter 19, *Performance and Flexibility,* describes the fundamental tradeoff between performance and flexibility. You can take advantage of Dylan's dynamic nature during the initial stages of development. Later on, when your application is nearing completion, you can optimize the performance of the program (and sacrifice flexibility, which presumably is no longer needed).

Chapter 20, *Exceptions,* describes how to use Dylan facilities to help create reliable programs in the face of exceptions — unexpected events that occur during program execution.

Chapter 21, *Macros,* describes how to define macros in Dylan. Macros can be used for abbreviation, abstraction, simplification, or structuring. They are also useful for delaying evaluation of arguments.

18

Multiple Inheritance

In the class relationships that we have defined so far, each class has only one direct superclass. When a class has a single direct superclass, the way in which that class inherits from its superclass is called **single inheritance**. In Dylan, a class can have more than one direct superclass. When a class has multiple direct superclasses, it inherits via **multiple inheritance**.

Why would we want to use multiple inheritance? Objects in the real world can have complicated behavior. As we make our software models more realistic, we often find that the behavior of the objects becomes more complicated as well. Multiple inheritance is useful when we can break down complicated behavior into sets of characteristics that do not interfere with one another. We might be able to define a class to represent each set of these characteristics. We can then define subclasses that combine sets of characteristics by inheriting from more than one of our superclasses. We give examples in this chapter.

Multiple inheritance does not change any of the rules of slot inheritance or method dispatch that we have learned so far. But it does require extensions to those rules. In this chapter, we explain how slot inheritance and method dispatch work in Dylan in the presence of multiple inheritance.

18.1 Example of multiple inheritance

In our airport example, we defined a **<vehicle>** class, and used it as a superclass for classes of aircraft. Figure 18.1 shows the hierarchy of vehicle classes that we defined.

So far, the only type of vehicle that we have defined is aircraft. Of course, there are many other kinds of vehicle: automobiles, ships, and spacecraft, to name a few. We have not needed these kinds of vehicles in the airport example so far, but we can easily see how we would need more vehicle classes if we made the example more realistic.

For example, aircraft need fuel before they can take off. An aircraft is typically fueled by a truck at the gate. If fuel is unavailable or fueling is delayed, the aircraft's departure from the gate is delayed as well. If we want to model the takeoff process more accurately, we should take account of the need for fuel, and specifically the need to get fuel trucks to aircraft preparing for takeoff.

We are not going to handle the fuel-supply problem in this book. However, in this section, we are going to modify the vehicle class hierarchy as a first step toward handling fuel trucks and other kinds of ground vehicles. In the process, we will develop an opportunity for using multiple inheritance in aircraft classes.

18.1.1 Modeling of ground vehicles

An obvious early step in modeling the behavior of fuel trucks would be to define a **<fuel-truck>** class. Presumably, we would want that class to inherit from

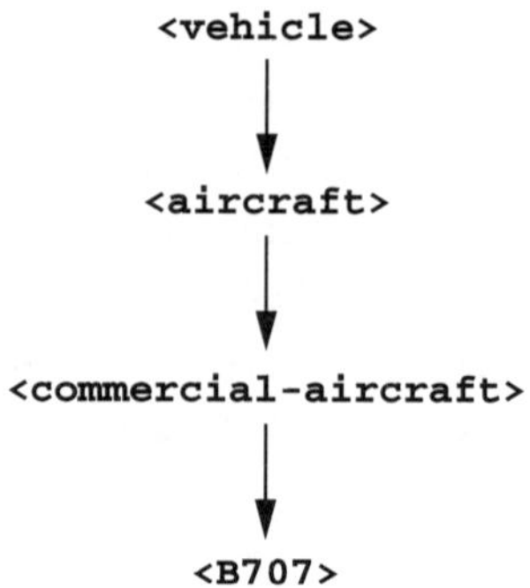

Figure 18.1 Hierarchy of vehicle classes.

<vehicle>. Let's look at our current definitions of both the **<vehicle>** class and its only direct subclass, **<aircraft>**:

```
// The class that represents all self-propelled devices
define abstract class <vehicle> (<physical-object>)
  // Every vehicle has a unique identification code
  slot vehicle-id :: <string>, required-init-keyword: id:;
  // The normal operating speed of this class of vehicle in miles per hour
  each-subclass slot cruising-speed :: <positive-integer>;
  // Allow individual differences in the size of particular aircraft, while
  // providing a suitable default for each class of aircraft
  each-subclass slot standard-size :: <size>;
end class <vehicle>;

// This class represents vehicles that normally fly for a portion of
// their trip
define abstract class <aircraft> (<vehicle>)
  slot altitude :: <integer>, init-keyword: altitude:;
  // Direction here is either #"inbound" or #"outbound".
  slot direction :: <symbol>;
  // The next transition that this aircraft might be able to make.
  slot next-transition :: <aircraft-transition>,
    required-init-keyword: transition:, setter: #f;
end class <aircraft>;
```

As a start, we can define a **<fuel-truck>** class as a subclass of **<vehicle>**. To operate on instances of this class, we will no doubt need to know how much aircraft fuel they contain. We define one initial slot, **aircraft-fuel-remaining**. We also need to provide initial values for the inherited slots **cruising-speed** and **standard-size**.

```
define class <fuel-truck> (<vehicle>)
  // Amount of aircraft fuel remaining in the tank
  slot aircraft-fuel-remaining :: <integer>,
    init-keyword: aircraft-fuel-remaining:, init-value: 0;
  inherited slot cruising-speed, init-value: 25;
  inherited slot standard-size,
    init-value: make(<size>, length: 30, width: 10, height: 10);
end class <fuel-truck>;
```

This definition serves our immediate purpose, but the class hierarchy is not as modular as it might be. Suppose that we want to take account of other vehicles on the ground, such as baggage carriers or fire trucks? We can anticipate that all ground vehicles might have common features, and we do not want each new class to be a direct subclass of **<vehicle>**. As a refinement, we define two intermediary classes, **<ground-vehicle>** and **<flying-vehicle>**:

```
define abstract class <ground-vehicle> (<vehicle>)
end class <ground-vehicle>;

define abstract class <flying-vehicle> (<vehicle>)
end class <flying-vehicle>;

define class <fuel-truck> (<ground-vehicle>)
  // How much aircraft fuel is left in the tank
  slot aircraft-fuel-remaining :: <integer>,
    init-keyword: aircraft-fuel-remaining:, init-value: 0;
  inherited slot cruising-speed, init-value: 25;
  inherited slot standard-size,
    init-value: make(<size>, length: 30, width: 10, height: 10);
end class <fuel-truck>;

define abstract class <aircraft> (<flying-vehicle>)
  slot altitude :: <integer>, init-keyword: altitude:;
  slot direction :: <symbol>;
  slot next-transition :: <aircraft-transition>,
    required-init-keyword: transition:, setter: #f;
end class <aircraft>;
```

At this point, we are going to leave the fuel-truck simulation. We do not model the fuel-supply problem further in this book. We do want to explore opportunities that our new class hierarchy presents for restructuring the aircraft classes.

18.1.2 Aircraft classes and multiple inheritance

It is obvious that an aircraft is a flying vehicle. In our airport model, however, we have to take account of an aircraft's behavior on taxiways and runways and at gates. In these situations, the aircraft is acting as a ground vehicle. Perhaps it makes sense to define our aircraft classes as subclasses of both **<flying-vehicle>** and **<ground-vehicle>**.

What could we gain by doing so? Consider cruising speed. When an aircraft is in the air, we need to take into account its flying cruising speed when estimating its time of arrival at its destination. When the aircraft is on the ground, we need to take into account the ground cruising speed when estimating how much time the aircraft will spend on a taxiway or runway. It makes sense to have both flying and ground cruising speeds. It also makes sense for flying cruising speed to be a property of flying vehicles — more specifically, aircraft — and for ground cruising speed to be a property of ground vehicles. After all, the notion of cruising speed can be useful in estimating how long a fuel truck will take to arrive at a given gate.

We now restructure our vehicle classes again, this time to make the aircraft classes be subclasses of both **<flying-vehicle>** and **<ground-vehicle>**. We need to remove the **cruising-speed** slot from the **<vehicle>** class, and to replace it by two slots: **ground-cruising-speed** for the **<ground-vehicle>** class and **flying-cruising-speed** for the **<flying-vehicle>** class. We can also take this opportunity to move the **altitude** slot from the **<aircraft>** class to the **<flying-vehicle>** class, because any flying vehicle is likely to need to keep track of its altitude. Finally, we introduce multiple inheritance by redefining the **<aircraft>** class to be a direct subclass of both **<flying-vehicle>** and **<ground-vehicle>**.

```
define abstract class <vehicle> (<physical-object>)
  // Every vehicle has a unique identification code
  slot vehicle-id :: <string>, required-init-keyword: id:;
  // The standard size of this class of vehicle
  each-subclass slot standard-size :: <size>;
end class <vehicle>;

define abstract class <ground-vehicle> (<vehicle>)
  // The normal operating speed of this class of vehicle
  each-subclass slot ground-cruising-speed :: <positive-integer>;
end class <ground-vehicle>;

define abstract class <flying-vehicle> (<vehicle>)
  // The normal operating speed of this class of vehicle
  each-subclass slot flying-cruising-speed :: <positive-integer>;
  slot altitude :: <integer>, init-keyword: altitude:;
end class <flying-vehicle>;

define abstract class <aircraft> (<flying-vehicle>, <ground-vehicle>)
  slot direction :: <symbol>;
  slot next-transition :: <aircraft-transition>,
    required-init-keyword: transition:, setter: #f;
end class <aircraft>;
```

Now, all aircraft classes have two slots for cruising speed: **ground-cruising-speed**, inherited from the **<ground-vehicle>** class, and **flying-cruising-speed**, inherited from the **<flying-vehicle>** class. We have to modify our **<B707>** class to provide default initial values for these slots.

```
define class <B707> (<commercial-aircraft>)
  inherited slot flying-cruising-speed, init-value: 368;
  inherited slot ground-cruising-speed, init-value: 45;
  inherited slot standard-size,
    init-value: make(<size>, length: 153, width: 146, height: 42);
end class <B707>;
```

Finally, to complete the example, we would change our **<fuel-truck>** class definition to provide a default initial value for **ground-cruising-speed**, instead of **cruising-speed**.

18.2 Multiple inheritance and slots

For the most part, using multiple inheritance does not present special problems in using slots. Recall that a class inherits all the slots of its superclasses. A subclass can also add slots of its own, but it cannot remove or replace any slots defined by its superclasses. A slot can appear only once in a class and in all that class's superclasses. Thus, a class's slots are the union of its slots and those of all its superclasses, and duplicate slot definitions are not permitted. This rule holds, regardless of whether a class has one direct superclass or more than one.

> **Comparison with C++**: In C++, a data member of the same name can appear in both a base class and a derived class. The name in the scope of the derived class hides the same name in the base class, but the base class slot can be accessed by qualifying its name.
>
> All access to Dylan class slots is through getter and setter methods, which are similar to C++ virtual functions. In Dylan, you can override access to an inherited slot by defining a getter or setter method specialized on the subclass (derived class).
>
> For more information on inheritance in C++, see Section B.2, page 386.

There are ways, however, in which subclasses and superclasses can have distinct effects on the same slot. One way is by providing default values for the slot. Even though duplicate slots are not permitted, a class can provide its own default value for a slot that it inherits from a superclass. The subclass can provide this default by supplying in its class definition an **inherited slot** option that includes an **init-value:** or **init-function:** specification, or an init expression.

Suppose that more than one class defines a default value for the same slot. Which default takes precedence? When each class has only one direct superclass, the answer is easy: the default value provided by the **most specific** class takes precedence. A default value for a subclass overrides a default value for a superclass.

But what if a class has more than one direct superclass, and each superclass provides a different default value for the same slot? Imagine, for example, that our **<vehicle>** class had a slot named **fuel-remaining**, and our **<ground-vehicle>** and **<flying-vehicle>** classes each had a different default value for the **fuel-remaining** slot, which they inherit from the common superclass **<vehicle>**:

```
define abstract class <vehicle> (<physical-object>)
  slot fuel-remaining :: <integer>;
  ...
end class <vehicle>;

define abstract class <ground-vehicle> (<vehicle>)
  inherited-slot fuel-remaining, init-value: 30;
  ...
end class <ground-vehicle>;

define abstract class <flying-vehicle> (<vehicle>)
  inherited-slot fuel-remaining, init-value: 3000;
  ...
end class <flying-vehicle>;

define abstract class <aircraft> (<flying-vehicle>, <ground-vehicle>)
  ...
end class <aircraft>;
```

Now neither the class **<ground-vehicle>** nor the class **<flying-vehicle>** is more specific than the other with respect to **<aircraft>**. So when we create an instance of **<aircraft>** that has both **<ground-vehicle>** and **<flying-vehicle>** as direct superclasses, what is the default initial value for the **fuel-remaining** slot: **30** or **3000**?

To answer this question, Dylan needs an additional way of ordering classes, called a **class precedence list**. In Section 18.3, we describe how Dylan constructs the class precedence list. The short answer to our question about default initial slot values is that Dylan uses the default value provided by the class that appears earlier in the class precedence list.

We shall see that the class precedence list is also important for method dispatch in the presence of multiple inheritance. Suppose, for example, that we had defined two getter or two setter methods for the **`fuel-remaining`** slot: one specialized on the **`<flying-vehicle>`** class, and the other specialized on the **`<ground-vehicle>`** class. Which method would be selected to get or set the slot value of an instance of **`<aircraft>`**? We return to the issue of method dispatch after we see how Dylan constructs the class precedence list.

18.3 The class precedence list

When each class has only one direct superclass, the relations among superclasses and subclasses form a **tree**. For every subclass in the tree, there is a well-defined ordering in terms of **specificity** for that class and all its superclasses. A subclass is always more specific than are any of its superclasses. When each class has only one superclass, we can order unambiguously any given class and all its superclasses, from **most specific** to **least specific**. Figure 18.1 illustrates part of such an ordering for our original, single-inheritance definitions of **`<vehicle>`** and **`<vehicle>`**'s subclasses.

With multiple inheritance, the relations among superclasses and subclasses can form a **graph**, which may not be a tree. We cannot always order a class and all its superclasses in terms of specificity. It is still true that a subclass is more specific than are any of its superclasses. But we cannot always order its superclasses in terms of specificity.

Figure 18.2 illustrates our current definitions of **`<vehicle>`** and of **`<vehicle>`**'s subclasses.

Consider **`<B707>`** and its superclasses. We can order **`<B707>`**, **`<commercial-aircraft>`**, and **`<aircraft>`** from more specific to less specific. But we cannot say that either **`<ground-vehicle>`** or **`<flying-vehicle>`** is more specific than the other, because neither class is a subclass of the other. We could order **`<B707>`** and its superclasses in two ways, from more specific to less specific:

```
<B707>, <commercial-aircraft>, <aircraft>,
  <flying-vehicle>, <ground-vehicle>, <vehicle>, <physical-object>, <object>
```

```
<B707>, <commercial-aircraft>, <aircraft>,
  <ground-vehicle>, <flying-vehicle>, <vehicle>, <physical-object>, <object>
```

Dylan needs a way to determine which of these orderings to use. It solves the problem by constructing a **class precedence list** for **`<B707>`** and its superclasses.

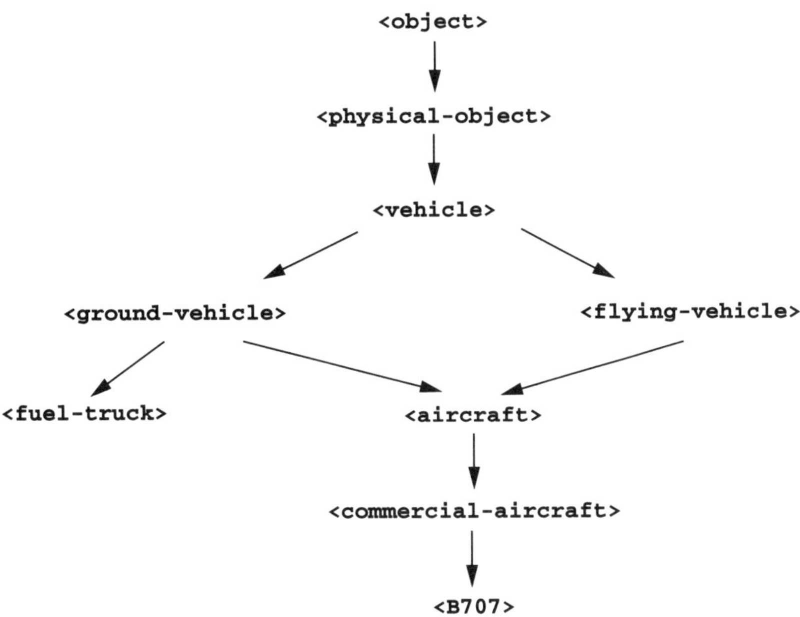

Figure 18.2 Graph of vehicle classes that use multiple inheritance.

18.3.1 Construction of the class precedence list

To understand how Dylan determines the class precedence list, recall that the **`define class`** form for a class includes a list of superclasses. Remember that we defined **`<aircraft>`** as follows:

```
define abstract class <aircraft> (<flying-vehicle>, <ground-vehicle>)
  ...
end class <aircraft>;
```

Here, we have listed the superclasses as **`<flying-vehicle>`** and **`<ground-vehicle>`**, in that order.

In creating the class precedence list for a class, Dylan uses the ordering of the list of direct superclasses in the **`define class`** form for that class. Dylan relies on the following rules:

1. The class being defined takes precedence over all its direct superclasses.
2. Each direct superclass in the list takes precedence over all direct superclasses that appear later in the list.

These rules establish an ordering of a class and its direct superclasses, called the **local precedence order**.

We listed **`<flying-vehicle>`** before **`<ground-vehicle>`** in the list of superclasses of **`<aircraft>`**, so, when we apply these rules, we see that, for the **`<aircraft>`** class, **`<flying-vehicle>`** must have precedence higher than that of **`<ground-vehicle>`**. The local precedence order for **`<aircraft>`** is as follows:

```
<aircraft>, <flying-vehicle>, <ground-vehicle>
```

The local precedence order for a class establishes an ordering of a class and its *direct* superclasses. But our goal is to produce an overall class precedence list, which establishes an ordering of the class and *all* its superclasses, direct and indirect. In constructing the class precedence list for a class, Dylan follows two steps:

1. Construct the local precedence order for the class and its direct superclasses, based on the order in which the direct superclasses appear in the **`define class`** form for the class.

2. Construct the overall class precedence list for the class by merging the class's local precedence order with the class precedence lists of the class's direct superclasses.

Notice that this procedure is recursive! But it is guaranteed to terminate, because no class can be its own superclass.

The resulting class precedence list must be consistent with the local precedence order of the class, and with the class precedence list of each direct superclass. If class **`<a>`** precedes class **`<b>`** in the class precedence list, then **`<b>`** cannot precede **`<a>`** in either the local precedence order or the class precedence list for any direct superclass. Because of the recursive procedure for constructing it, the class precedence list must be consistent with the local precedence orders and class precedence lists of *all* the class's superclasses, rather than just with those of the direct superclasses.

We can now see how Dylan computes the class precedence list for the **`<B707>`** class:

1. Construct the local precedence order for **`<B707>`** and its only direct superclass, **`<commercial-aircraft>`**. The result is as follows: **`<B707>`**, **`<commercial-aircraft>`**.

2. Merge the local precedence order with the class precedence list of the only direct superclass, **`<commercial-aircraft>`**.

Dylan must now use these rules, recursively, to compute the class precedence list of **<commercial-aircraft>**. In doing so, Dylan must compute recursively the class precedence list of the only direct superclass of **<commercial-aircraft>**: **<aircraft>**. This process continues until Dylan has recursively computed the class precedence lists for all superclasses of **<B707>**. Finally, Dylan finishes constructing the class precedence list for **<B707>** itself. Table 18.1 shows the results.

One implication of this procedure is that, if a class inherits a superclass via two different paths, the superclass in common must have precedence lower than that of any of its subclasses. For example, the **<object>** class is a superclass of

Class	Local precedence order	Class precedence list
<object>	<object>	<object>
<physical-object>	<physical-object>, <object>	<physical-object>, <object>
<vehicle>	<vehicle>, <physical-object>	<vehicle>, <physical-object>, <object>
<ground-vehicle>	<ground-vehicle>, <vehicle>	<ground-vehicle>, <vehicle>, <physical-object>, <object>
<flying-vehicle>	<flying-vehicle>, <vehicle>	<flying-vehicle>, <vehicle>, <physical-object>, <object>
<aircraft>	<aircraft>, <flying-vehicle>, <ground-vehicle>	<aircraft>, <flying-vehicle>, <ground-vehicle>, <vehicle>, <physical-object>, <object>
<commercial-aircraft>	<commercial-aircraft>, <aircraft>	<commercial-aircraft>, <aircraft>, <flying-vehicle>, <ground-vehicle>, <vehicle>, <physical-object>, <object>
<B707>	<B707>, <commercial-aircraft>	<B707>, <commercial-aircraft>, <aircraft>, <flying-vehicle>, <ground-vehicle>, <vehicle>, <physical-object>, <object>

Table 18.1 Class precedence lists for **<B707>** and its superclasses.

every class (except itself). This class must have lower precedence than any of its subclasses, so it appears last in every class precedence list. The class precedence list is consistent with the rule that a subclass is more specific than are any of its superclasses.

18.3.2 More complicated class precedence lists

Sometimes, more than one class precedence list is consistent with the procedure that we have outlined so far. Suppose, for example, that we had defined two additional classes, **`<wheeled-vehicle>`** and **`<winged-vehicle>`**, with the class relations illustrated in Figure 18.3.

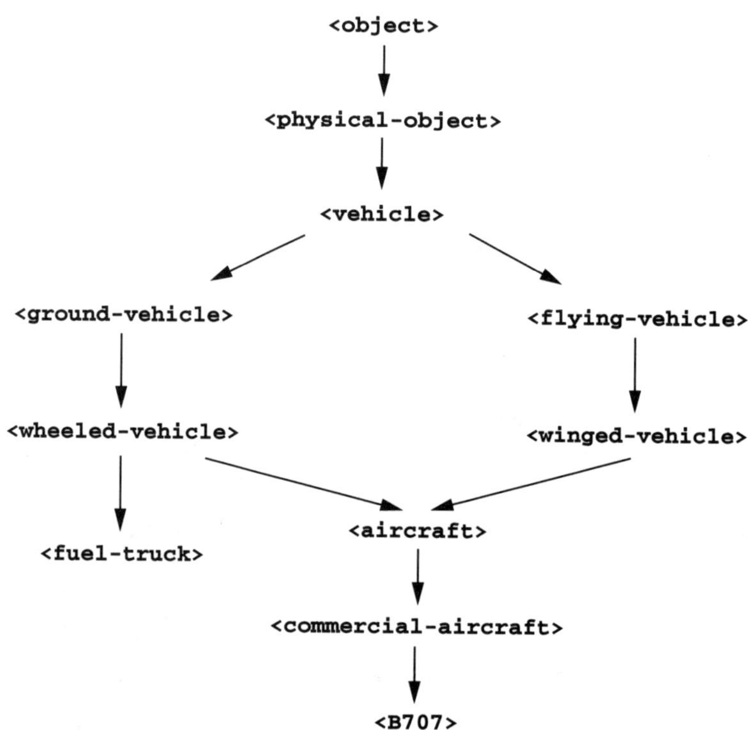

Figure 18.3 Expanded graph of vehicle classes that use multiple inheritance.

Let's assume that the **define class** form for **<aircraft>** lists **<winged-vehicle>** before **<wheeled-vehicle>** in its list of direct superclasses. Now, three class precedence lists for **<B707>** are consistent with the procedures that we have discussed so far:

```
<B707>, <commercial-aircraft>, <aircraft>, <winged-vehicle>,
  <flying-vehicle>, <wheeled-vehicle>, <ground-vehicle>, <vehicle>,
  <physical-object>, <object>
```

```
<B707>, <commercial-aircraft>, <aircraft>, <winged-vehicle>,
  <wheeled-vehicle>, <flying-vehicle>, <ground-vehicle>, <vehicle>,
  <physical-object>, <object>
```

```
<B707>, <commercial-aircraft>, <aircraft>, <winged-vehicle>,
  <wheeled-vehicle>, <ground-vehicle>, <flying-vehicle>, <vehicle>,
  <physical-object>, <object>
```

In this case, Dylan uses an algorithm that tends to keep together, in the class precedence list, nonoverlapping superclass-to-subclass chains.

Look at this situation another way: The algorithm Dylan uses to construct the class precedence list in effect builds the list one class at a time, from highest to lowest precedence. The class precedence list under construction for **<B707>** is unambiguous from **<B707>** through **<winged-vehicle>**. At that point, Dylan could insert either **<flying-vehicle>** or **<wheeled-vehicle>** into the list. It chooses the class that has a *direct subclass rightmost* in the partial class precedence list that it has already constructed. In this case, **<flying-vehicle>** has a direct subclass **<winged-vehicle>**, and **<wheeled-vehicle>** has a direct subclass **<aircraft>**. Because **<winged-vehicle>** is rightmost in the partial list already constructed, Dylan chooses **<flying-vehicle>** as the next entry in the list. Once that decision has been made, the resulting class precedence list must be the first of the three possible orderings that we listed:

```
<B707>, <commercial-aircraft>, <aircraft>, <winged-vehicle>,
  <flying-vehicle>, <wheeled-vehicle>, <ground-vehicle>, <vehicle>,
  <physical-object>, <object>
```

Note that it is not always possible to compute a class precedence list. Consider the three classes defined as follows:

```
define class <a> (<object>)
  ...
end class <a>;
```

```
define class <b> (<a>)
  ...
end class <b>;

define class <c> (<a>, <b>)
  ...
end class <c>;
```

No class precedence list is possible for class **<c>** in this example, because the ordering of classes **<a>** and **<b>** conflicts in the local precedence lists for classes **<b>** and **<c>**. Dylan signals an error when it tries to compute a class precedence list and finds that it cannot do so.

To examine the class precedence list for a class, we use the **all-superclasses** function, which returns the class and its superclasses in the same order as they appear in the class precedence list:

```
? all-superclasses (<B707>)
#[{class <B707>}, {class <commercial-aircraft>}, {class <aircraft>},
  {class <winged-vehicle>}, {class <flying-vehicle>},
  {class <wheeled-vehicle>},{class <ground-vehicle>}, {class <vehicle>},
  {class <physical-object>}, {class <object>}]
```

The details of the algorithm that Dylan uses to construct class precedence lists are complicated, and are beyond the scope of this book. For most uncomplicated uses of simple inheritance, the most important points to remember about the class precedence list are that the list of direct superclasses in a **define class** form is ordered, and each direct superclass in the list takes precedence over all direct superclasses that appear later in the list. In general, if more than one superclass defines a behavior, the subclass behaves most like the first superclass in its class precedence list that defines that behavior.

18.4 Multiple inheritance and method dispatch

Now that we have seen how Dylan constructs the class precedence list, we return to the issue of how multiple inheritance affects method dispatch. Recall that, when a generic function is called, Dylan chooses the **most specific applicable method** to call. For simplicity, let's consider a generic function that has one specialized parameter. As we have seen, Dylan chooses which method to dispatch by comparing the type of the required **argument** to the generic function with the type of the corresponding specialized **parameter** for each method, using the following procedure:

1. Find all the applicable methods. A method is applicable if the required argument is an instance of the type of the specialized parameter.
2. Sort the applicable methods in order of specificity. A method is more specific than another if the type of its specialized parameter is a proper subtype of the type of the other method's specialized parameter.
3. Call the most specific method.

In the presence of multiple inheritance, it is possible to have two or more methods that are applicable, but that cannot be sorted by specificity because neither parameter type is a subtype of the other. By following only the rules that we have seen so far, Dylan cannot choose either method to call.

18.4.1 Class precedence and method dispatch

To see how this problem for method dispatch can arise, we return to our airport example. Recall that we now have two slots representing vehicle cruising speed: **ground-cruising-speed** for **<ground-vehicle>** and **flying-cruising-speed** for **<flying-vehicle>**. Let's define a generic function, **say-cruising-speed**, to report the applicable cruising speed for each class:

```
define generic say-cruising-speed (vehicle :: <vehicle>);

// Method 1
define method say-cruising-speed (vehicle :: <flying-vehicle>)
  format-out("Flying cruising speed: %d\n", vehicle.flying-cruising-speed);
end method say-cruising-speed;

// Method 2
define method say-cruising-speed (vehicle :: <ground-vehicle>)
  format-out("Ground cruising speed: %d\n", vehicle.ground-cruising-speed);
end method say-cruising-speed;

// Method 3
define method say-cruising-speed (vehicle :: <vehicle>)
  format-out("No cruising speed defined for type <vehicle>\n");
end method say-cruising-speed;
```

Now, suppose that we call **say-cruising-speed** on an instance of **<B707>**. Which method does Dylan call? All three methods are applicable. Both method 1 and method 2 are more specific than is method 3. But Dylan cannot order methods 1 and 2 by specificity.

In this case, Dylan consults the class precedence list for the class of the argument. In our example, the class of the argument is **<B707>**. The **<flying-vehicle>** class takes precedence over the **<ground-vehicle>** class, because **<flying-vehicle>** precedes **<ground-vehicle>** in the list of direct superclasses for **<aircraft>**. Dylan calls method 1, which produces the following output:

```
Flying cruising speed: 368
```

Note that, if we had happened to list **<ground-vehicle>** before **<flying-vehicle>** in the list of direct superclasses for **<aircraft>**, Dylan would have called method 2, and we would have seen the following output:

```
Ground cruising speed: 45
```

In defining classes of aircraft, we did not intend for **<flying-vehicle>** characteristics to override **<ground-vehicle>** characteristics. But for method dispatch to work in the presence of multiple inheritance, Dylan must order subclasses and superclasses whenever it can.

How can we change our example to make **<flying-vehicle>** behavior add to, rather than override, **<ground-vehicle>** behavior? By using **next-method** in our **say-cruising-speed** methods for **<flying-vehicle>** and **<ground-vehicle>**, we can report all applicable kinds of cruising speed for any combination of either or both of those classes. To make this behavior work, we also change the **say-cruising-speed** method for **<vehicle>**, which will always be called last, to have no effect:

```
// Method 1
define method say-cruising-speed (vehicle :: <flying-vehicle>)
  format-out("Flying cruising speed: %d\n", vehicle.flying-cruising-speed);
  next-method();
end method say-cruising-speed;

// Method 2
define method say-cruising-speed (vehicle :: <ground-vehicle>)
  format-out("Ground cruising speed: %d\n", vehicle.ground-cruising-speed);
  next-method();
end method say-cruising-speed;

// Method 3
define method say-cruising-speed (vehicle :: <vehicle>)
end method say-cruising-speed;
```

Recall that, when Dylan decides which method to call, the result is a list of methods, sorted by specificity. When **say-cruising-speed** is called on an instance of

<B707>, the list of methods is sorted in the following order: method 1, method 2, method 3. Dylan calls method 1. Then, as a result of the call to **next-method** in method 1, Dylan calls method 2. Finally, as a result of the call to **next-method** in method 1, Dylan calls method 3. The output we see is as follows:

```
Flying cruising speed: 368
Ground cruising speed: 45
```

Note that, if we called **say-cruising-speed** on an instance of **<fuel-truck>**, we would see the following output:

```
Ground cruising speed: 25
```

18.4.2 Refined rules for method dispatch

In summary, the effect of multiple inheritance on method dispatch is to refine the rule for sorting methods according to specificity:

> A method is **more specific** than another if the type of its specialized parameter is a proper subtype of the type of the other method's specialized parameter. (For definitions of proper subtype, see Section 9.3, page 111.) If one type is not a proper subtype of the other, a method is more specific if the class of its specialized parameter precedes the class of the other method's specialized parameter in the class precedence list of the argument to the generic function. Otherwise, the methods are **unordered** for that parameter.

If the generic function has more than one required argument, Dylan uses this augmented rule for determining specificity in the usual way for sorting applicable methods with more than one argument. In essence, Dylan orders the applicable methods separately for each required argument, and then constructs an overall ordering by comparing the separate sorted lists. In the overall method ordering, a method is more specific than another if it satisfies two constraints:

1. The method is *no less specific* than the other method for *all* required parameters. (The two methods might have the same types for some parameters.)
2. The method is *more specific* than the other method for *some* required parameter.

Note that one method might be more specific than another for one parameter, but less specific for another parameter. These two methods are **ambiguous** in specificity and cannot be ordered. If the method-dispatch procedure cannot find any method that is more specific than all other methods, Dylan signals an error.

> **Comparison with C++:** Multiple inheritance in C++ is different from multiple inheritance in Dylan. In C++, unless a base class is virtual, it is inherited multiple times if there is more than one path to the base class as a result of multiple inheritance. In Dylan, all base classes are effectively virtual.
>
> C++ has nothing like Dylan's class precedence list for determining the precedence of two superclasses, neither of which is derived from the other. There is no implicit ordering of virtual members defined for such classes. C++ also has nothing like Dylan's **`next-method`** for invoking the next most specific virtual function. A C++ programmer must often explicitly provide the sort of method dispatch and combination that Dylan implements automatically.
>
> For examples of similar Dylan and C++ programs that use multiple inheritance, see Section B.2, page 386.

> **Comparison with Java:** Java formalizes the concept of a **protocol** with its **interfaces**. An interface is like an abstract class and a set of required generic functions. A class that **implements** an interface must define methods for each of the generic functions specified by that interface. In a sense, an interface is like a specification for multiple inheritance, without the implementation. A class that implements an interface is considered to be of the interface type, but it must implement all the behaviors directly, rather than inheriting them from the interface — which may mean that code has to be duplicated, rather than shared and reused.

18.5 Use of multiple inheritance

Multiple inheritance is likely to be most useful when you can separate the characteristics of objects into **orthogonal** sets, in which the characteristics of one set do not depend on the characteristics of other sets. If you can define a class to represent each set of characteristics, you can use multiple inheritance to build complex classes with different combinations of characteristics. We gave a glimpse of how to create such a design by starting to segregate characteristics of flying and ground vehicles, and then noting that certain vehicles, like such as aircraft, can combine both sets of characteristics.

Another approach that can be useful for various applications is to create one or more **base** superclasses, which define common characteristics of subclasses, and a number of **mix-in** classes, each of which adds a set of orthogonal characteristics. A mix-in class is like an addition, such as chocolate chips or nuts, that might be mixed into an ice-cream base. Another way to think about this approach is to imagine the base class as a noun and the mix-in classes as adjectives that modify or specialize the noun. You can then construct concrete subclasses by using multiple inheritance. For each concrete subclass, one or more mix-in classes typically precede a single base class in the list of superclasses.

18.5.1 Use of a mix-in class

In our airport example, four classes now define slots that serve as names or strings that represent identifiers for objects:

```
define abstract class <vehicle-storage> (<physical-object>)
  slot identifier :: <string>, required-init-keyword: id:;
  ...
end class <vehicle-storage>;

define abstract class <vehicle> (<physical-object>)
  slot vehicle-id :: <string>, required-init-keyword: id:;
  ...
end class <vehicle>;

define class <airport> (<physical-object>)
  slot name :: <string>, init-keyword: name:;
  ...
end class <airport>;

define class <airline> (<object>)
  slot name :: <string>, required-init-keyword: name:;
  ...
end class <airline>;
```

Our example would be more unified and maintainable if we had a single representation for these identifiers.

There are several ways that we could improve the example using single inheritance. One way to do that in principle would be to define a **name** slot in a common superclass. In this case, we cannot use this solution, because the only common superclass is the built-in class **<object>**. This approach would work if all named classes inherited from **<physical-object>** — we could add a **name** slot to **<physical-object>**. But then all subclasses of **<physical-object>** would inherit the **name** slot, whether or not those subclasses need names. Some objects might be inappropriately named, and those instances would be larger than they need to be.

Another approach would be to define two new subclasses to contain the **name** slot: a **<named-object>** subclass of **<object>**, and a **<named-physical-object>** subclass of **<physical-object>**. We would then use **<named-physical-object>** as the superclass for **<vehicle-storage>**, **<vehicle>**, and **<airport>**, and we would use **<named-object>** as the superclass for **<airline>**. That would work, too, although the **name** slot would be defined in two classes, rather than in one.

Suppose, however, that we later find that some, but not all, subclasses need another attribute, such as a unique identifier. Perhaps **<airport>, <vehicle>**, and **<airline>** need unique identifiers, but **<vehicle-storage>** does not. Extending this model, we might have to define new classes **<unique-object>**, **<unique-named-object>**, **<unique-physical-object>**, and **<unique-named-physical-object>**. We now have eight base classes to represent the possible combinations of name and unique identifier. If we add a third attribute, we end up with many more classes. We soon have an unmanageable proliferation of base classes.

Multiple inheritance provides a solution to these problems. We can define a mix-in class, **name-mix-in**, whose only purpose is to contain the **name** slot:

```
define abstract class <name-mix-in> (<object>)
  slot name :: <string>, init-keyword: name:;
end class <name-mix-in>;
```

Now, we redefine our **<vehicle-storage>**, **<vehicle>**, **<airport>**, and **<airline>** classes to have two direct superclasses: **<name-mix-in>**, and either **<object>** or **<physical-object>**:

```
define abstract class <vehicle-storage> (<name-mix-in>, <physical-object>)
  // identifier slot removed
  required keyword name:;
  ...
end class <vehicle-storage>;
```

```
define abstract class <vehicle> (<name-mix-in>, <physical-object>)
  // vehicle-id slot removed
  required keyword name:;
  ...
end class <vehicle>;

define class <airport> (<name-mix-in>, <physical-object>)
  // name slot removed
  keyword name:, init-value: "Anonymous Airport";
  ...
end class <airport>;

define class <airline> (<name-mix-in>, <object>)
  // name slot removed
  required keyword name:;
  ...
end class <airline>;
```

We use the **required keyword** option to make the **name:** keyword required when we create an instance of **<vehicle-storage>**, **<vehicle>**, or **<airline>**. If we provided an **init-value:** or **init-function:** for the **name** slot in the definition of **<name-mix-in>**, Dylan would ignore that option when we created an instance of any of these subclasses.

We also use the **keyword** option with an **init-value:** to provide a default initial value for the **name:** initialization argument and for the **name** slot for instances of **<airport>**.

Of course, we also have to change other code in our example to use the name **name** and the init keyword **name:** when referring to the slot.

Multiple inheritance provides several advantages in solving the name problem:

1. We localize in a single class the characteristic of having a name.
2. Subclasses can still customize aspects of the name attribute, such as what that attribute's initial value is, and whether or not it is required.
3. We can give a subclass a name attribute without redefining any of its superclasses.
4. The only subclasses that have a name attribute are those for which that is appropriate.

18.5.2 Pros and cons of multiple inheritance

There is debate about the value of using multiple inheritance in object-oriented programs. Some people think that multiple inheritance in appropriate applications can improve modularity and can make it easier to reuse code. Other people think that the complications and pitfalls of multiple inheritance make program maintenance difficult, and thus outweigh the possible advantages.

We have presented examples of multiple inheritance that show that it can have advantages when you can separate object characteristics into nonoverlapping sets. Multiple inheritance then lets you create complex classes using only the characteristics that you need, without a proliferation of base classes.

Multiple inheritance does complicate method dispatch and impose additional requirements on an application. It is essential to be aware of dependencies on subclass–superclass ordering, particularly in method selection and slot initialization. In general, classes that are intended to be multiple direct superclasses of the same subclass should depend on one another as little as possible. Protocols involving multiple inheritance may need more documentation than do those involving single inheritance.

18.6 Summary

In this chapter, we covered the following:

- We introduced the concept of multiple inheritance: inheritance from more than one direct superclass.
- We discussed the implications of multiple inheritance for slot initialization.
- We described how Dylan constructs the class precedence list for a class. The class precedence list is an ordering of a class and all its superclasses.
- We showed how Dylan uses class precedence lists in sorting methods by specificity when a generic function is called.
- We developed extensions of the airport example using multiple inheritance.
- We discussed advantages and disadvantages of using multiple inheritance.

19

Performance and Flexibility

This chapter covers the advanced topic of balancing performance and flexibility in a Dylan program. If you are writing a stand-alone program and are comfortable with using type constraints as you would in a static language, you do not need to read this chapter carefully. You may want to skim the chapter, so that you have an idea of what options are available to you in the future for larger or more complex projects.

We start out by describing what Dylan's execution model is, and what we mean by an *efficiency model*. The efficiency model can help a programmer to choose the appropriate language features for a particular problem. We also explore advanced features of Dylan that will let the programmer negotiate with the compiler to trade away part of the flexibility of the execution model for enhanced performance.

19.1 Execution model

Dylan is a dynamic language — everything in Dylan is defined in terms of a dynamic **execution model**. As we saw in Section 5.5, page 63, the execution model of how a method is chosen when a generic function is called with a particular set of arguments is highly dynamic: the arguments are evaluated; the types of the arguments are determined; the applicable methods are found and sorted according to specificity; and, finally, the most specific, applicable method is called.

This model implies that values and types can change, and that methods can be added right up until the generic function is called, and any of these changes still have an effect on which method is ultimately chosen. This dynamism — the model that value, number, and type of arguments; return values; applicable method; and method choice and execution are all determined at the last possible moment — is what gives the Dylan language its power.

You might think that this dynamism also means that Dylan must perform poorly, because the only way to obey its execution model is to do a lot of extra computation at run time. But not every program makes use of dynamic features. Most functions accept and return a fixed number of values (often they return only one), and those values are often of a fixed or constrained type. Even programs that do use dynamism will not require it everywhere. So, a good Dylan compiler will identify the static parts of a program, and will compile them statically (that is, in a manner that is competitive with what a compiler of any good static language would do). To do that, the compiler uses a technique called **partial evaluation** — operations that can be evaluated at compile time (that the compiler knows can have only one outcome), will be done at compile time. Thus, even though the programmer can continue to think and program in terms of Dylan's dynamic execution model, the compiler will generate efficient code when it can show that it can obtain the same return value without carrying out the full process at run time.

For small projects — projects that can fit in a single library — the compiler can analyze the entire project and generate code that is competitive with any static language. If type constraints are used for all module variables, slots, parameters, and return values (as they would be in a static language), the compiler can generate code equivalent to that generated by compilers for static languages. In the remainder of this chapter, we examine how we can use type constraints, limited types, open classes, open generic functions, domain sealing, and primary classes to balance performance and flexibility in Dylan programs.

19.2 Efficiency model

Dylan is a powerful language: Many of the built-in, or primitive, language operations are high-level operations, such as the method-dispatch mechanism, the collection facility, and the exception mechanism. Because of Dylan's powerful features, it can be hard for the programmer to develop an **efficiency model** — a model of the absolute or relative cost of different approaches to a problem.

In contrast, in other languages, such as C, every language construct can be explained directly in terms of a small number of machine instructions. Although it may be easy to understand the performance of a C program in terms of a simple model, programming in C is more work for the programmer — the higher-level abstractions are not provided, and must often be built from scratch.

For example, a C programmer expects that the run-time cost of calling a function is the cost of possibly saving registers on a stack, passing the arguments, executing a machine instruction for jumping to a subroutine, and then executing a return instruction at the end of the function; if it is a call through a function pointer, or a C++ virtual function, the cost of an indirect jump must be added. In Dylan, the story is more complicated, because Dylan has a more sophisticated execution model: A call to a generic function might be much more expensive in a dynamic situation, because computing the most specific method could take much longer than would execution of the method itself.

To write efficient programs in Dylan, you have to understand what constructs in the language can be expensive in time or space, and how you can reduce those costs in common cases. This understanding is based on an **efficiency model** — a conceptual model of how a program in Dylan runs at a low level.

One problem with developing an efficiency model is that there is no single way to implement many Dylan operations. Different compilers do things in different ways, and certain compilers have multiple techniques for compiling the same piece of code, depending on circumstances. Nonetheless, we shall try to give an intuitive feel for which features of Dylan are costly, and which features enable the compiler to make optimizations.

19.3 Type constraints

In Dylan, variables, parameters, return values, and slots can all have type constraints. Dylan's dynamic nature means that type constraints can be looser than is typical of a static language, or can even be deferred altogether, in support of rapid prototyping or evolutionary development. Type constraints in a dynamic language serve three primary purposes:

1. Type constraints are required for method dispatch: the methods of a generic function are distinguished by the types of their required arguments. The generic function chooses the applicable methods by sorting them according to the type constraints of their parameters.

2. Type constraints can be used optionally to enforce program restrictions. The compiler ensures that a variable, parameter, return value, or slot will never take on a value that is incompatible with the type constraint of the parameter, return value, or slot. (If the compiler cannot prove at compile time that an incorrect type is impossible, it inserts a run-time check to enforce the type constraint.)
3. Type constraints allow the compiler to generate better code, because they are a contract between the programmer and the compiler that the variable, parameter, return value, or slot in question will never take on a value that is incompatible with its type constraint; hence, the compiler needs only to generate code for dealing with the declared type.

Many Dylan compilers use **type inferencing** to determine the possible types of variables, parameters, and slots that do not have explicit type constraints. Within a library, the compiler essentially knows everything about the variables and functions that are not exported at the library interface — it can analyze all uses of variables, and all callers and callees of functions. Through this analysis, the compiler can develop a worst-case scenario of the possible types of every variable, parameter, return value, and slot. As a result, these compilers generate efficient code even if the programmer does not fully declare all types (as would be required in most static languages).

Comparison with C: Static languages such as C have little need for type inferencing, because the type of every value must be declared, and the types can be checked easily at compile time. On the other hand, when a problem domain is ill-specified, the program is evolving through development, or a value may take on one of several types, the programmer must construct union types, and must use variant records or other bookkeeping to track the actual type of the value manually.

Dylan automatically handles this bookkeeping and uses type inferencing to minimize the associated overhead. At the same time, when the type of a variable can change at run time, Dylan also automatically tracks the changing type.

Some compilers have a facility for generating **performance warnings**, which inform you when type inferencing is not able to determine types sufficiently to generate optimal code. Some compilers have a facility for generating **safety warnings**, informing you when type inferencing is not able to determine types sufficiently to omit run-time type checking. As an example, consider these definitions (which are similar to, but not exactly the same as, the definitions on which we settled in Chapter 14, *Four Complete Libraries*):

```
define abstract open class <sixty-unit> (<object>)
  slot total-seconds :: <integer> = 0, init-keyword: total-seconds:;
end class <sixty-unit>;

define method decode-total-seconds
    (sixty-unit :: <sixty-unit>)
 => (hours :: <integer>, minutes :: <integer>, seconds :: <integer>)
  let total-seconds = abs(sixty-unit.total-seconds);
  let (total-minutes, seconds) = truncate/(total-seconds, 60);
  let (max-unit, minutes) = truncate/(total-minutes, 60);
  values (max-unit, minutes, seconds);
end method decode-total-seconds;
```

Because we made the choice to store **total-seconds** as an integer, and because **60** is an integer constant, the compiler can infer that the **truncate/** calls are for an integer divided by integer. There is no need to consider whether to use floating-point or integer division.

If we were more concerned with testing out ideas, we might have left unspecified the type of the **total-seconds** slot (implicitly, its type would then be **<object>**), or, if we wanted to keep the option of having times more accurate than just seconds, we might have specified that its type was **<real>**, allowing for the possibility of using floating-point numbers, which can express fractional seconds.

If we left the type of the **total-seconds** slot unspecified, the compiler would need to check the arguments to **truncate/**, on the off chance that an argument was not numeric at all. In some compilers, you would be able to get a compile-time safety warning stating that a run-time type error is possible (which, if unhandled, will result in program failure), and that the check, and the possibility of a run-time error, could be avoided if the compiler knew that **total-seconds** was a **<real>**.

What is a safe program? Dylan is always safe in that a programming error cannot cause a corruption of the program (or of other programs). For example, an out-of-bound array access or passing an argument of incompatible type simply cannot happen. The compiler will either prove that the requested action is impossible, or will insert code to verify bounds or type at run time, and will signal an error if the bounds or type is incorrect.

When we discuss safety in this section, we are referring to whether or not such errors will be visible to the user. If we have not provided for a recovery action, signaling of an error will halt the program. See Chapter 20, *Exceptions*, for an example of how run-time errors can be handled by the program.

Comparison with Java: Java recognizes the need for safe operations, and has eliminated many of the unsafe practices of C and C++, adding such checks as array-bounds checks and type-cast checks at run time. However, Java retains the C mathematical model that trades performance for correctness. Java integers are of a fixed size, and computations that cannot be represented in that size silently overflow. In contrast, Dylan requires numeric operations to complete correctly or to signal an error. Several Dylan implementations are also expected to provide libraries for infinite-precision numerical operations.

If we specified the type of the **`total-seconds`** slot as **`<real>`**, the compiler would have to dispatch on the type of **`total-seconds`**, using either floating-point or integer division as necessary. In some compilers, we would be able to get a compile-time performance warning stating that this dispatch could be omitted if the compiler knew that **`total-seconds`** was of a more restricted type.

Note that the type of the return value of **`decode-total-seconds`** can be inferred: **`max-unit`** and **`minutes`** must be **`<integer>`** (inferred from the definition of **`truncate/`**), and **`seconds`** must have the same type as **`total-seconds`** (**`<integer>`**, in our example); thus, the compiler does not have to insert any type checks on the return values of **`decode-total-seconds`**. Dylan enforces declared return types in the same way as it enforces parameter types, by eliminating the check where type inferencing can show it is not needed, and using the enforced types to make further inferences.

From this example, you can see how the compiler can get a lot of mileage from a small number of constraints, and how it can point you to the places where further clarification will produce the most performance and safety benefits. At the same time, Dylan does not require that you have all your types thought out in advance of compiling the program; the dynamic nature of the language allows Dylan to defer considering type information until the program is actually running. In good Dylan development environments, there is support for resolving and continuing from run-time type errors during program development (rather than requiring editing of the code and recompilation).

Remember that your code is more suited to reuse when it has fewer and more general type constraints. If you have a compiler that can issue safety and performance notes, try to generalize and minimize your type constraints, being guided by your safety and performance requirements. Often, just the constraints required to specify method applicability will be sufficient for good safety and performance. Declaring the types of module variables, slots, and return values of functions is also useful and can help to document your program. Declaring types for constants and local variables can be useful for enforcing program correctness, but is unlikely to create optimization opportunities, and might actually reduce performance, because the compiler will insert type checks to enforce such constraints if they are overly restrictive.

19.4 Limited types

Some of Dylan's built-in types are extremely general. When these types are used, the compiler's type inferencing is thwarted, and less efficient code will be generated. The place where this situation is most obvious is in the **`<collection>`** types, where the elements of a collection are essentially like multiple slots, all with the same type constraint. For the built-in collections, elements typically have a general default type (often simply **`<object>`**), and there can be an arbitrary number of them. The **`limited`** mechanism is a way to specify that you expect to store objects of a particular type in the collection, and to specify how many elements will be in the collection.

As an example, in Section 17.2, page 259, the **`generate-gates`** method returns a **`<vector>`**. Without further information, the compiler must assume that that vector might contain objects of any types. As a result, the following code in the **build-simple-airport** method from Section 17.5, page 277, will be inefficient:

```
let gates = generate-gates(gates-per-terminal, capacity);
...
for (gate in gates)
  gate.connected-to := taxiway-vector;
end for;
```

Because the compiler can infer only that **gates** is a **<vector>**, it must generate extra code to determine whether each **gate** has a **connected-to** method on it. We can use limited types to constrain **gate-instances** as follows:

```
define constant <gate-vector> = limited(<vector>, of: <gate>);

define method generate-gates
    (gates-per-terminal :: <vector>, default-gate-capacity :: <size>)
 => (gates :: <gate-vector>)
  let result = make(<gate-vector>, size: reduce1(\+, gates-per-terminal));
  ...
  values(result);
end method generate-gates;
```

With the limited constraint of the return value of **generate-gates**, the compiler can ensure that only gate objects will ever be stored in the vector; hence, it can be sure that each **gate** will be a **<gate>** and will have a **connected-to** method.

Note that limited-collection types are instantiable types; that is, you can make an object of a limited type. This capability is different from similar constructs in certain other languages, in which those constructs are only an assertion about the range or type of values to be stored in the collection. Having declared the return value of **generate-gates** to be a **<gate-vector>**, it would be an error to return a **<vector>** instead; hence, we changed the argument to **make** when constructing **result** to be **<gate-vector>** instead of the original **<vector>**.

If **<gate>** and **connected-to** are not **open** (as described in Section 19.9 and Section 19.10), the compiler can infer that **connected-to** is used here to set a slot in the gate instance and to further optimize the code generated. We do not delve into the exact details of what the compiler has to know to make this optimization, but it is worth noting that, if either the class or the generic function were open, the optimization could not be made.

> **Comparison with C++:** The Dylan limited-collection types provide a capability similar to that offered by the C++ template classes. Unlike in C++, the base type of a limited-collection type (the equivalent of a C++ class template — in the example above, **`<vector>`**) is also a valid type. Dylan's dynamic capabilities mean that Dylan can defer determining the element type of a collection until run time, in effect adapting the class template as it goes along. By using a limited type, the compiler can generate more efficient code.

Another use of limited types is to allow compact representations. We can use **`limited`** with the built-in type **`<integer>`** to specify numbers with a limited range that can be stored more compactly than integers. It is especially useful to use a limited range in combination with a limited collection; for example,

```
define constant <signed-byte-vector>
  = limited(<simple-vector>,
           of: limited(<integer>, min: -128, max 127));
```

In the preceding example, we define a type that can be represented as a one-dimensional array of 8-bit bytes.

> **Comparison with C:** C provides efficient data representations, because its data types typically map directly to underlying hardware representations. A drawback of C is that its efficient data representations are often not portable: The size of a **`short int`** may vary across platforms, for instance. Dylan takes the more abstract approach of describing the requirements of a data type, and letting the compiler choose the most efficient underlying representation. A drawback of the Dylan approach is that it cannot easily be used for low-level systems programming, where data structures must map reliably to the underlying hardware. Most Dylan systems provide a foreign-function interface to allow calling out to C or some other language more suitable to these low-level tasks. Some Dylan systems augment the language with machine-level constructs that provide the level of control necessary while staying within the object model as much as possible.

> **Comparison with Java:** Java recognizes that portable programs need well-defined data types, rather than types that map to the particular underlying hardware differently in each implementation. However, Java retains some of C's concreteness in simply specifying four distinct sizes of integer (in terms of how many binary digits they hold), and forcing the programmer to convert integer types to objects manually, when object-oriented operations are to be performed. In contrast, Dylan's limited-integer types specify, at the program level, the abstract requirements of the type, giving the compiler freedom to map the program requirements as efficiently as possible to the underlying architecture.

19.5 Enumerations

Many languages provide enumeration types both to enforce program correctness and to provide more compact representation of multiple-choice values. Dylan does not have a built-in enumeration type, but you can easily construct enumerations using the **type-union** and **singleton** type constructors.

For example, consider the **<latitude>** and **<longitude>** classes, where there are only two valid values for the **direction** slot in each class. Rather than enforcing the restrictions programmatically, as we did in Section 10.6, page 128, we can create types that do the job for us:

```
define abstract class <directed-angle> (<sixty-unit>)
  slot direction :: <symbol>, required-init-keyword: direction:;
end class <directed-angle>;

define constant <latitude-direction>
  = type-union(singleton(#"north"), singleton(#"south"));

define class <latitude> (<directed-angle>)
  keyword direction:, type: <latitude-direction>;
end class <latitude>;

define constant <longitude-direction>
  = type-union(singleton(#"east"), singleton(#"west"));

define class <longitude> (<directed-angle>)
  keyword direction:, type: <longitude-direction>;
end class <longitude>;
```

Here, the abstract superclass specifies that the read-only slot **direction** must be a **<symbol>**, and that it must be initialized when an instance is created with the keyword **direction:**. The constant **<latitude-direction>** is a type specification that permits only the symbol **#"north"** or the symbol **#"south"**. The class **<latitude>** specifies that, when an instance of **<latitude>** is made, the initial value must be of the **<latitude-direction>** type. We handled the longitude case similarly.

The use of **type-union** and **singleton** to create enumeration types in this fashion is common enough that the function **one-of** is usually available in a utility library as a shorthand:

```
define constant one-of
  = method (#rest objects)
      apply(type-union, map(singleton, objects))
    end method;
```

With this abbreviation, the direction types can be written more compactly:

```
define constant <latitude-direction> = one-of(#"north", #"south");

define constant <longitude-direction> = one-of(#"east", #"west");
```

Some Dylan compilers will recognize the idiomatic use of **type-union** and **singleton** to represent such enumerations more compactly. For instance, a compiler could represent the direction slot of a latitude or longitude as a single bit, using the getter and setter functions to translate back and forth to the appropriate symbol.

19.6 Direct methods

The definition of the **one-of** constant is a method called a **direct method** or **bare method**. It is the equivalent of a function in other languages. A bare method does not create an implicit generic function, and invoking a bare method does not use method-dispatch procedure, but rather calls the method directly. We choose to use a bare method here because we are sure that **one-of** will never need method dispatch: it performs the same operation independent of the types of its arguments. The bare method serves to document this intent. If there were some possibility of additional methods, it would be more perspicuous to use a generic function, even if there is initially only one method. Most Dylan compilers will generate equally efficient code for a bare method and for a generic function with only one method, so the choice of which to use should be based on whether or not it would ever make sense to have additional methods that discriminate on parameter types.

19.7 Tail calls

The most important construct in the Dylan execution model is the function call, because function calls are the most common operation in the language. Remember that all slot accesses and assignments, arithmetic operations, and collection accesses obey the execution model of function calls, even if the syntax for them does not look like that of function calls.

We have already discussed how Dylan compilers can optimize away runtime checking of argument types and the overhead of method dispatch, and that good compilers will generate equally efficient code for calls to single-method generic functions or direct methods.

There is one additional optimization that good Dylan compilers will make, which is enabled by a particular style of programming. If the final operation in a method is a call to another function (called a **tail call**) then the calling function can jump directly to the called function, rather than using a call-and-return sequence. Thus, the return from the called function returns to its caller's caller.

As an example, consider this **decode-total-seconds** method:

```
define method decode-total-seconds
    (sixty-unit :: <sixty-unit>)
 => (hours :: <integer>, minutes :: <integer>, seconds :: <integer>)
  decode-total-seconds(sixty-unit.total-seconds);
end method decode-total-seconds;
```

The inner call to **decode-total-seconds** can be a direct jump rather than a function call, because the compiler can infer which method should be called and that the return values already have the correct constraints.

19.8 Typed generic functions

In addition to specifying the types of the parameters and return values of methods, you can specify the types of the parameters and return values of a generic function. You usually restrict the parameter types of a generic function to establish the **contract** of the generic function — that is, to define the domain of arguments that the generic function is intended to handle, and the domain of the values that it will return.

If we define a method without also defining a generic function, Dylan creates an implicit generic function with the most general types for each parameter and return value that are compatible with the method. For example, assume that we defined a method for **next-landing-step**, and did not explicitly create a generic function for it. The method is as follows:

```
define method next-landing-step
    (storage :: <sky>, aircraft :: <aircraft>)
 => (next-class :: false-or(<class>), duration :: false-or(<time-offset>))
  ...
  end if;
end method next-landing-step;
```

When we define a method without also defining a generic function, the compiler will generate an implicit generic function for us, which, in this case, will be as though we had defined the generic function like this:

```
define generic next-landing-step (o1 :: <object>, o2 :: <object>)
 => (#rest r :: <object>);
```

In Section 17.4, page 267, where we did define a generic function, we used a simple definition, just documenting the number of arguments, and giving them mnemonic names:

```
define generic next-landing-step (container, vehicle);
```

Because we did not specify types of the arguments or return values, they default to **<object>**, just as they did in the preceding implicit generic function.

Although the generic function that we wrote does prevent us from defining methods with the wrong number of arguments, it does not constrain the types of those arguments or the format or type of return values in any way. A sophisticated compiler may be able to make inferences based on the methods that we define, but we could both aid the compiler and more clearly document the protocol of **next-landing-step** by specifying the types of the parameters and return values in the definition of the generic function:

```
define generic next-landing-step
    (storage :: <vehicle-storage>, aircraft :: <aircraft>)
 => (next-storage :: <vehicle-storage>, elapsed-time :: <time-offset>);
```

Now, the compiler can help us. If we define a method whose arguments are not a subclass of **`<vehicle-storage>`** and a subclass of **`<aircraft>`** (for example, if we provided the arguments in the wrong order), the compiler will report the error. Furthermore, the compiler can use the value declaration to detect errors in the return values (for example, if we returned only a single value or returned a value of the wrong type). Finally, the compiler can be asked to issue a warning if there is a subclass of the argument types for which no method is applicable.

In addition to establishing a contract, specifying the types of the parameters and return values of generic functions can allow the compiler to make additional inferences, as described in Section 19.3 with regard to **`truncate/`**. In the absence of other information, the compiler is limited in the optimizations that it can make based solely on the parameter types in the generic function, so it is generally best not to restrict artificially the types of a generic function, but rather to use the restricted types to document the generic function's protocol.

19.9 Open generic functions

By default, generic functions are **sealed**. When you use **`define generic`**, that is the same as using **`define sealed generic`**. No other library can add methods to a sealed generic function — not even on new classes that they may introduce. Methods cannot be added to, or removed from, the generic function at run time. The only methods on a sealed generic function are the methods that are defined in the library where the generic function itself is defined. Because of the restrictions on a sealed generic function, the compiler, using type-inference information, can usually narrow the choice of applicable methods for any particular call to the generic function, eliminating most or all of the overhead of run-time dispatching that would normally be expected of a dynamic language.

We saw in Chapter 13, *Libraries and Modules*, that we must define a generic function that is part of a shared protocol using **`define open generic`**, so that libraries sharing the protocol can implement the protocol for the classes that they define, by adding methods. If we do not define the generic function to be open, other libraries are prohibited from adding methods to the generic function, which would make it useless as a protocol. Unfortunately, a generic function that is open cannot be optimized. Even when the compiler may be able to infer the exact types of the arguments to the generic function in a particular call, because an open generic function may have methods added or removed, even at run time, the compiler must produce code to handle all these possibilities.

Because open generic functions cannot be optimized, you should use them only when necessary. You need to balance the division of your program into libraries against the need to export and open more generic functions if the program is too finely divided. This balance is illustrated by the considerations we made in designing a protocol in Section 13.9, page 214. When we chose to split the **time** and **angle** libraries, we were forced to create the **say** protocol library and open the generic function **say**. In Section 19.11, we show how to regain certain optimizations when you decide that opening a generic function is required.

Note that generic functions that are defined implicitly in a library — such as those that are defined when you define only a single method, or those that are defined for slot accessors — are sealed by default. If you expect other libraries to add methods to one of these implicit generic functions, you must define the generic function explicitly to be open using **define open generic**.

19.10 Open classes

By default, classes are **sealed**. When you use **define class**, that is the same as using **define sealed class**. Other libraries cannot directly subclass a sealed class — they cannot define new classes that have your sealed class as a direct superclass. The only direct subclasses of the class are those subclasses that are defined in the library where the class itself is defined. Extensive optimization opportunities occur when the methods of a sealed generic function are specialized on sealed classes. In this case, the compiler can usually choose the correct method of the generic function to call at compile time, eliminating any run-time overhead for using a generic function.

We saw in Chapter 13, *Libraries and Modules*, that we must define a class that is a shared substrate, such as **<sixty-unit>**, using **define open class**, if the libraries sharing the substrate are expected to subclass the class. If we did not define the class to be open, other libraries would be prevented from subclassing it — which might be reasonable if the substrate were not intended to be extended by subclassing.

Unlike an open generic function, an open class does not prevent all optimization. If a generic function has a method applicable to an open class, but the generic function is sealed, then the compiler might still be able to optimize method dispatch if that compiler can infer the types of the arguments to the generic function at a particular call. Sometimes, the dispatch code will be slightly less optimal, because it must allow for arbitrary subclasses, rather than a fixed set of subclasses; in general, however, opening a class is less costly than is opening a generic function.

Note that, although you cannot directly subclass a sealed class from another library, you can subclass a sealed class in the library that defines the sealed class. It may not be obvious, but a corollary of this rule of sealing is that you can define an **open subclass** of a sealed class in the library that defines the sealed class. Using a sealed class with an open subclass is one simple way to get both flexibility and efficiency — the classes in the sealed branch will be optimized by the compiler, while the open subclass can be exported for other libraries to build on and extend.

19.11 Sealed domains

When you define a protocol that is meant to be extended by many libraries, both the base classes and the generic functions that make up the protocol must be open. This simple exigency might make it seem that there is no hope of optimizing such a protocol — however, there is hope. You use the **`define sealed domain`** form to seal selectively subsets or **branches** of the protocol, permitting the compiler to make all the optimizations that would be possible if the classes and generic functions were sealed, but only for the particular subset or branch in question.

> **Advanced topic:** Sealed domains are one of the most difficult concepts of the Dylan language to understand fully. It is reasonable to defer careful reading of this section until you are faced with a situation similar to the example — an imported open class and generic function that will be specialized by your library.

As an example, consider the **`say`** protocol as used in the **`time`** library. Because the **`say`** generic function is defined to be open, even if the compiler can infer that the argument to **`say`** is a **`<time>`** or **`<time-offset>`**, it must insert code to choose the appropriate method to call at run time on the off chance that some other library has added or removed methods for **`say`**. The solution is to add the following definition to the **`time`** library:

```
// Declare the say generic function sealed, for all time classes
define sealed domain say (<time>);
```

This statement is essentially a guarantee to the compiler that the only methods on **say** that are applicable to **<time>** objects (and also to **<time-of-day>** and **<time-offset>** objects, because **<time-of-day>** and **<time-offset>** are subclasses of **<time>**) are those that are defined explicitly in the **time** library (and in any libraries from which that one imports). Thus, when the compiler can prove that the argument to **say** is a **<time-offset>**, it can call the correct method directly, without any run-time dispatch overhead.

Another way to get the same effect as a sealed domain, which is also self-documenting, is to use **define sealed method** when defining individual methods on the protocol. So, for instance, in the case of the **time** library, we might have defined the two methods on **say** as follows:

```
define sealed method say (time :: <time>)
  let (hours, minutes) = decode-total-seconds (time);
  format-out("%d:%s%d", hours, if (minutes < 10) "0" else " " end, minutes);
end method say;

define sealed method say (time :: <time-offset>) => ()
  format-out("%s ", if (time.past?) "minus" else "plus" end);
  next-method();
end method say;
```

Defining a sealed method is the same as defining the generic function to be sealed over the domain of the method's specializers. In effect, this technique says that you do not intend anyone to add more specific methods in that domain, or to create classes that would change the applicability of the sealed methods.

With either the **define sealed domain** form or the sealed methods, the use of **say** on **<time>** objects will be as efficient as it would be were **say** not an open generic function after all. At the same time, other libraries that create new classes can still extend the **say** protocol to cover those classes.

Sealed domains impose restrictions on the ability of other libraries to create new methods, to remove new methods, and to create new classes:

You cannot add methods to an open generic function imported from another library that would fall into the sealed domain of *any* other library. You can avoid this restriction by ensuring that at least one of the specializers of your method is a subtype of a type defined in your library.

> **Comparison with C++:** A C++ compiler could optimize out the dispatching of a virtual function by analyzing the entire scope of the argument on which the virtual function dispatches, and proving that argument's exact class. Unfortunately, that scope is often the entire program, so this optimization often can be performed only by a linker. Even a linker cannot make this optimization when a library is compiled, because the classes of a library can be subclassed by a client. The complexity is compounded for dynamic-link libraries, where there may be multiple clients at once. As a result, this optimization is rarely achieved in C++.
>
> In Dylan, sealed classes, sealed generic functions, and sealed domains explicitly state which generic functions and classes may be extended, and, more important, which cannot. The library designer plans in advance exactly what extensibility the library will have. The Dylan compiler can then optimize dispatching on sealed generic functions and classes and within sealed domains with the assurance that no client will violate the assumptions of the optimization. The sealing restrictions against subclassing or changing method applicability are automatically enforced on each client of a Dylan library.

When you seal a domain of a generic function imported from another library, you will not cause conflicts with other libraries, as long as both of the following conditions hold:

1. At least one of the types in the sealed domain is a subtype of a class defined in your library
2. No additional subtypes can be defined for any of the types in the sealed domain

In the case of a type that is a class, the first condition means that you must have defined either the class or one of its superclasses in your library. The second condition means that the classes in the domain must not have any open subclasses (a degenerate case of which is a leaf class — a class with no subclasses at all).

If you need to seal a domain over a class that has open subclasses, you will need a thorough understanding of the sealing constraints detailed in *The Dylan Reference Manual*, but these two simple rules should handle many common cases.

In our example, we obeyed both rules of thumb: our methods for **say** are on classes we defined, and our sealing was over classes that will not be further subclassed. The rules of thumb not only keep you from violating sealing constraints, they make for good protocol design: a library that extends a protocol really should extend it only for classes it fully understands, which usually means classes it creates.

As an example of the restriction on subclassing open classes involved in a sealed domain, if the **<time>** class were an open class, we still could not add the following class in a library that used the **time** library:

```
define class <place-and-time> (<position>, <time>)
end class <place-and-time>;
```

As far as the compiler is concerned, it "knows" that the only **say** method applicable to a **<time>** is the one in the **time** library. (That is what we have told it with our **sealed domain** definition.) It would be valid to pass a **<place-and-time>** object as an argument to a function that accepted **<time>** objects, but within that function the compiler might have already optimized a call to **say** to the method for **<time>** objects (based on **<time>** being in the sealed domain of **say**). But there is also a method for **say** on **<position>**, and, more important, we probably will want to define a method specifically for **<place-and-time>**. Because of this ambiguity, the class **<place-and-time>** cannot be defined in a separate library, and the compiler will signal an error.

Note that the class **<place-and-time>** could be defined in the **time** library. The compiler can deal correctly with classes that may straddle a sealed domain, if they are known in the library where the sealed domain is defined. It would also be valid to subclass **<time>** in any way that did not change the applicability of methods in any sealed generic-function domains that include **<time>**. The actual rule involved depends on an analysis of the exact methods of the generic function, and the rule is complicated enough that you should just rely on your compiler to detect illegal situations.

19.12 Slot accessors

Dylan does allow you to omit definition of a generic function. As we mentioned earlier, if you define a method without also defining a generic function, Dylan implicitly creates a generic function with the most general types for the parameters and return values that are compatible with the method. The most common case of implicit generic functions is for the slot-accessor methods that are created when a new class is defined. Because these generic functions typically have only a single method and are **sealed** by default (see Section 19.9), the compiler can make extensive optimizations for slot accessors, ideally making slot access no more expensive than an array reference or structure-member access in other languages.

Even when a slot is inherited by subclassing, a good Dylan compiler will use a **coloring algorithm** to assign slots to the same offset in each subclass, keeping the cost of slot access to a minimum. You can use primary classes (see Section 19.13) to guarantee efficient slot access.When a program defines explicit methods for a slot getter or setter generic function, of course, the overhead is greater.

> **Comparison with C++:** Dylan classes are similar to virtual base classes with virtual data members in that the offsets of their data members are not fixed, and access to the data members can be overridden. See Section B.2 in Appendix B, *Dylan Object Model for C and C++ Programmers*, for a more detailed analogy.

In the **<sixty-unit>** class, we specified an initial value for **total-seconds**; hence, there is no need to check that the slot has been initialized before it is accessed. In some situations, it may not be feasible to give a default or initial value for a slot. Dylan permits this omission and will ensure that the slot is initialized before that slot is used; of course, this check does not come for free, so it is preferable to provide initial values where possible. In fact, because we always expect to initialize the **total-seconds** slot when we make a new **<sixty-unit>**, it would be more accurate to specify **<sixty-unit>** as follows:

```
define open abstract class <sixty-unit> (<object>)
  slot total-seconds :: <integer>,
    required-init-keyword: total-seconds:,
end class <sixty-unit>;
```

That is, rather than giving the slot an initial value of **0** and an optional **init-keyword:**, we simply require that the slot be initialized when we make a **<sixty-unit>** object. Of course, the initial value must obey the type constraint of **<integer>**. The compiler can still make the inference that the slot will always be initialized and will always have an integer value.

> **Comparison with C:** Dylan always ensures that a slot is initialized before that slot is accessed, automatically inserting a run-time check when it cannot prove at compile time that the slot is always properly initialized. C puts this burden of safety on the programmer, and that can be the source of subtle bugs. A number of debugging and analysis tools are available as addons to C, to help the programmer with this task.

Always initializing slots, either with a default value or required init-keyword, will make slot access efficient.

Finally, in many cases, slots hold values that will not change over the lifetime of each instance (although they may be different values for each instance). In the case of the **<sixty-unit>** class, we never change the value of **total-seconds**. When adding two instances, we create a new one to hold the new value, rather than changing one of the argument instances (that way, we do not have to worry about changing an instance that may still be in use by some other part of the program). In such cases, declaring the slot to be **constant** both documents and enforces this intent. Furthermore, the compiler can often make additional optimizations for slots that are known never to be modified. The final definition of **<sixty-unit>** is as follows:

```
define open abstract class <sixty-unit> (<object>)
  constant slot total-seconds :: <integer>,
    required-init-keyword: total-seconds:,
end class <sixty-unit>;
```

(The **constant** declaration is simply shorthand for the slot option **setter: #f**, meaning that there is no way to set the slot.)

19.13 Primary classes

Classes have one additional variation that you can use to optimize performance. A class that is defined as **primary** allows the compiler to generate the most efficient code for accessing the slots defined in the primary class (whether the accessor is applied to the primary class or to one of that class's subclasses). However, a primary class cannot be combined with any other primary class (unless one is a subclass of the other). This restriction implies that you should delay declaring a class to be primary until you are sure of your inheritance design. Also, because sealed classes are already highly optimized, the **primary** declaration is of most use for open classes.

As an example, consider the class **<sixty-unit>**, and its slot **total-seconds**, as used in this method for **decode-total-seconds**:

```
define method decode-total-seconds
    (sixty-unit :: <sixty-unit>)
 => (hours :: <integer>, minutes :: <integer>, seconds :: <integer>)
  decode-total-seconds(sixty-unit.total-seconds);
end method decode-total-seconds;
```

Although the generic function for the slot accessor **total-seconds** is sealed, and it is trivial for the compiler to infer that its argument is a **<sixty-unit>** in the call **sixty-unit.total-seconds**, because **<sixty-unit>** is declared open, the compiler cannot emit the most efficient code for that call. Because an open class could be mixed with any number of other classes, there is no guarantee that the slots of every object that is a **<sixty-unit>** will always be stored in the same order —there is no guarantee that **total-seconds** will always be the first slot in an object that is an indirect instance of **<sixty-unit>**, for instance.

Declaring a class **primary** is essentially making a guarantee that the compiler can always put the primary class's slots in the same place in an instance, and that any other superclasses will have to adjust:

```
define abstract open primary class <sixty-unit> (<object>)
  constant slot total-seconds :: <integer>,
    required-init-keyword: total-seconds:;
end class <sixty-unit>;
```

By adding the **primary** declaration to the definition, any library that subclasses **<sixty-unit>** is guaranteed to put **total-seconds** at the same offset. Hence, the compiler can turn the call **sixty-unit.total-seconds** into a single machine instruction (load with constant offset), without concern over which subclass of **<sixty-unit>** was passed as an argument.

> **Comparison with C++:** A primary class is like an ordinary base class in C++. Because only one primary class is allowed as a base class, its data members can be assigned the same fixed offset for all derived classes. See Appendix B.2, *The concept of classes*, for a more detailed analogy.

It is permissible to make subclasses of a primary class also primary, essentially freezing the assignment of all the slots in the subclass too. What is not permissible is to multiply inherit from more than one primary class; as you can see, such behavior would lead to a conflict between the fixed slot assignments.

Because primary classes restrict extension in this way, you should use them sparingly in libraries intended to be software components. Primary classes are of most benefit in large, modular programs, where all the clients of each component are known, and the need for extensibility is bounded; typically that occurs toward the end of a project, when you are tuning for performance.

19.14 Additional efficiency information

In this section, we review additional techniques that compilers can use to generate code that obeys the Dylan execution model, but is more efficient than a straightforward implementation of that model might suggest. Knowing about these techniques can help you to evaluate different vendors' compilers. You will have to consult the documentation of your particular implementation to discover whether or not these techniques are used.

19.14.1 Efficiency of generic function calls

In addition to using type inferencing and sealed domains, another way to speed up generic function calls when they must dispatch at run time is to cache the return values of previous calls. So, for example, the first time that a given generic function is called with certain classes of arguments, the full sorted sequence of applicable methods is computed; after that, however, it only to be only looked up in a table. Thus, if the generic function is called often with the same type of arguments, most calls will be fast. This technique is used in other object-oriented languages, such as Smalltalk and CLOS, and is useful for speeding up completely dynamic situations. Most good Dylan compilers will use some form of cached dispatching.

A second form of cached dispatching is called **call-site caching**. Although a generic function may have many calls throughout a program, often the types of arguments passed are directly related to where (that is, in what other method) the call is made. Some Dylan compilers will cache the types and methods of each call at the point of call, and will use this cache to avoid dispatch if the same types are passed as arguments in a subsequent call from the same place.

19.14.2 Efficiency of keyword arguments and of multiple values

Keyword arguments are a powerful and flexible, but potentially expensive, feature of Dylan. The processing of keywords and values at run time can be an expensive operation, especially if many keywords are used. A Dylan compiler can pass keyword arguments as efficiently as it can required arguments, if the called function is known at compilation time.

Returning multiple values again raises performance issues. In some implementations of Dylan, there is an extra cost for returning more than one value; in others, the cost is associated with calling a function that does not declare how many values it returns. When the compiler knows what function is being called, these costs usually can be eliminated, but certain costs may still exist — for example, certain implementations may not optimize tail calls between functions that return different numbers of arguments.

19.14.3 Memory usage

Dylan uses automatic storage-management; thus, programmers explicitly allocate objects, and hence memory, but deallocation is automatic and occurs after all references to an object are gone. The process of reclaiming memory when objects are no longer in use is known as **garbage collection**.

There are strong advantages to automatic storage-management. With manual storage-management, small program bugs, such as freeing of an object that is still in use, can cause subtle bugs that lead to crashes in parts of the program unrelated to where the real problem lies. Dylan is able to guarantee that all programs fail in disciplined ways, usually with exceptions, because the type system and memory management are safe.

But automatic storage-management may create performance concerns. Although early implementations of garbage collection were infamously slow, modern garbage collectors are usually fast enough that using one should not raise concerns for most programs. But some programs with specialized or tuned use of memory may run slower with automatic management.

Whether storage management is automatic or manual, the use of memory raises performance issues. Every allocation of memory takes time, including the time to reclaim unused memory; either the programmer must free it explicitly, or the garbage collector has to do more work.

It is obvious that calling a function such as **`make`**, **`vector`**, or **`pair`** in Dylan allocates memory, but there are operations that implicitly use memory. For example, creating a closure (see Section 12.3.6, page 183) will usually cause Dylan to allocate memory for the closure.

On the other hand, sometimes the compiler is able to prove that an object is never used after the function that creates it returns. In a good compiler, such objects are allocated on the stack, and are reclaimed automatically when the function exits.

A good Dylan development environment will have tools that help you to meter and profile memory usage, so that you can adjust your program to utilize memory efficiently.

19.14.4 Inlining, constant folding, and partial evaluation

One optimization that is common in many computer languages is **inlining**. Inlining replaces a call to a known function with the body of the function. Inlining is an important optimization in Dylan, because almost all Dylan operations — slot access, array indexing, and collection iteration — involve function calls.

All good Dylan compilers, when compiling for speed, can be aggressive about inlining any computations, as long as doing so would not make a program grow too large. Constant folding (evaluating expressions involving constant values at compile time) and inlining are just two of the **partial-evaluation** techniques that you should expect to find in any good Dylan compiler.

> **Comparison with C:** A programmer familiar with the optimizations done in C compilers can think of partial evaluation as an extreme combination of inlining and constant folding. One way in which Dylan has an advantage over C for partial evaluation is that it hard for a compiler to evaluate expressions that involve dereferencing pointers. For example, in C, it is difficult to evaluate partially a call to **`malloc`**, but Dylan compilers can often evaluate a call to **`make`** at compile time.

19.14.5 Type inference

The quality of type inference can vary greatly among Dylan compilers. Type inference — like most forms of program analysis — works best with simple, straightforward code. Some constructs that are typically difficult for type inference are assignment and calling of block exit functions outside of the method that defines the block exit functions.

One other way in which type constraints can be helpful is that they permit the compiler to choose efficient representations for objects. Most Dylan objects contain enough information for Dylan to determine their class — this one is an important feature for the dynamic aspects of the language. But, suppose we have a 1000x1000 **`limited(<array>, of: <single-float>)`**. There is no reason that each of the numbers in that array should also contain a reference to the **`<single-float>`** class; the one reference in the limited type is sufficient. (Note that, if we had used **`of: <real>`** or **`of: <float>`**, we would have needed more information, since multiple classes would have been possible.)

When an object is represented in such a way, often many of the operations on it can be optimized. For example, the conventional representation of **`<double-float>`** will usually require an indirect-memory-reference machine instruction to get at the actual number, so adding two such objects is one floating-point machine instruction and two load-from-memory machine instructions; if a direct representation is used, just the add machine instruction is needed. Further, if the return value is saved in a variable for which type information is not available, it may be necessary to allocate memory dynamically to store the return value.

Types that may have more efficient representations include certain integer classes, the floating-point classes, characters, and Booleans. Precise declarations about these types, especially in slots and limited collections, can lead to significant improvements in both the time and memory needed to run a program.

19.15 Summary

The most important point about performance is that it is important to pay attention to efficiency during the entire design and development cycle of a project. During the design phase, try to ensure that the algorithms chosen have the right asymptotic behavior and constant factors, and that it is possible to implement the needed operations efficiently. During the implementation phase, use the language constructs that most clearly express what the program is doing. Once the program is working correctly, it is then time to add type and sealing declarations, and to use metering and profiling tools to find and rewrite heavily used, slow parts of the program, in order to improve the performance.

One of the most important considerations when programming is not to worry about performance too soon. It is always more important that your design and implementation be clear and correct, first. There is no value in arriving at an answer with lightning speed, if it turns out to be the wrong answer.

In this chapter, we covered the following:

- We showed how Dylan can balance performance and flexibility to support a range of programming requirements.
- We showed how type constraints affect performance.
- We showed how limited types can improve performance.
- We showed how open generic functions provide modularity and flexibility.
- We showed how open classes provide modularity and flexibility.
- We showed how sealed generic function domains mitigate the performance penalty of open classes and generic functions.
- We showed how primary classes permit efficient slot access.
- We presented both an execution and efficiency model that provides a conceptual model of how a program in Dylan runs, and what the relative cost of different program elements are.
- We examined the method constructs for flexibility and performance available in Dylan; see Table 19.1.

Construct	Effects
direct method	highly optimizable no method dispatch
sealed generic function on a sealed class	highly optimizable not extensible by other libraries
sealed generic function on an open class	optimizable other libraries can subclass
open generic function on an open class in a sealed domain	highly optimizable other libraries can add methods other libraries can subclass
open generic function on an open class	not optimizable methods can be added at run time subclasses can be created at run time

Table 19.1 Methods: flexibility versus performance.

- We discussed the constructs that can have type constraints, and the influence on performance or flexibility of using such a declaration; see Table 19.2.

Construct	Effects
module constants	enforce program correctness
module variables	permit type inferencing
required parameters	required for method dispatch permit type inferencing

Table 19.2 Type constraint: flexibility versus performance.

Construct	Effects
optional parameters	permit type inferencing
return values	enforce program correctness permit type inferencing
limited types	permit type inferencing permit compact data representation
slots	permit type inferencing

Table 19.2 Type constraint: flexibility versus performance. *(continued)*

20

Exceptions

An **exception** is an unexpected event that occurs during program execution (as opposed to problems detected during program compilation). One common type of exception is a violation of the contract of a function, such as attempting to divide a number by zero. Another example is an attempt to access an uninitialized slot, or certain cases of an attempt to violate the type constraint on a slot or variable (those that cannot be detected at compile time). Dylan detects all these exceptions itself. Sometimes, an application detects a violation of a contract that it defines. For example, in Section 10.6, page 128, we defined methods that detected attempts to specify a longitude direction of anything other than east or west. (In Section 19.5, page 318, we changed the application such that this particular application-detected exception was transformed into one that is detected by Dylan.)

When an an unusual event occurs in an application, there are many options available for responding to that event. The application can try to handle the situation in its own particular way, or it can use the **exception protocol** defined by Dylan. In this chapter, we explore several approaches to providing an exception protocol between parts of an application.

20.1 An informal exception protocol

Our goal is to modify the method that adds a **`<time-offset>`** instance to a **`<time-of-day>`** instance. We redefine that method to detect overflow beyond the

24-hour period covered by a time of day, and to take special action in that case. In this section, we show a simple way to indicate and handle exceptions, without using the Dylan exception protocol. We then discuss the problems with this informal approach. In Section 20.2, we achieve the same goal using Dylan conditions, and discuss the advantages of that approach.

20.1.1 The + method using informal exceptions

First, we redefine the method for adding **<time-offset>** and **<time-of-day>** (this method was last defined in Section 14.3.2, page 228). The method now returns an error string in the event that the computed sum is beyond the permitted 24-hour range:

```
define method \+ (offset :: <time-offset>, time-of-day :: <time-of-day>)
 => (sum :: type-union(<time-of-day>, <string>))
  let sum
    = make(<time-of-day>,
           total-seconds: offset.total-seconds + time-of-day.total-seconds);
  if (sum >= $midnight & sum < $tomorrow)
    sum;
  else
   "time boundary violated";
  end if;
end method \+;
```

We have altered the + method in two important ways. First, we have modified the original values declaration, **(sum :: <time-of-day>)**, to allow the return of either a **<time-of-day>** instance or a string describing a problem. Second, we have added code that checks the computed time of day, and returns an error string if the sum is out of bounds.

To illustrate further how the informal exceptions work, we define a method that calls the + method defined in this section. We define a method, **correct-arrival-time**, that adds predicted weather and traffic delays to an arrival time; and we define **say-corrected-time**, which calls **correct-arrival-time** and displays the results:

```
define method correct-arrival-time
    (arrival-time :: <time-of-day>, weather-delay :: <time-offset>,
     traffic-delay :: <time-offset>)
 => (sum :: type-union(<time-of-day>, <string>))
  let sum1 = weather-delay + arrival-time;
  // Check whether the result of + was a string representing an error
  if (instance?(sum1, <string>))
    sum1;
  else
    // Otherwise, if there is no error, compute the second part of the sum
    traffic-delay + sum1;
  end if;
end method correct-arrival-time;

define constant $no-time = make(<time-offset>, total-seconds: 0);

define method say-corrected-time
    (arrival-time :: <time-of-day>,
     #key weather-delay :: <time-offset> = $no-time,
     traffic-delay :: <time-offset> = $no-time)
 => ()
  let result = correct-arrival-time(arrival-time, weather-delay,
                                    traffic-delay);
  // Check whether the result of + was a string representing an error
  if (instance?(result, <string>))
    format-out("Error during time correction: %s", result);
  else
    // Otherwise, if there is no error, display the result
    say(result);
  end if;
end method say-corrected-time;
```

20.1.2 Problems with the informal exception protocol

There are several significant problems with the approach used in Section 20.1.1:

- As we saw in the **`correct-arrival-time`** method, most callers of the **`+`** function must check the type of the value returned. This type checking breaks up the normal flow of control, and gives as much weight to the unusual case (the exception) as it does to the usual case. If a caller fails to check the return value to see whether that value is a string, then a different error will occur later in the program (such as adding a string and time together), when it might be hard to trace back the problem to the original point of failure. Note that both direct callers of **`+`** (**`correct-arrival-time`**) and indirect callers of **+** (**say-corrected-time**) must understand and use this error protocol correctly.

- For other methods that might return any object (including strings, for example), an additional return value would have to be used to indicate that an exception occurred. It would be easy to forget to check the extra return value and such failure could easily go undetected, causing unpredictable program behavior. If the method is being added to a generic function in another library, it might be impossible to add a second return value indicating failure, because the generic function might limit the number of return values.

- A casual reader of the code could become easily confused about this ad hoc error protocol. Someone might inadvertently write code that did not obey this ad hoc protocol. Also, if all programmers use their own error protocols, it will be hard to remember which convention to obey at the call site; programmers will have to check the convention in the source code or programmer documentation.

- In this example, the ability to restrict the return value to only **<time-of-day>** is lost. This loss might prevent compile-time error checking that could catch errors that would be difficult or inconvenient to catch at run time. It might also prevent the compiler from optimizing code that uses the results of this function, thus decreasing performance of the application.

- We are limited in how we can respond to the error. The context in which the error was detected has been lost. There is no state we can examine to gather more details about the error, and to determine why the error occurred. We also cannot correct whatever caused the problem, then continue from the point where the error occurred.

20.2 A simple Dylan exception protocol

In Sections 20.2.1 through 20.2.4, we show how to modify the three methods in Section 20.1.1 to use the basic tools that Dylan provides for indicating and responding to exceptional situations.

20.2.1 Signaling conditions

Dylan provides a structured mechanism for indicating that an unusual event or exceptional situation has occurred during the execution of a program. Using this mechanism is called **signaling a condition**. A **condition** is an instance of the `<condition>` class, which represents a problem or unusual situation encountered during program execution.

To signal a condition, we need to take these steps:

1. Define a condition class, which must be a subclass of `<condition>`. The condition class should have slots that are appropriate for the application. In this example, we define a condition class named `<time-error>` to be a direct subclass of `<error>`. Note that `<error>` is a subclass of `<condition>`. We defined `<time-error>` to inherit from `<error>`, because in case our application does not handle the exception, we want Dylan always to take some action, such as entering a debugger. If `<time-error>` inherited from `<condition>` and the application failed to handle the exception, then the exception might simply be ignored.
2. Modify the functions that might detect the exception. These functions must make an instance of the condition class, and must use an appropriate Dylan function to initiate the signaling process. In this example, we redefine the `+` method to signal the condition with the `error` function.

In the following code, we define a condition named `<time-error>` to represent any kind of time error, and we define a condition named `<time-boundary-error>` to represent violations of time-of-day bounds.

```
define abstract class <time-error> (<error>)
  constant slot invalid-time :: <time>, required-init-keyword: invalid-time:;
end class <time-error>;

define method say (condition :: <time-error>) => ()
  format-out("The time ");
  say(condition.invalid-time);
  format-out(" is invalid.");
end method say;
```

```
define class <time-boundary-error> (<time-error>)
  // Inclusive bound
  constant slot min-valid-time
    :: <time>, required-init-keyword: min-time:;
  // Exclusive bound
  constant slot valid-time-limit
    :: <time>, required-init-keyword: time-limit:;
end class <time-boundary-error>;

define method say (condition :: <time-boundary-error>) => ()
  next-method();
  format-out("\nIt must not be less than ");
  say(condition.min-valid-time);
  format-out(" and must be less than ");
  say(condition.valid-time-limit);
  format-out(".");
end method say;
```

We redefine the + method to signal the **<time-boundary-error>** condition (instead of returning an error string) to indicate that this problem has occurred:

```
define method \+ (offset :: <time-offset>, time-of-day :: <time-of-day>)
  => (sum :: <time-of-day>)
  let sum
    = make(<time-of-day>,
           total-seconds:
             offset.total-seconds + time-of-day.total-seconds);
  if (sum >= $midnight & sum < $tomorrow)
    sum;
  else
    error(make(<time-boundary-error>, invalid-time: sum,
               min-time: $midnight, time-limit: $tomorrow));
  end if;
end method \+;
```

We create the condition with **make**, just as we create instances of other classes. We call the **error** function to signal the condition. The **error** function is guaranteed never to return to its caller.

Now we can specify an exact return value for the + method, because we are no longer returning an error string to indicate a problem with the addition.

In previous chapters (for example, in Section 6.1.3, page 78), we called the **error** function with a string. Given a string as its first argument, the **error** function creates a general-purpose condition named **<simple-error>** and stores its arguments in the condition instance. In the preceding example, however, we created an instance of a condition that is customized for our program (**<time-**

boundary-error>), and then supplied that condition to the **error** function. This approach provides information that is more readily accessible to the code that will handle the condition. Conditions, like any other Dylan class, can use inheritance, and can participate in generic function dispatch. For example, we define **say** methods for our errors, so that our handlers can provide a reasonable error message to the user. (Unfortunately, Dylan debuggers do not yet have a standard way to know about our **say** generic function. We expect that Dylan will eventually support such a mechanism.)

Supplying a specific condition to the **error** function brings the full power of Dylan's object-oriented programming capabilities to the task of signaling and handling exceptional situations.

Once the **error** function receives a condition instance, or makes an instance of **<simple-error>** itself, Dylan begins a process of attempting to resolve the situation represented by the condition. We present the details of condition resolution in the next section.

20.2.2 Simple condition handling

A **handler** can potentially resolve an exceptional situation, although a handler can decline to resolve a particular exception. If an application provides no handlers, then the generic function **default-handler** is called on the condition. There is a method on **<condition>** that just returns false, and there is a method on **<serious-condition>** (a superclass of **<error>**) that causes some kind of implementation-specific response to be invoked. Most development environments provide a debugger that deals with any serious conditions not handled by the application. Typically, the debugger describes the serious condition being signaled, and might provide any number of options for recovery (or might provide no recovery options). In a sense, the debugger is the handler of final resort.

In the following example, we establish a handler for the condition that we want to resolve, before calling the code that might signal that condition. We redefine the **correct-arrival-time** and **say-corrected-time** methods to take advantage of the Dylan exception protocol.

```
define method correct-arrival-time
    (arrival-time :: <time-of-day>, weather-delay :: <time-offset>,
     traffic-delay :: <time-offset>)
 => (sum :: <time-of-day>)
  traffic-delay + (weather-delay + arrival-time);
end method correct-arrival-time;
```

```
define method say-corrected-time
    (arrival-time :: <time-of-day>,
     #key weather-delay :: <time-offset> = $no-time,
     traffic-delay :: <time-offset> = $no-time)
 => ()
  block ()
    say(correct-arrival-time(arrival-time, weather-delay, traffic-delay));
  // We establish the handler in the following two lines
  exception (condition :: <time-error>)
    say(condition);
  end block;
end method say-corrected-time;
```

The **exception** clause of **block** establishes a handler for a condition, and all that condition's subclasses, for any code in the **block** body, and for any code called by the **block** body. We say that the handler is established within the **dynamic scope** of the **block** body. When an exception is signaled, Dylan starts a search to find the nearest handler available that matches the condition signaled, and that accepts the exception. The **nearest handler** is the one that was most recently established in the dynamic scope of the signaler. The handler matches the condition if the class associated with the handler (the handler class) is the same as the condition, or if the handler class is a superclass of the condition. You can associate a test with the handler so that the handler can selectively accept the condition. By default, a matching handler always accepts. If a handler established by the **exception** clause of **block** matches and accepts, then a nonlocal exit from the signaler occurs, with execution continuing in the body of the exception clause, which is executed in the context of the very beginning of the block. All the locals defined by the block are gone, but the exit procedure (if there is one) is still available. If there is relevant local state, it may be captured in slots of the condition prior to signaling of the condition. The code within the exception clause body is executed, and the value of the last statement in that body is then returned as the value of the block.

In this example, the **+** method (called by **correct-arrival-time**) may signal a **<time-boundary-error>** condition using the **error** function during the execution of **say-corrected-time**. If this error is signaled, then the handler established by the **block** for **<time-error>** will match the **<time-boundary-error>** condition. This **exception** clause will always accept the condition, so a nonlocal exit will occur, and will terminate execution of the **error** function, the **+** method, and the **correct-arrival-time** method. Within the context of the beginning of the **block**, the variable **condition** is bound to the condition instance being signaled (the instance supplied to **error**); then, execution resumes with the code inside the body of the **exception** clause. The body calls the **say** generic function on the condition instance, which causes an appropriate error message (instead of the time) to be displayed to the user. Execution then continues normally after the end of the block; in this case, that results in the normal exit from the **say-corrected-time** method. Figure 20.1 shows the state of execution when **error** is called, and after the execution of the **exception** clause body for **<time-error>** begins. Figure 20.1 is a simplified diagram of the internal calling stack of a hypothetical Dylan implementation. It is similar to what a debugger might produce when asked to print a backtrace at these two points in the execution of the example. The **error** function called within the **+** method signals the **<time-boundary-error>** error, and the **exception** clause of **block** in the **say-corrected-time** method establishes the handler for that error. Once the handling of the exception is in progress, the handler selected is no longer established. If there is relevant local state, it may be captured in slots of the condition being signaled.

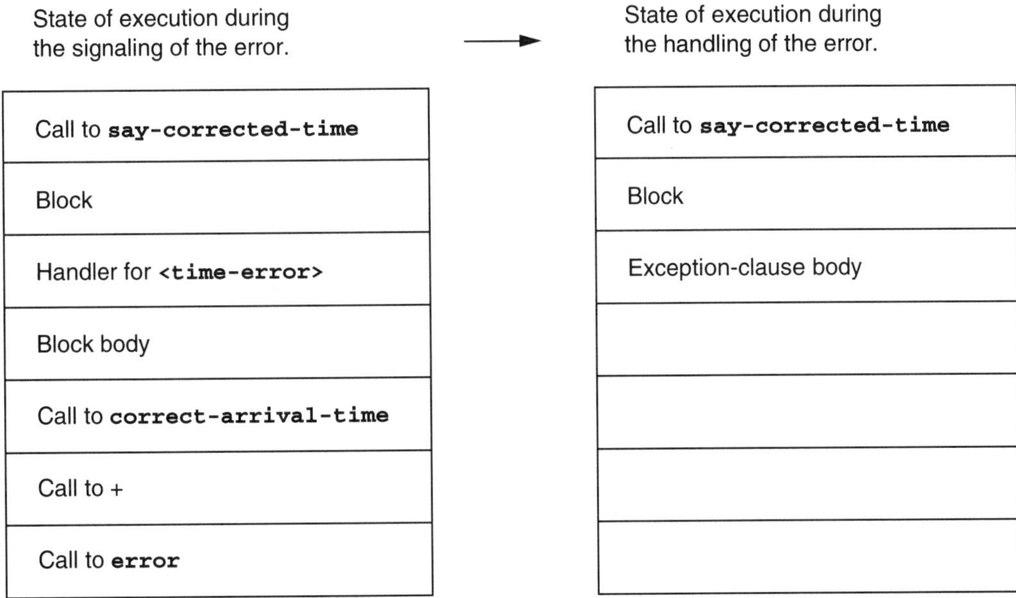

Figure 20.1 Context transition from signaler to handler.

The advantages of this structured approach to signaling and handling conditions are significant:

- The method focuses on the normal flow of control, and the exceptional flow of control appears only where necessary. For example, the **correct-arrival-time** method does not need to be aware of the potential exceptions at all. The Dylan condition system makes it easier to reuse code that might not know about, or care to participate in, your application-specific exception recovery code.
- Because **correct-arrival-time** does not need to participate in the exception-recovery protocol, it can also have a specific return value; thus, like the + method, it might allow better compiler optimizations and better compile-time error checking.
- We allow room for expansion in the code. For example, at some point, **correct-arrival-time** might do more sophisticated computations with time, which might signal other kinds of time errors. As long as these new time errors inherit from **<time-error>**, they can be resolved by the same handler established by **say-corrected-time**. As the application evolves, we can build various families of error conditions, and can provide application-specific handlers that perform the correct recovery actions for those families.
- Because we are using the signaling and handling protocol defined by Dylan, casual readers of the code should be able to understand our intent.
- Because the handler has access to the condition object, the handler can perform intelligent recovery actions based on the information captured in the condition object when the exception occurred. For example, the handler may examine various slots of the condition object, and perform different actions based on information stored in those slots.

Dylan supports two models of handler execution. The **exception** clause of **block** implements the exit model. When you establish handlers by the **exception** clause of **block**, you do not have the ability to restart a computation in the context of the signaler, or in a context closer to the signaler than the handler. In Section 20.2.3, we explore the calling model of handler execution, which allows you to recover from an exception without a nonlocal exit back to the point where the handler was established.

20.2.3 Definition of a recovery protocol

With the new definition of our **+** method on **<time-offset>** and **<time-of-day>**, if we add 5 hours to 10:00 P.M., a condition instance is signaled. The **say-corrected-time** method handles that condition, and prints a suitable error message. By the time the handler in **say-corrected-time** takes control, the addition that we were performing has been aborted. In fact, we are no longer even executing within the **correct-arrival-time** method. We have ceased executing there because handlers established using the **exception** clause of **block** perform nonlocal exits out of the current computation back to the block where the handler was established. Suppose that we, instead of aborting the addition, wanted to continue with the addition, perhaps modifying the value returned by the **+** method such that it would still be within the correct 24-hour range for **<time-of-day>** instances. In this section, we modify **say-corrected-time** to use a different technique for establishing a handler that does not abort the computation in progress, and we modify the **+** method for **<time-offset>** and **<time-of-day>** to offer and implement a way to modify the value returned to be a legal time of day.

First, we must find a way to execute a handler in the context of the signaler, instead of at the point where the handler was established. Then, we must find a way to activate special code in the **+** method to return a legal **<time-of-day>** instance as a way of recovering from the time-boundary exception.

- The **let handler** local declaration provides a way to establish a handler that will execute in the context of the signaler, just as though the handler was invoked with a normal function call by the signaler.
- The restart protocol provides a structured way for a handler to recover from the exception, and to continue with the computation in progress.

In this case, continuing with the computation means that the **+** method will return a legal **<time-of-day>** instance to **correct-arrival-time**, and **correct-arrival-time** will finish any additional processing and return normally to its caller.

To recover from an exception, we use a signaling and handling technique as similar to that we used to indicate the exception in the first place. This time, we signal a particular condition that is a subclass of **<restart>**, to indicate how the exception handler wishes to recover. We use a **restart handler** to implement the particular recovery action. You can think of a restart as a special condition that represents an opportunity to recover from an exception. Establishing a restart handler is a way to offer such an opportunity to other handlers, and to specify the implementation of the restart. Any handler, when activated, might signal a restart to request that a particular recovery action take place. Restart signaling and handling connects recovery requests with recovery actions.

For example, adding 5 hours to 10:00 P.M. is an error for **<time-offset>** and **<time-of-day>** instances. One way to recover from this error would be to wrap around the result to 3:00 A.M. Here, we define the restart class **<return-modulus-restart>**, which represents an offer to return from a time-of-day computation by wrapping the result:

```
define class <return-modulus-restart> (<restart>)
end class <return-modulus-restart>;
```

Using the **exception** clause of **block**, we redefine the **+** method to establish and implement the restart handler:

```
define constant $seconds-per-day = $hours-per-day * $seconds-per-hour;

define method \+ (offset :: <time-offset>, time-of-day :: <time-of-day>)
 => (sum :: <time-of-day>)
  let sum
    = make(<time-of-day>,
           total-seconds: offset.total-seconds + time-of-day.total-seconds);
  block ()
    if (sum >= $midnight & sum < $tomorrow)
      sum;
    else
      error(make(<time-boundary-error>, invalid-time: sum,
                 min-time: $midnight, time-limit: $tomorrow));
    end if;
  // Establish restart handler
  exception (restart :: <return-modulus-restart>)
    make(<time-of-day>,
         total-seconds: modulo(sum.total-seconds, $seconds-per-day));
  end block;
end method \+;
```

If a handler (established with **let handler**) signals a **<return-modulus-restart>** during the handling of the **<time-boundary-error>** exception, then the sum will be wrapped around so that it will stay within the bounds of the time-of-day specification, and the result will be returned from the **+** method.

Next, we want to write a handler using **let handler** that will invoke the restart. However, before we invoke the restart, we want to confirm that the restart is currently established. Signaling a restart that is not currently established is an error. The **available-restart** method that follows returns an instance of a a given restart, if that restart is currently established; otherwise, **available-restart** returns false:

```
define method available-restart
    (restart-class :: <class>, exception-instance :: <condition>)
 => (result :: false-or(<restart>))
  block (return)
    local method check-restart (type, test, function, initargs)
      // Make an instance of the restart, so we can see whether it matches
      // our search criteria
      if (subtype?(type, restart-class))
        let instance = apply(make, type, condition:, exception-instance,
                             initargs | #[]);
        if (test(instance)) return(instance); end;
      end if;
    end method;
    // The built-in Dylan function do-handlers will call check-restart
    // for every handler currently established, in order (first is nearest
    // to the signaler)
    do-handlers(check-restart);
    #f;
  end block;
end method available-restart;
```

Dylan provides the **do-handlers** function, which iterates over all the currently established handlers, calling its argument (a function) on all the relevant information about the handler, including all the information necessary to instantiate a restart instance for restart handlers. The **check-restart** local method returns from **available-restart** with a restart instance only when a matching restart that accepts is found. All restarts take a **condition** init-keyword argument, which, if supplied, should be the original exception that occurred. If the handler that created the restart provided the original exception condition as an init-keyword argument, then restart handlers can handle restart conditions for only particular exceptions. If none of the established handlers match and accept the restart that we seek, then **available-restart** returns false. Note that you should establish restart handlers for instantiable restart classes only, because the restart classes will be instantiated by restart-savvy handlers. If the restart classes cannot be instantiated, then the recovery process will not operate correctly.

Next, we need to define a method to be called by the exception handler to invoke the restart whether it is available. If the restart is not available, the method will call the **next-handler** method, which will allow another handler the opportunity to decide if it will handle the exception. In other words, if the **<return-modulus-restart>** restart is not established, the handler for **<time-error>** established by **say-corrected-time** will **decline** to handle the **<time-boundary-error>** condition being signaled.

```
define method invoke-modulus-restart-if-available
    (condition :: <time-error>, next-handler :: <function>)
  let restart = available-restart(<return-modulus-restart>, condition);
  if (restart) error(restart); else next-handler(); end;
end method invoke-modulus-restart-if-available;
```

No return values are declared for **invoke-modulus-restart-if-available**, because we cannot be certain what **next-handler** might return. Our handler method must be prepared to return any number of objects of any types. Next, we establish a handler using the **let handler** local declaration:

```
define method say-corrected-time
    (arrival-time :: <time-of-day>,
     #key weather-delay :: <time-offset> = $no-time,
     traffic-delay :: <time-offset> = $no-time)
 => ()
  let handler (<time-error>) = invoke-modulus-restart-if-available;
  say(correct-arrival-time(arrival-time, weather-delay, traffic-delay));
end method say-corrected-time;
```

The **let handler** local declaration establishes a handler for the **<time-error>** condition and for all that condition's subclasses. When the **error** function inside the **+** method signals the **<time-boundary-error>** condition instance, Dylan conducts a search for the nearest matching handler that accepts. In this case, the nearest matching handler that accepts is the handler established by **say-corrected-time**. Because this handler was established by a **let handler** local declaration, instead of by the **exception** clause of **block**, no nonlocal exit takes place. Instead, the function specified in the **let handler** local declaration is invoked in the context of the signaler. The **error** function essentially performs a regular function call on the function associated with the nearest matching handler. The function is passed the condition instance being signaled, and the **next-handler** function that might be used to decline handling this condition. In our example, the **invoke-modulus-restart-if-available** function will be called from **error**. Once called, **invoke-modulus-restart-if-available** will first see whether the **<return-modulus-restart>** restart is established. If the restart is established, we will invoke it by signaling an instance of the restart. If the restart is not established, we decline to process the **<time-boundary-error>** condition in this handler. Assuming that no other handlers exist, the debugger will be invoked.

If the restart is signaled, a nonlocal exit to the restart exception clause in **+** method is initiated, which returns the sum suitably wrapped such that it lies within the 24-hour boundary.

Figure 20.2 shows the state of execution after the handler function for **<time-error>** is invoked, and the state after the restart handler function for **<return-modulus-restart>** is invoked. As you can see, although establishing a handler with **let handler** can be far removed from the signaler, the handler function itself is executed in the context of the signaler.

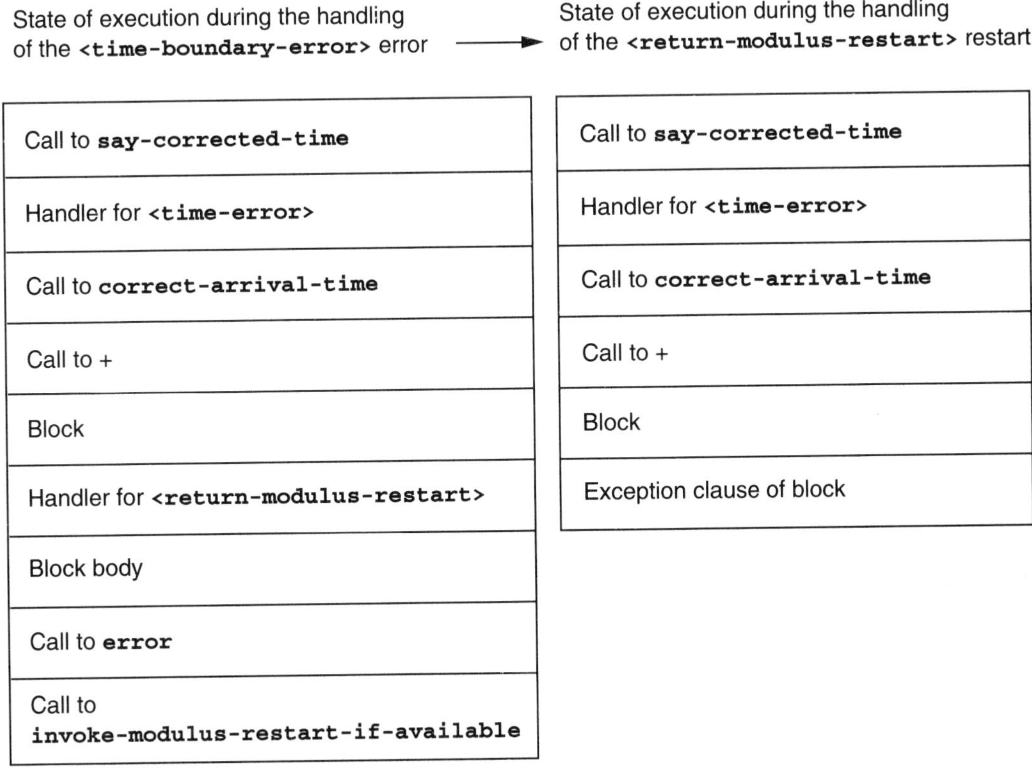

Figure 20.2 Context transition from handler to restart handler.

20.2.4 Continuation from errors

The restart mechanism just described is exceedingly general, and may provide several different ways to recover from exceptional situations. Sometimes, however, there is just one main way to recover. Under certain circumstances, Dylan provides a way for handlers simply to return to their callers, allowing execution to continue after the signaler. Here, we present a simpler (but less flexible) implementation for recovering from the time-of-day overflow exception:

```
define method return-24-hour-modulus
    (condition :: <time-error>, next-handler :: <function>)
 => (corrected-time :: <time>)
  make(type-for-copy(condition.invalid-time),
       total-seconds: modulo(condition.invalid-time.total-seconds,
                             $seconds-per-day));
end method return-24-hour-modulus;


define method return-allowed? (condition :: <time-error>)
  #t;
end method return-allowed?;


define method return-description (condition :: <time-error>)
  "Returns the invalid time modulo 24 hours.";
end;


define method say-corrected-time
    (arrival-time :: <time-of-day>,
     #key weather-delay :: <time-offset> = $no-time,
     traffic-delay :: <time-offset> = $no-time)
 => ()
  let handler (<time-error>) = return-24-hour-modulus;
  say(correct-arrival-time(arrival-time, weather-delay, traffic-delay));
end method say-corrected-time;
```

```
define method \+ (offset :: <time-offset>, time-of-day :: <time-of-day>)
 => (sum :: <time-of-day>)
  let sum
    = make(<time-of-day>,
           total-seconds: offset.total-seconds + time-of-day.total-seconds);
  block ()
    if (sum >= $midnight & sum < $tomorrow)
      sum;
    else
      // If a handler returns, it must return a valid <time-offset>
      signal(make(<time-boundary-error>, invalid-time: sum,
                  min-time: $midnight, time-limit: $tomorrow));
    end if;
  end block;
end method \+;
```

The **return-allowed?** and **return-description** generic functions are provided by Dylan. When the generic function **return-allowed?** returns true for a given condition, introspective handlers know that they can return successfully back to the signaler. When returning is allowed, such introspective handlers may call the **return-description** generic function to find out what values to return, if there are any. This description can be especially useful for interactive handlers, such as debuggers.

The **return-24-hour-modulus** method has been generalized compared to the exception-specific restart defined in Section 20.2.3. This method may return either an instance of **<time-of-day>** or **<time-offset>**, depending on the class of time that overflowed. Thus, it could be reused for exception handling in other parts of the application.

In this implementation approach, there is an implicit contract between the signaler in the **\+** method and any handler that matches and accepts **<time-boundary-errors>**. The contract is that the handler will always return a valid **<time>** value, or will never return at all. If any handler violates this implicit contract, then the reliability of the program will be placed at risk. It is important to document these error-handling contracts.

Note that, in the **\+** method, we must use the **signal** function to signal the exception, because it is illegal for a handler to return from exceptions signaled with the **error** function.

20.3 Additional exception mechanisms

We do not cover the entire Dylan exception protocol in this book. Here, we mention briefly certain other techniques that we do not discuss further in this book:

- You can signal conditions with **`cerror`**, and **`break`**, in addition to with the **`error`** and **`signal`** functions. The **`cerror`** function establishes a simple restart, then signals an error in a manner similar to **`error`**. The **`break`** function directly invokes the debugger without signaling.
- The **`exception`** clause of **`block`** and **`let handler`** takes several options that, among other things, can facilitate restart signaling and handling.
- There are additional protocols for attaching a user interface to returning or restarting (**`return-query`**, **`restart-query`**), which could be used with handlers that act like interactive debuggers.

See *The Dylan Reference Manual* for more information.

20.4 Protected operations and the `block` construct

In this section, we describe how to use **`block`** to protect sections of Dylan code from unexpected nonlocal exits. Dylan provides powerful ways to execute nonlocal exits from a given execution context. An application might signal a condition that might cause a handler to execute a nonlocal exit, or an application might call an exit procedure named by the first argument to **`block`**. Sometimes, it is necessary to add behavior to the nonlocal exit, to keep the application's execution environment in good shape.

20.4.1 Protected objects

Suppose that you want to design a class of objects that could be accessed only when a lock for that object is granted. You might use instances of such a class to avoid conflicting concurrent access in a multithreaded implementation of Dylan, or you might use instances of such a class to represent files or other operating-system objects that might be accessed reliably by only one process at a time. Let's assume that the **`<lock>`** class and the **`get-lock`** and **`release-lock`** functions are supplied by an external library. The **`get-lock`** function atomically obtains the lock if that lock is available; otherwise, it waits until the lock becomes free, and then obtains the lock. The **`release-lock`** function frees the lock so that some other process can acquire the lock. Given this locking library, how would we define the following?

- A class that represents a protected object
- A **call-using-lock** function, which acquires a lock associated with a protected object, calls an arbitrary function, and then releases the lock

We could define the class as follows:

```
define abstract class <protected-object> (<object>)
  slot object-lock :: <lock> = make(<lock>);
end class <protected-object>;
```

Each subclass of **<protected-object>** would inherit an **object-lock** slot. The lock instance stored in this slot must be acquired prior to any operation on the protected object, and released when the operation is complete. One naive way to implement **call-using-lock** would be as follows:

```
define method call-using-lock
    (object :: <protected-object>, function :: <function>, #rest args)
 => (#rest results)
  get-lock(object.object-lock);
  apply(function, object, args);
  release-lock(object.object-lock);
end method call-using-lock;
```

The approach in the preceding example has two serious problems. First, **call-using-lock** does not return the values returned by calling **function**. Second, if **function** executes a nonlocal exit past **call-using-lock**, the **release-lock** call will never be executed, and after that point no process will be able to acquire the lock for the protected object. Thus, subsequent attempts to use the protected object will wait forever, because the lock was not properly released. We could add a handler that would release the lock if any condition is signaled, but that might be incorrect, because certain conditions might be handled within the dynamic scope of **function**, and might never perform a nonlocal exit past **call-using-lock**. Thus, the lock might be released prematurely, possibly causing the integrity of the protected object to be violated. Also, calling an exit procedure performs a nonlocal exit without signaling a condition at all.

To solve exactly this sort of problem, Dylan provides the **cleanup** clause of **block**. Code within the body of a **cleanup** clause is guaranteed to be executed before the **block** is exited, even if it is a nonlocal exit that causes the **block** to terminate. The value of this **block** will be the result of calling **function**. The **cleanup** clause does not affect what the **block** returns.

```
define method call-using-lock
    (object :: <protected-object>, function :: <function>, #rest args)
 => (#rest results)
  block ()
    get-lock(object.object-lock);
    apply(function, object, args);
  cleanup
    release-lock(object.object-lock);
  end block;
end method call-using-lock;
```

The **cleanup** clause of **block** provides a powerful tool for ensuring the integrity of applications that use nonlocal exits.

20.5 Summary

In this chapter, we covered the following:

- We described how to define condition classes, and to signal them.
- We explored establishing simple error handlers using the **exception** clause of **block**.
- We showed how to design and implement a introspective recovery protocol using **let handler**, **do-handler**, and restarts.
- We demonstrated how a handler can simply return to the signaler with cooperation from that signaler.
- We showed how we can protect sections of code from unexpected nonlocal exits by using the **cleanup** clause provided by **block**.

You can use these techniques to control the handling of exceptional situations when they arise. By designing your condition classes carefully and handling those conditions correctly, you make your program significantly more robust, without interrupting the normal flow of control. By providing recovery protocols, you make it possible to continue cleanly after a problem has been detected. By protecting critical code against unexpected nonlocal exits, you enhance the reliability of your applications.

21

Macros

The term **macro**, as used in computer programming, originally stood for **macro-instruction**, meaning an instruction that represented a sequence of several machine (or micro) instructions. Over time, the term has evolved to mean any word or phrase that stands for another phrase (usually longer, but built of simpler components). Macros can be used for abbreviation, abstraction, simplification, or structuring. Many application programs, such as word processors or spreadsheets, offer a macro language for writing scripts or subroutines that bundle a number of simpler actions into one command.

Many computer languages support a macro facility for creating shorthand notations for commonly used, longer phrases. They range from simple, text-based abbreviations to full languages, permitting computed replacements. Macros are processed before the program is compiled by **expanding** each macro into its replacement phrase as that macro is encountered until there are no more macros. You can use macros to extend the base language by defining more sophisticated phrases in terms of simpler, built-in phrases.

The primary use of macros in programming languages is to extend or adapt the language to allow a more concise or readable solution for a particular problem domain. A simple program rarely needs macros. More complicated programs, including the implementation of a Dylan compiler and run-time system, will use macros often. Macros have no visible run-time cost or effect — they are transformations that take place during the compilation of a program (hence, they *can* increase compilation time). Although macros may take the form of function calls, they are not functions — they cannot be passed as functional arguments, and they cannot be invoked in a run-time image as a function can. Although macros may have parameters, they do not take arguments the way functions do. The arguments to a macro are not evaluated; they are simply program phrases that can be substituted in the replacement phrase.

Dylan provides a macro facility that is based on pattern matching and template substitution. This facility is more powerful than is a simple textual substitution facility, but is simpler than a *procedural-macro* facility, which allows arbitrary computations to construct replacement phrases. Dylan's macro facility is closely integrated with the Dylan language syntax, and permits most macro needs to be satisfied. Dylan designers have also planned for a full procedural macro capability, so that it can be added compatibly at a later time if there is sufficient demand.

> **Comparison with C and C++:** C and C++ macros are text substitutions, performed by a preprocessor. The preprocessor has no understanding of the language; it simply splices together text fragments to create replacement phrases.
>
> Dylan macros are written in terms of Dylan language elements; the macros choose their transformation by pattern matching, and they substitute program fragments.
>
> Language-based macros are more powerful than — and avoid a number of common pitfalls of — text-substitution macros. These pitfalls are described in later comparisons in this chapter.

21.1 Patterns and templates

A Dylan macro consists of a set of **rules**. Each rule has two basic parts: a **pattern** that is matched against a fragment of code, and a **template** that is substituted for the matched fragment, perhaps including pieces of the original fragment. When a macro is invoked, each rule is tried in order until a matching pattern is found. When a match is found, the macro is replaced by the matching template. If no match can be found, an error occurs.

Dylan macros are recognized by the compiler because they fit one of three possible formats: the function macro, the statement macro, and the defining macro. The macro format determines the overall fragment that is matched against the macro's rules at each macro invocation.

The simplest macro format that the compiler can match is that of a function call. A **function macro** is invoked in exactly the same way that a function is invoked. The name of the macro is a module variable that can be used anywhere a function call can occur. Typically, it is simply the name followed by a parenthesized list of arguments, but recall that slot-style abbreviations and unary and binary operators are also function calls.

The most important use of function macros is to rearrange or delay evaluation of arguments. The fragment that is matched against the function macro's rules is the phrase that represents a function's arguments. The function macro can then rearrange the function arguments, perhaps adding code. When a macro rearranges its arguments, its action has the effect of delaying the evaluation of the arguments (as opposed to a function call, where the argument expressions are evaluated and then passed to the function).

One simple use of delaying evaluation is to write a functionlike construct similar in spirit to C's `?:` operator:

```
define macro if-else
  { if-else (?test:expression, ?true:expression, ?false:expression) }
 => { if (?test) ?true else ?false end }
end macro if-else;
```

We could not write `if-else` as a function, because both the true and false expressions would be evaluated before the function was even called:

```
? define variable *x* = 0;

? define variable *y* = 0;

? *y* := if-else(*y* == 0, *x* := 1, *x* := -1);
1

? *y*;
1

? *x*;
1
```

If we had defined `if-else` as a function, `*x*` would have been `-1`, rather than `1`, because both assignments to `*x*` would have been evaluated, before `if-else` was called. When a macro is used, the assignments are just substituted into the template `if`, which evaluates the first clause only when the condition is true.

Looking at the macro definition of `if-else`, we can infer basic ideas about macros. A macro is introduced by `define macro`, followed by the **macro name** —

in this case, **`if-else`**. The definition of the macro is a **rule** that has two parts: a **pattern** enclosed in braces, `{}`, that mimics the fragment that it is to match, and a **replacement**. Macro parameters, called **pattern variables**, are introduced in the pattern by `?`. They match fragments with particular **constraints** — in this case, `:expression`. They are delimited by punctuation — in this case, the open and close parentheses, `()`, and the comma, `,`.

The replacement part of the rule, the **expansion**, is indicated by `=>` and is defined by a **template**, also enclosed in braces. The template is in the form of a code fragment, where pattern variables are used to substitute in the fragments they matched in the pattern. Note that matching and replacement are language based, so required and optional whitespace is treated exactly as in Dylan. We have used optional whitespace to improve the legibility of the macro definitions presented here.

Most Dylan development environments provide a way to view code after all macros have been expanded. This view can be helpful in debugging macros that you write. For example, showing the expanded view of an expression like

```
*y* := if-else(*y* == 0, *x* := 1, *x* := -1);;
```

might yield

```
*y* := if (*y* == 0) *x* := 1 else *x* := -1 end;
```

The exact format of the expanded view of the macro depends on the particular development environment. Here, we show the code that comes from the macro template in ***underlined italic***, whereas the fragments matched by the pattern variables and substituted into the template are presented in our conventional `code font`. Note that the **`if-else`** macro we have defined is just syntactic sugar — Dylan's built-in **`if`** statement is perfectly sufficient for the job.

Another reason to delay evaluation is to change the value of an argument — for example, to implement an operator similar in spirit to C's `++` and `+=` operators:

```
define macro inc!
  { inc! (?place:expression, ?by:expression) }
 => { ?place := ?place + ?by; }
  { inc! (?place:expression) }
 => { ?place := ?place + 1; }
end macro inc!;
```

This macro might be used as follows:

```
? define variable *x* = 0;
```

```
? inc!(*x*, 3);
3

? *x*;
3

? inc!(*x*);
4

? *x*;
4
```

In this macro, it is important to delay the evaluation of the first argument because we want to be able to assign to the variable or slot it is stored in, rather than simply to manipulate the value of the variable or slot.

The `inc!` macro demonstrates the use of multiple rules in a macro. They are tried in order until an appropriate match is found. This allows the `inc!` macro to have two forms. The one-argument form increments the argument by 1. The two-argument form allows the increment amount to be specified.

21.2 Macro hygiene

Displaying the code fragments inserted by the macro in ***underlined italics*** both helps to show exactly what the macro has done to our code, and draws attention to an important feature of Dylan macros — they are hygienic macros. A **hygienic** or **referentially transparent** macro system is one that prevents accidental collisions of macro variables with program variables of the same name. Consider the following macro, which is used to exchange the values of two variables:

```
define macro swap!
  { swap! (?place1:expression, ?place2:expression) }
 => { let value = ?place1;
      ?place1 := ?place2;
      ?place2 := value
    }
end macro swap!;
```

The local variable `value` is created by the macro. There is a possibility that this variable could conflict with another variable in the surrounding code. Consider what might happen if we were to expand `swap!(value, x)`:

```
let value = value;
value := x;
x := value
```

With simple textual substitutions, **swap!** would have no effect in this case. Dylan's hygienic macros solve this problem by differentiating between the ***value*** introduced by the macro and any other **value** that might appear in the original code.

> **Comparison with C:** Because C (and C++) macros are simply text substitutions performed by a preprocessor that has no understanding of the C language, they are inherently unhygienic. C macro writers reduce this problem by choosing unusual or unlikely names for local variables in their macros (such as **_swap_temp_value**), but even this workaround can be insufficient in complex macros. Dylan macros in effect automatically rename macro variables on each expansion to guarantee unique names.

21.3 Evaluation in macros

Dylan's template macros do no evaluation. In particular, the pattern variables of a macro are unlike function parameters. They name fragments of code, rather than naming the result of the evaluation of a fragment of code.

If we were trying to write an operation like C's || (one that would evaluate expressions and would return the value of the first nonzero expression without evaluating any subsequent expressions), we could not write it as a function:

```
define method or-int (arg1, arg2) if (arg1 ~= 0) arg1 else arg2 end end;
```

When a function is invoked, all its arguments are evaluated first, which defeats our purpose. If we model our macro on our function idea, however, we will not get the ideal result either:

```
define macro or-int
  { or-int (?arg1:expression, ?arg2:expression) } =>
    { if (?arg1 ~= 0) ?arg1 else ?arg2 end }
end macro or-int;
```

The expansion of **or-int (x := x + 1, y := y - 1)** is probably not what we want:

```
if (x := x + 1 ~= 0) x := x + 1 else y := y - 1 end
```

We see a common macro error — the expression **x := x + 1** will be evaluated twice when the resulting substitution is evaluated, leaving **x** with an incorrect (or at least unexpected) value. There is no magic technique for avoiding this error — you just have to be careful about repeating a pattern variable in a template. Most often, if you are repeating a pattern variable, you should be using a local variable instead, so that the fragment that the pattern represents is evaluated only once:

```
define macro or-int
  { or-int (?arg1:expression, ?arg2:expression) }
 => {
      let arg1 = ?arg1;
      if(arg1 ~= 0) arg1 else ?arg2 end
    }
end macro or-int;
```

Another potential pitfall arises if the pattern variables appear in an order in the template different from the one in which they appear in the pattern. In this case, unexpected results can occur if a side effect in one fragment affects the meaning of other fragments. In this case, you would again want to use local variables to ensure that the fragments were evaluated in their natural order.

These rules are not hard and fast: The power of macros is due in a large part to the ability of macros to manipulate code fragments without evaluating those fragments, but that power must be used judiciously. If you are designing macros for use by other people, those people may expect functionlike behavior, and may be surprised if there are multiple or out-of-order evaluations of macro parameters.

> **Comparison with C:** Because it is more difficult to introduce local variables in C macros than it is in Dylan macros, most C programmers simply adopt the discipline of never using an expression with side effects as an argument to a macro. The problem of multiple or out-of-order evaluations of macro parameters is inherent in all macro systems, although some macro systems make it easier to handle.

21.4 Constraints

So far, in our macros, we have seen the constraint **expression** used for the pattern variables. Except for a few unusual cases, pattern variables must always have a constraint associated with them. Constraints serve two purposes: they limit the fragment that the pattern variable will match, and they define the meaning of the pattern variable when it is substituted. As an example, consider the following **statement macro**, which we might find useful for manipulating the decoded parts of seconds:

```
define macro with-decoded-seconds
  {
    with-decoded-seconds
        (?max:variable, ?min:variable, ?sec:variable = ?time:expression)
      ?:body
    end
  }
 => {
       let (?max, ?min, ?sec) = decode-total-seconds(?time);
       ?body
    }
end macro;
```

The preceding macro might be used as follows:

```
define method say (time :: <time>)
  with-decoded-seconds(hours, minutes, seconds = time)
    format-out("%d:%s%d",
                 hours, if (minutes < 10) "0" else "" end, minutes);
  end;
end method say;
```

A statement macro can appear anywhere that a **begin/end;** block can appear. A statement macro introduces a new **begin word** — in this case, **with-decoded-seconds** — and is matched against a fragment that extends up to the matching **end**.

The pattern and the constraints on the pattern variables limit what the macro will match; they define the syntax of this particular statement. In the case of **with-decoded-seconds**, the syntax of this statement begins with a parenthesized list of

- Three **variable** expressions (that is, **name :: <type>**, where the type is optional)
- The literal token **=**
- An **expression** (any Dylan expression yielding a value)

After the parenthesized list comes a **body** (any sequence of expressions separated by **;**, just as would be valid in a **begin/end;** block). Note the use of the abbreviation **?:body**, to mean **?body:body** (a pattern variable, **body**, with the constraint **body**).

The constraints are similar to type declarations on variables: They limit the acceptable values of the pattern variables, and they help to document the interface of the macro. The constraints also serve a second purpose: Once the compiler has recognized a fragment under a particular constraint, it will ensure the correct behavior of that fragment when that fragment is substituted in a template. For example, suppose that we define a function macro:

```
define macro times
  { times (?arg1:expression, ?arg2:expression ) } =>
    { ?arg1 * ?arg2 }
end macro times;
```

We might use the macro as follows:

```
times(1 + 3, 2 + 5);
```

Here is the expanded macro:

```
1 + 3 * 2 + 5
```

We can see that, if the macro were a simple text-substitution macro, the result would be 12, rather than the 28 we were expecting. But because, in Dylan, the constraint is maintained when a pattern variable is substituted (that is, the expression that makes up each of the pattern variables remains a single expression), the result is as though the macro automatically inserted parentheses, and the expansion were

```
(1 + 3) * (2 + 5)
```

Some development environments may display the implicit parentheses of an expression constraint. Thus, the macro will yield the expected result of 28.

> **Comparison with C:** Because C macros are simple textual substitutions, the macro writer must be sure to insert parentheses around every macro variable when it is substituted, and around the macro expansion itself, to prevent the resulting expansion from taking on new meanings.

21.5 More complex rules

The macros shown so far have all been simple: a single pattern transformed into a single template. To get a flavor of the full power of the Dylan macro system, consider this **defining macro**:

```
define macro aircraft-definer
  { define aircraft ?identifier:name (?type:name) ?flights end }
   => { register-aircraft(make("<" ## ?type ## ">", id: ?#"identifier"));
        register-flights(?#"identifier", ?flights) }
flights:
  { }
   => { }
  { ?flight; ... }
   => { ?flight, ... }
flight:
  { flight ?id:name, #rest ?options:expression }
   => { make(<flight>, id: ?#"id", ?options) }
end macro aircraft-definer;
```

We might use the macro **define aircraft** as follows:

```
define aircraft UA4906H (DC10)
  flight UA11, from: #"BOS", to: #"SFO";
  flight UA12, from: #"SFO", to: #"BOS";
end aircraft UA4906H;
```

This macro shows a number of the more esoteric features of Dylan macros. First, notice the pattern variable **?flights**, which has no constraint, but rather is called out as an **auxiliary rule**. When the compiler matches this macro, it will try each of the auxiliary rule's patterns listed under **flights:** for a match. When it finds a match, it will assign the pattern variable **?flights** to the fragment resulting from the matching pattern's template substitution. In effect, auxiliary rules give a way of writing new constraints, combined with the effect of a subroutine for matching and substitution.

In this particular case, we use the auxiliary rule to map yet another auxiliary rule, **flight**, over a sequence of flight descriptions that look similar to the slot descriptions in a class. The mapping is signaled by the points of ellipsis (**...**) which means that the rule should be applied recursively (that is, the current rule is matched again to the fragment that matches **...**). Note that **flights** must have a rule to cover the case of there being no flight; that rule also handles the end of the recursion when the final flight has been matched.

The **flight** rule simply converts each flight name and its options into the appropriate call to **make**, to create the flight. We could extend this rule to allow a more natural specification for flight origin, destination, and time.

We do the work of defining an aircraft by calling the helper functions **register-aircraft** and **register-flights** (which are not given here), but the macro takes care of getting the arguments in order. The substitution **"<" ## ?type ## ">"** turns the name **DC10** into the name **<DC10>** by using **concatenation**, allowing a more concise format for our definer while maintaining our convention for naming types. The substitution **?#"identifier"** turns the name **UA1306** into the symbol **#"UA1306"** by using **coercion**; the program can use the symbol **#"UA1306"** to look up an aircraft in the registry by name. The template for **flights** collects all the individual flights into a comma-separated list that is passed to **register-flights** as a **#rest** argument.

21.6 More hygiene

We shall make one more note about hygiene: In a textual substitution macro, there is a chance that the global variables that the macro uses (in this case, the helper function **define-aircraft**) could be confused with a surrounding local variable of the same name where the macro is called. This confusion does not happen in a Dylan macro. The global variables used in a Dylan macro always denote what they denoted at the time that the macro was defined, rather than at the time that the macro is called. It is as though the variables were automatically renamed so that conflicts will be avoided.

You will also notice this feature if you export a macro from a module. Only the macro needs to be exported. Its global references still refer to the proper (module-private) values that they had at the time the macro was defined, just as occurs when a function exported from a module calls module-private subroutines.

Occasionally, you will want to circumvent macro hygiene. You may want to define a macro that creates a variable that *is* visible at the macro call. Here is a simple statement macro that repeats its body until you ask it to **stop!**:

```
define macro repeat
  { repeat ?:body end }
 => { block (?=stop!)
        local method again() ?body; again() end;
        again();
      end }
end macro repeat;
```

The term **?=stop!** says that the local variable **stop!**, which is the block exit variable, will be visible when the macro is called exactly as **stop!**; there will be no hygienic renaming. Here is an example that uses the macro to count to 100:

```
begin
  let i = 0;
  repeat
    if (i == 100) stop!() end;
    i := i + 1;
  end;
end;
```

Note that the **body** constraint invokes the Dylan parser to match the code properly between the **repeat** and the corresponding **end**. It is not confused by the **end** of the **if** statement, as a text-based macro might be. The expanded view of the preceding code might look like this:

```
begin
  let i = 0;
  block (stop!)
    local method again()
      if (i == 100) stop!() end;
      i := i + 1;
       again()
    end;
    again();
  end;
end;
```

Note that we have shown the local variable **stop!** introduced by the macro **block** in **code font** rather than in ***underline italic***, because it is visible to the body and is exactly the **stop!** called in the **if** to stop the repetition. The local variable ***again***, on the other hand, is not visible to the body code. We could use **again** instead of **i** as our repetition count without a problem.

> **Comparison with C:** All C macros have the syntax of function calls, making it impossible to write language extensions such as **repeat**. By using language-based constraints, such as the **body** constraint used here, Dylan macros can match language forms, and thus can create extensions that are consistent with the base language.

Note that we would have to document how **repeat** works for other users, or they might be surprised if they tried to use **stop!** instead of **i** in the example.

21.7 Auxiliary macros

One difficulty with the aircraft macro that we defined in Section 21.5 is this: suppose that we want each flight object to know the type of equipment used, rather than our having to look up the type in the aircraft registry. What looks like the obvious approach does not work:

```
define macro aircraft-definer
  { define aircraft ?identifier:name (?type:name) ?flights end }
   => { register-aircraft(make("<" ## ?type ## ">", id: ?#"identifier"));
        register-flights(?#"identifier", ?flights) }
flights:
  { }
   => { }
  { ?flight; ... }
   => { ?flight, ... }
flight:
  { }
   => { }
  { flight ?id:name, #rest ?options:expression }
   => { make(<flight>, equipment: ?"type", id: ?#"id", ?options) }
end macro aircraft-definer;
```

When we are processing the **flight** auxiliary rules, we would like to be able to reference the pattern variable **?type** (coercing it to a string) from the main rules, but it is not **in scope** — it is inaccessible to the auxiliary rules. We could have **register-flights** set the **equipment** slot after the flight is created, but we would prefer to initialize the slot at the time we create the **<flight>** object. There is a workaround, an **auxiliary macro**:

```
define macro aircraft-definer
  { define aircraft ?identifier:name (?type:name) ?flights:* end }
   => { register-aircraft (make("<" ## ?type ## ">", id: ?#"identifier"));
        define flights (?#"identifier", ?"type")
          ?flights
        end }
end macro aircraft-definer;
```

```
define macro flights-definer
  { define flights (?craft:name, ?equipment:name) end }
   => { }
  { define flights (?craft:name, ?equipment:name) ?flight ; ?more:* end }
   => { register-flights
          (?craft, make(<flight>, equipment: ?equipment, ?flight)) ;
        define flights (?craft, ?equipment) ?more end }
flight:
  { }
   => { }
  { flight ?id:name, #rest ?options:expression }
   => { id: ?#"id", ?options }
end macro flights-definer;
```

Here, we have essentially broken out the work that used to be done by the auxiliary rule **flights** into a separate definition macro. Where **flights** used points of ellipsis to walk over each flight, the definition macro uses a **wildcard** constraint **?more:***, explicitly calling itself again (that is, the macro appears in the substitution, and will be expanded again), as long as there are more flights to be processed.

Here is an example use of the **flights-definer** macro:

```
define aircraft UA4906H (DC10)
  flight UA11 from: #"BOS", to: #"SFO";
  flight UA12 from: #"SFO", to: #"BOS";
end aircraft UA4906H;
```

Expanding that code would result in the following:

```
register-aircraft (make(<DC10>, #"UA4096H"));
register-flights (#"UA4096H",
                  make(<flight>, equipment: "DC10",
                       id: #"UA11" from: #"BOS", to: #"SFO");
register-flights (#"UA4096H",
                  make(<flight>, equipment: "DC10",
                       id: #"UA12" from: #"SFO", to: #"BOS");
```

(Note that this example is a hypothetical one used to illustrate macro expansion. The **define aircraft** statement cannot be compiled in the airport example.)

21.8 Summary

In this chapter, we introduced macros by explaining their purpose as a language-extension tool, and by showing a range of Dylan macros. Macros can be useful when you want to tailor the language to express a particular problem domain more concisely.

Table 21.1 summarizes how constraints control pattern-variable matches.

Constraint	Matches
token	a lexeme (a Dylan word), including literal strings, symbols, and numbers and punctuation
name	a Dylan identifier, including reserved identifiers, such as **define**, **end**, and operators such as **+**, or *****
variable	either **variable** or **variable :: <type>**, useful for macros that mimic variable binding (automatically drops the **:: <type>**, as appropriate on substitution)
expression	a well-formed Dylan expression -- a constant, such as **37**; a variable, such as ***my-position***; a function call, such as **get-current-time()**; a statement, such as **if (test) 12 else try() end**; or a binary operand series, such as **x + y * z**
body	a well-formed Dylan body — a sequence of semicolon-separated constituents, each constituent being either a definition, local declaration, or expression
case-body	a Dylan **case** statement body
*****	any sequence of Dylan tokens and parsed forms

Table 21.1 Pattern constraints.

Appendix A

Resources on Dylan

A.1 World Wide Web pages for this book and its examples

Both Addison-Wesley and Harlequin maintain Web pages about this book, including the source code of the program examples, and excerpts from the book. The address of the Addison-Wesley Web page for computer science and engineering is

```
http://www.aw.com/cseng/
```

The address of Harlequin's Web page is

```
http://www.harlequin.com/
```

A.2 Newsgroup

The name of the newsgroup about Dylan is

```
comp.lang.dylan
```

The newsgroup is also available as an Internet mailing list

```
info-dylan@cambridge.apple.com
```

To subscribe to **info-dylan**, send a message to

```
info-dylan-request@cambridge.apple.com
```

A.3 Harlequin

Harlequin's initial Dylan product is a Dylan implementation for Windows 95 and Windows/NT. Harlequin will offer Dylan implementations on the three major platforms: Windows, UNIX, and the Macintosh. Harlequin will provide a native Dylan development environment and technical support.

Harlequin's Dylan Web site contains a great deal of useful information about Dylan, including the FAQ, *The Dylan Reference Manual*, and pointers to public-domain implementations of Dylan and to the **`comp.lang.dylan`** newsgroup. The address of Harlequin's Dylan Web page is

`http://www.harlequin.com/full/dylan.html`

Harlequin's main Web site is located at

`http://www.harlequin.com/`

Harlequin's main telephone numbers are
United States.: 617-374-2400
United Kingdom: 44 (0) 1223 873800

Harlequin's main addresses are:
Harlequin Incorporated
One Cambridge Center
Cambridge, MA 02142 USA

Harlequin Limited
Barrington Hall
Barrington
Cambridge
United Kingdom
CB2 5RG

A.4 Carnegie Mellon University

Carnegie Mellon provides a public-domain implementation called **Mindy**, which stands for "Mindy Is Not Dylan Yet." Mindy is an experimental byte-compiler and interpreter written in C. Mindy implementations are available for UNIX, WindowsNT, OS/2, and the Macintosh (both 68000 and PowerPC).

Carnegie Mellon's Gwydion and Dylan Web site contains a great deal of useful information about Dylan, including the FAQ, *The Dylan Reference Manual*, the **`comp.lang.dylan`** newsgroup, and releases of Mindy. Carnegie Mellon's Web site about Gwydion and Dylan is located at

```
http://legend.gwydion.cs.cmu.edu/gwydion/
```

The address of Carnegie Mellon's Gwydion and Dylan ftp site is

```
ftp://legend.gwydion.cs.cmu.edu/usr/gwydion/ftp/
```

Carnegie Mellon's main Web site is located at

```
http://www.cmu.edu/
```

Carnegie Mellon's electronic mail address for Gwydion is:

```
gwydion-group@cs.cmu.edu
```

A.5 Apple Computer, Inc.

Apple Computer sells the Apple Dylan Technology Release. That release is a low-cost product, which provides the opportunity for programmers to become familiar with the Dylan language and the Apple Dylan development environment. The software is unfinished, and will not be supported or updated by Apple.

Apple's Dylan Web page contains much useful information about Dylan, including the FAQ, *The Dylan Reference Manual*, mail archives, newsgroup archives, articles about Dylan, and pointers to public-domain implementations of Dylan:

```
http://www.cambridge.apple.com/
```

Apple's Dylan ftp site is located at

```
ftp://ftp.cambridge.apple.com/pub/dylan/
```

You can order the Apple Dylan Technology Release from the Apple Developer Catalog Online, located at

```
http://www.devcatalog.apple.com/
```

The telephone numbers for the Apple Developer Catalog Online are:

U.S.: 1-800-282-2732
Canada: 1-800-637-0029
International: 1-716-871-6555

Apple's main Web site is located at

```
http://www.apple.com/
```

Apple's main address is:

Apple Computer, Inc.
1 Infinite Loop
Cupertino, CA 95014

A.6 Digitool, Inc.

Digitool ported the Apple Dylan Technology Release to run natively on the Power Macintosh. You can obtain this version from Apple Computer directly.

Digitool's main Web site is located at

`http://www.digitool.com/`

Digitool's telephone number is
617-441-5000

Digitool's address is

Digitool, Inc.
One Main Street — 7th Floor
Cambridge, MA 02142

A.7 Marlais

Marlais is an experimental Dylan interpreter in the public domain as "copylefted" software. Marlais is available on UNIX, the Macintosh, and Windows. It was originally developed by Brent Benson of Harris Computer Systems, and new versions were developed by Joseph N. Wilson, at the University of Florida. Patrick Beard developed the Macintosh implementation of Marlais.

The address of the Web site for Marlais is

`http://www.cise.ufl.edu:/~jnw/Marlais/`

The Web site for the Computer and Information Science and Engineering Department of the University of Florida is located at

`http://www.cise.ufl.edu/`

The telephone number of the department where Marlais is being developed is
904-392-1200

The address of the department where Marlais is being developed is

Computer & Information Science & Engineering
Room E301 CSE Building
PO Box 116120
University of Florida
Gainesville, FLA 32611-6120

Appendix B

Dylan Object Model for C and C++ Programmers

In this appendix, we discuss certain areas where Dylan's object model differs significantly from the object model of C and C++.

B.1 The concept of pointers

If you are familiar with a language with explicit pointers, such as C, you may be confused initially by Dylan's object model. Although there is no "pointer-to" operation in Dylan, there are pointers in the implementation. If you are trying to imagine how Dylan objects are implemented, it is better to think in terms of always manipulating a pointer to the object: A Dylan variable (or slot) stores a pointer to an object, rather than a copy of the object's slots. Similarly, assignment, argument passing, and identity comparison are in terms of pointers to objects.

Even characters and numbers can be *considered* as objects that are pointed to (objects with an unmodifiable value slot), making the object model uniform. But compilers optimize away the indirection for these built-in classes.

Note that = comparison defaults to pointer comparison, but can be customized by class. There are sensible customizations built-in for characters, numbers, collections, sequences, and lists. You can add your own customizations for classes that you create.

Consider this Dylan code:

Dylan object example.

```
define class <color> (<object>)
  slot red :: <integer> = 0, init-keyword: red:;
  slot green :: <integer> = 0, init-keyword: green:;
  slot blue :: <integer> = 0, init-keyword: blue:;
end class <color>;

define constant black = make(<color>);

define constant white
  = make(<color>, red: 2 ^ 24 - 1, green: 2 ^ 24 - 1, blue: 2 ^ 24 - 1);

define method whiteness-test(color :: <color>)
  if (color = white) format-out("It's white!\n") end;
end method whiteness-test;

define variable color = black;

color := white;
whiteness-test(color);
```

The equivalent C code is as follows:

C equivalent of Dylan object example.

```
typedef struct _color
  { int red, green, blue; }
Color;

static Color _black = {0, 0, 0};
Color* const black = &_black;

static Color _white = {16777215, 16777215, 16777215};
Color* const white = &_white;

void whitenessTest(Color* const color) {
  if (color == white) { printf("It's white!\n"); }
}

void main () {
  Color* color = black;

  color = white;
  whitenessTest(color);
}
```

The benefit of the Dylan model is that the final two statements are a single pointer assignment and a passing of a single pointer as a parameter. The comparison in **whitenessTest** is a single pointer comparison. Another possible C implementation — one more typical of C style, but *not* equivalent to the Dylan implementation — is as follows:

C-style example, without pointers.

```
typedef struct _color
  { int red, green, blue; }
Color;

Color const black = {0, 0, 0};
Color const white = {16777215, 16777215, 16777215};

void whitenessTest(Color const color) {
  if (color.red == white.red &&
      color.green == white.green &&
      color.blue == white.blue)
  { printf("It's white!\n"); }
}

void main () {
  Color color = black;

  color = white;
  whitenessTest(color);
}
```

In the C-style example, without pointers, the final two statements consist of three integer assignments (as the **Color** structure is copied), and a passing of a three-slot structure (the equivalent of three arguments) as an argument. The comparison in **whitenessTest** is three integer comparisons (as the two **Color** structures are compared, slot by slot).

The drawback of the Dylan object example is shown here:

```
color.blue := 0;
```

The preceding call makes **white** yellow! In the C-style example, without pointers, you would make only **color** yellow. You can prevent people from changing defined colors to other colors in Dylan by not allowing the slots of **<color>** objects to be modified once they are initialized — in other words, by making **<color>** objects *immutable*:

Dylan object example, with immutable objects.

```
define class <color> (<object>)
  constant slot red :: <integer> = 0, init-keyword: red:;
  constant slot green :: <integer> = 0, init-keyword: green:;
  constant slot blue :: <integer> = 0, init-keyword: blue:;
end class <color>;

define constant black = make(<color>);

define constant white
  = make(<color>, red: 2 ^ 24 - 1, green: 2 ^ 24 - 1, blue: 2 ^ 24 - 1);

define variable color = black;

define method whiteness-test(color :: <color>)
  if (color = white) format-out("It's white!\n") end;
end method whiteness-test;

color := white;
whiteness-test(color);
```

You can consider Dylan as always using pointers, even to objects such as integers and characters. Integers and characters are, by definition, immutable objects: There are no slots that you can change in an integer or character object. Thus, there is no danger of setting 6 to 9. Built-in immutable objects can have their pointers optimized away by the compiler: The compiler just has to arrange that 6 = 6 and 9 = 9, whether there is only one 6 object pointed to by all the variables with the value 6, or copies of 6 are stored in each of those variables (saving the need for a pointer).

Another difficulty in the Dylan model is this potentially embarrassing situation:

```
color := make(<color>, red: 2 ^ 24 - 1, green: 2 ^ 24 - 1, blue: 2 ^ 24 - 1);
if (color = white) format-out("It's white!\n") end;
```

The preceding expression might not say "It's white!", because **make** might return a new object with white RGB values, and that object would not be **=** to the object named **white**. The equivalent C code would be:

```
Color* make_color(int r, int g, int b) {
  Color* c = (Color*)malloc(sizeof(Color));
  c->red = r; c->green = g; c->blue = b;
  return c;
}

static Color _white = {16777215, 16777215, 16777215};
Color* const white = &_white;

Color* color = make_color(16777215, 16777215, 16777215);
if (color == white) { printf("It's white!\n"); };
```

Because the preceding code is comparing the pointer stored in **white** to the pointer stored in **color**, it will clearly not say "It's white!". The default implementation of = in Dylan is to compare pointers.

There are several solutions to this difficulty in Dylan. One is to customize the = comparison operator for our class to do a comparison more thorough than the default comparison:

```
define method \= (o1 :: <color>, o2 :: <color>)
  o1.red = o2.red & o1.green = o2.green & o1.blue = o2.blue;
end method \=;
```

Now, using = will compare colors by checking their individual RGB components, and our whiteness test will work.

Note that Dylan also provides the == comparison operator, which always compares pointers. This comparison is useful when you want to check object identity. But, as we have seen, it is not always the appropriate default for comparison of equality of objects. The compiler can avoid calling our \= method altogether if the same object is compared to itself. It can do so because, with the exception of IEEE NaNs (nonnumbers), values that are == must also be =.

Another approach that you can use if your objects are immutable is to make sure that they are unique. The **make** function is not required to return a new object each time, as shown in the Dylan object example, with unique, immutable objects.

This advanced use of **make** and tables ensures that there is always only one instance of each color. Thus, when we make another white, it will always be *the* white, and our whiteness test will work with the default = comparison. The choice of solution depends on whether you will be doing more making or more comparing.

Dylan object example, with unique, immutable objects.

```
define class <color-table> (<table>)
end class <color-table>;

define method table-protocol(<color-table>)
  local method color-hash(color :: <color>)
    let (red-id, red-state) = object-hash(color.red);
    let (grn-id, grn-state) = object-hash(color.green);
    let (blu-id, blu-state) = object-hash(color.blue);
    let (merge-id, merge-state) =
      merge-hash-codes(red-id, red-state,
                       grn-id, grn-state, ordered: #t);
    merge-hash-codes(merge-id, merge-state,
                     blu-id, blu-state, ordered: #t);
  end;
  local method color-test(o1 :: <color>, o2 :: <color>)
    o1.red = o2.red & o1.green = o2.green & o1.blue = o2.blue;
  end;
  values(color-test, color-hash)
end method table-protocol;

define variable color-table = make(<color-table>);

define method make(class == <color>, #key red, green, blue)
  let prototype = next-method();
  element(color-table, prototype, default: #f) |
    (color-table[prototype] := prototype);
end method make;
```

B.2 The concept of classes

If you are familiar with the class concepts of C++, you may be confused by Dylan's class model. In Dylan, all base classes are effectively virtual base classes, with "virtual" data members. When a class inherits another class more than once (because of multiple inheritance), only a single copy of that base class is included. Each of the multiple-inheritance paths can contribute to the implementation of the derived class. The Dylan class model favors this mix-in style of programming.

Here is an example of such a program, followed by the equivalent C++:

Mix-in example in Dylan.

```
define class <window> (<object>)
  slot width :: <integer>;
  slot height :: <integer>;
end class <window>;

define class <border-window> (<window>)
  slot border-width :: <integer>;
end class <border-window>;

define method width(window :: <border-window>)
  next-method() - 2 * window.border-width;
end method width;

define method height(window :: <border-window>)
  next-method() - 2 * window.border-width;
end method height;

define class <label-window> (<window>)
  slot label-height :: <integer>;
  slot label-text :: <string>;
end class <label-window>;

define method height(window :: <label-window>)
  next-method() - window.label-height;
end method height;

define class <border-label-window>
    (<border-window>, <label-window>, <window>)
end class <border-label-window>;
```

The example is a greatly simplified sketch of a computer-display windowing system, where a window may have a border (outline decoration), or a title (such as the title bar of a window), or both. (We omit any further detail, such as scroll bars.) One chore in such a system is to compute the available display area of a window from that window's overall size and from the sizes of the window's components.

Note that calling **height** on an instance of **<border-label-window>** will automatically perform the actions appropriate for a window with a border and a label. First, the method for **<border-window>** will be called, subtracting out the border width; when it calls **next-method**, to get the underlying window width, the method for **<label-window>** will be called, subtracting out the label height;

finally, when it calls **next-method**, the method for getting the value of the **height** slot in the underlying window will be called.

This example is a classic one of the mix-in style — the full functionality of the **<border-label-window>** class is the result of the combination of the individual pieces of **<border-window>** and **<label-window>** functionality.

C++ equivalent of the mix-in example.

```
class Window {
private:
  int _width;
  int _height;
public:
  virtual int width() { return _width; }
  virtual int height() { return _height; }
};

class BorderWindow : public virtual Window {
private:
  int _border_width;
public:
  virtual int border_width() { return _border_width; }
  virtual int width();
  virtual int height();
};

int BorderWindow::width() {
  return Window::width() - 2 * border_width();
}

int BorderWindow::height() {
  return Window::height() - 2 * border_width();
}

class LabelWindow : public virtual Window {
private:
  int _label_height;
  char *_label_text;
public:
  virtual int label_height() { return _label_height; }
  virtual char* label_text() { return _label_text; }
  virtual int height();
};

int LabelWindow::height() {
  return Window::height() - label_height();
}
```

C++ equivalent of the mix-in example. *(continued)*

```
class BorderLabelWindow :
  public virtual BorderWindow,
  public virtual LabelWindow,
  public virtual Window {
public:
  virtual int height();
};

  // Have to generate "combined" method by hand in C++
int BorderLabelWindow::height() {
  return Window::height() - 2 * border_width() - label_height();
}
```

It may be helpful for C++ programmers to consider that:

- Dylan base classes are always virtual.
- In Dylan, data members are accessed through virtual functions, so it is always possible to override access to a data member in a derived class, and to modify the returned value (or, by overriding the setter, to modify the value to be stored).
- Dylan's **next-method** allows you to use automatic method combination when you are programming in a mix-in style.

Note that the C++ equivalent of the mix-in example is incomplete. It is intended only as a guide to how you can think of Dylan classes. In particular, we have not modeled the slot setter virtual functions that Dylan classes define automatically, and we have not gone into how instances of the classes are constructed. In Dylan, we would simply give init-keywords for each of the slots, and the automatically generated constructor would fill them in for any of the derived classes. In contrast, constructors for virtual base classes are a particularly difficult aspect of C++: They make it hard to model what is done in Dylan accurately. In general, the mix-in style of programming is more difficult to do in C++, because that language's support for it is quite limited.

Note also that the C++ code is provided only as a model of Dylan execution, so that you can understand the semantics of Dylan classes in C++ terms. Good Dylan compilers use library compilation, type inferencing, and partial evaluation to optimize out the overhead normally associated with virtual classes and virtual functions, while preserving the dynamic execution semantics.

Glossary

abstract class

A class that cannot have direct instances. To define an abstract class, you provide the `abstract` class adjective in the `define class` form. All superclasses of an abstract class must also be abstract.

allocation

The allocation of a slot determines where the storage for the slot's value is allocated, and determines which instances share the value of the slot. There are four kinds of allocation: instance, class, each-subclass, and virtual.

ambiguous methods

Methods that cannot be ordered as more specific or less specific than one another, in the method dispatch.

assignment

The act of setting the value of an existing variable or slot, or of setting an element of a collection. The assignment operator is `:=`.

binding

An association between a name and an object. For example, there is a binding that associates the name of a constant and the object that is the value of the constant. The names of functions, module variables, and local variables are also bindings.

body

A region of program code that delimits the scope of all local variables declared inside it. Bodies can be nested. An body is begun implicitly with `define method`, and is ended by the corresponding `end`. You can define a body explicitly by using `begin` to start it and `end` to finish it. A local variable has scope extending from its declaration to the end of the smallest body that surrounds it.

built-in class

A class provided by Dylan, such as `<object>`, `<integer>`, or `<string>`.

class

A definition of a type of other objects, which are called its instances. A class defines the slots of its instances. Dylan provides built-in classes, and users can define new classes. When you define a class, you specify its name, its direct superclasses, and its slots.

class precedence list

For a particular class, a list of the class and all its superclasses, ordered from most specific (the class itself) to least specific (the `<object>` class).

closure

A method that closes over some local variables. The closure can access the local variables which existed when the closure was created. The ability to dynamically create and return closures that can access lexical state is one of the important dynamic aspects of Dylan.

collection

A kind of container that can hold zero or more objects. Dylan provides the usual kinds of collections, including arrays, vectors, strings, singly linked lists, queues, hash tables, and so on. In Dylan, a collection is an instance of a class. For example, the `<array>` class represents arrays, and the `<vector>` class represents vectors.

concrete class

A class that can have direct instances. By default, a class is concrete.

condition

An instance (direct or indirect) of the **<condition>** class, that represents a problem or unusual situation encountered during program execution.

constant (also called **module constant**)

An unchanging binding whose scope is its module. You define a constant explicitly with **define constant**, and implicitly with **define class**, **define generic**, **define macro**, or possibly **define method**. You must initialize the value of a constant, and you cannot assign another value to a constant during the execution of a Dylan program.

constituent

A definition, a local declaration, or an expression.

constructor

A function that creates an instance. A constructor provides a shorthand means for calling **make**. For example, you can call the constructor function **vector** to create a vector, and to initialize that vector with data.

contract

An agreement between a generic function and its methods. The generic function defines the terms of the contract, and the methods must obey the contract; particularly, the methods' parameters and value declarations must be congruent with the generic function's parameters and value declarations.

definition

A declaration of a piece of program structure, such as a library, module, class, generic function, or method. A definition usually establishes a module variable or constant. Definitions include **define variable**, **define class**, and **define method**.

development environment

A collection of tools for Dylan programmers that can include an editor custom-tailored for Dylan code, a browser, a compiler, a debugger, and a listener that enables you to enter expressions and to see their values. The features of any development environment are defined by the implementation, rather than by Dylan itself.

direct instance

An object is a direct instance of class A if the object's class is class A. You can use **`object-class`** to find out the class of which an object is a direct instance.

direct subclass

A class is the direct subclass of all its direct superclasses. "Direct" means there is no class intervening between the class and its subclass in the inheritance graph.

direct superclass

The direct superclasses of a class appear in the **`define class`** form for that class. Direct means that there is no class intervening between the class and its superclass in the inheritance graph.

`dylan` **library**

A library that contains modules that contain the elements of the core Dylan language.

`dylan` **module**

A module that contains the elements of the core Dylan language.

`dylan-user` **module**

The special bootstrapping module in which you define the modules and libraries that make up your program.

exception

An unexpected event that occurs during program execution.

expression

A piece of code that, when executed, can return (zero or more) values and can have side effects. Expressions include (among others) literals, references to variables or constants, function calls, and statements (such as **`if`**, **`while`**, and **`case`**).

`#f`

The canonical false value. This object is the only object that represents false in Dylan.

general instance

A member of a class. An object is a general instance of a class if it is either a direct or an indirect instance of that class. The term *instance* is equivalent to the term *general instance*.

generic function

A kind of function. A generic function defines an interface, and contains methods that implement that generic function. When a generic function is called, it chooses the method to call based on the types of its required arguments.

getter

A method that retrieves the current value of a slot in an object. Each slot in a class automatically has a getter defined for it. The getter's name is the same as the name of the slot.

handler

A function that can potentially resolve an exceptional situation.

implicit generic function

A generic function created by Dylan if a method is defined by **`define method`** or (for a slot getter or setter) by **`define class`** and if no generic function of the same name exists. An implicit generic function has the most general parameter and result types that are compatible with the method.

indirect instance

An object is an indirect instance of class A if the object's class has class A as a superclass.

infix function

A function whose calling syntax has the function appearing between the arguments. The arithmetic functions `+`, `-`, `*`, `/`, `<`, `>`, and so on are infix functions, as is the assignment operator, `:=`. An example of the calling syntax is: `3 + 2`.

information hiding

A principle of minimizing the information that is passed among components in a system; it reduces the interdependencies of components.

inheritance

The ability to arrange for classes that are logically related to one another to share the behaviors and data attributes that they have in common. Each class inherits from one or more other classes, called its superclasses. If no other class is an appropriate superclass, the class inherits from the class **`<object>`**.

init expression

A technique for initializing slots. An init expression provides an expression that yields a default value. Every time that an instance is made and the slot needs a default value, this expression is evaluated, and its value is used as the default. The slot receives its default initial value when no init keyword is defined, or when the caller does not supply the init-keyword argument to **`make`**.

init function

A function of zero arguments that is to be called to return a default initial value for the slot. The function is called every time that an instance is created if no init keyword is defined, or if the caller does not supply the init keyword argument to **`make`**. To define an init function for a slot, use the **`init-function:`** slot option in the class definition.

init keyword

A keyword that can be given to **make** to provide an initial value for a slot. To define an init keyword for a slot, you use the **init-keyword:** or **required-init-keyword:** slot option in the class definition.

init value

A default initial value for a slot, obtained by evaluating an expression once, before the first instance of the class is made. To define an init value for a slot, use the **init-value:** slot option in the class definition.

initialize

To provide an initial value for something that you are creating, such as a slot or a variable.

initialize method

A method for the **initialize** generic function. The purpose of initialize methods is to initialize an instance before that instance is returned by **make**.

instance

A member of a class. An object is an instance of a class if it is either a direct or an indirect instance of that class. The term *instance* is equivalent to the term *general instance*.

instantiable class

A class that can be used as the first argument to **make**. All concrete classes are instantiable. You can make an abstract class be instantiable by defining a **make** method for the class; the **make** method must return an instance of a concrete subclass of the abstract class.

interchange format

A format that all Dylan implementations accept for publishing and exchanging source code by means of files. In this format, each file contains a single source record. The file must have a header at the front, consisting of pairs of keywords and values. One required keyword is **module:**; its value is the name of the module in which the source record of the file resides.

keyword

A symbol name followed by a colon, such as **`total-seconds:`**.

keyword argument

An optional argument to a function consisting of a keyword followed by that keyword's value. You can give keyword arguments in any order. Keyword arguments can be useful for functions that take many arguments — when you call the function, you do not need to remember the order of the arguments. Keyword parameters enable a method to accept optional arguments that are keyed to a name. Keyword parameters appear after **`#key`** in the parameter list.

library

A Dylan library defines a software component, which is a separately compilable unit that can be either a stand-alone program or a component (library) of a larger program. A library contains modules.

library-interchange definition (LID) file

A file that enumerates all the files that make up a library. Most Dylan implementations support LID files, but these files are not required to by the core language.

limited type

A type that is a more restricted version of its base type. For example, a limited-integer type is based on **`<integer>`**, but has a given minimum or maximum value. Another example of a limited type is a limited-collection type, which is a collection type that specifies the type of elements, and/or the size of the collection. Limited types are created via **`limited`**.

listener

A tool that enables you to enter Dylan expressions, executes the expressions, and displays any values and output produced by them.

literal constant

An object whose contents are known completely at compile time.

local declaration

A declaration that establishes a local variable, local method, or local condition handler. Local declarations include **`let`**, **`local`**, and **`let handler`**.

local variable

A binding whose scope extends from its definition to the end of the smallest body that surrounds it. You establish and use local variables within a body. Once the program exits the body, the local variables are no longer defined, and an attempt to access them is an error.

macro

A word or phrase that stands for another phrase (usually longer, but built of simpler components). Macros can be used for abbreviation, abstraction, simplification, or structuring. The primary use of macros in programming is to extend or adapt the language to allow a more concise or readable solution for a particular problem domain.

method

A kind of function that can belong to a generic function. Although methods are independent of classes, they operate on instances of classes. A method states the kinds of objects that it handles by the types of its required arguments.

module

A unit that contains a portion of the definitions of a library. Each module specifies an independent namespace for Dylan constants and variables, and controls the visibility of the names within a module from outside the module. You can use modules both to do information hiding and to prevent name clashes between constants and variables.

module constant (see **constant**)

module variable

A binding whose scope is its module. A module variable is much like a global variable in other languages. You define a module variable with **`define variable`**. When you define a module variable, you must initialize it (that is, provide an initial value for it). If a module variable is not exported from the module that defines it, then it is accessible only within the module. If the module variable is exported by the module that defines it, and is imported or used by another module, then it is accessible within that other module as well.

multiple inheritance

Inheritance of a class from more than one direct superclass.

`<object>` class

The class from which all classes inherit, either directly or indirectly.

object

An individual datum. Also called an *instance.*

parameter list

A list of specifications for the arguments to a function. A parameter list can specify required and optional arguments. The optional arguments can be keyword arguments, each of which is passed to the function as a keyword followed by a value. Each parameter has a name, which is bound to the corresponding argument within the function's body when the function is called. Required parameters and a method's keyword parameters can include type constraints. The parameter lists of a generic function and all its methods must be congruent.

parameter specializer

The type of a required parameter of a method.

predicate

A function that returns true or false. False is always represented as **`#f`**. True is represented by the canonical true value, **`#t`**, and by any value other than **`#f`**.

protocol

The interface definition of a software component. The purpose of establishing protocols is to define a uniform interface that clients can use, even if the implementation of a component is enhanced or modified.

recursion

A technique in which a function calls itself.

required parameter

A parameter corresponding to an argument that must be provided in the call to the function. Required parameters appear before any rest or keyword parameters in a parameter list. Required parameters are ordered, and the required arguments must be given in the same order.

rest parameter

Parameters that enable a method to accept any number of optional arguments. Any arguments provided in the call after the required arguments are collected in a sequence, which is the value of the rest parameter. A rest parameter, if one exists, appears after `#rest` in the parameter list.

restart

A special condition that represents an opportunity to recover from an exception.

restart handler

A function used to implement the particular recovery action for a restart condition.

value declaration

A list of the values returned by a function, and of the types of the values. The name of a return value is used purely for documentation purposes. When you provide a value declaration for a function, Dylan signals an error if the function tries to return a value of the wrong type. The compiler can check receivers of the results of the method for correct type, and can usually produce more efficient code. The value declarations of a generic function and all that function's methods must be congruent.

root

The starting point of Dylan class inheritance — the class `<object>`, from which all Dylan classes inherit, either directly or indirectly.

setter

A method that stores a value in a slot. By default, each slot in a class has a setter defined for it automatically.

signature

The parameter list and the values declaration of a function.

singleton type

A type whose only member is one particular instance. Singleton types are created via **`singleton`**.

single inheritance

Inheritance in a class that has only one direct superclass.

slot

A unit of data associated with an instance. A slot is like a structure member or a field in other languages. Information about a slot is specified in the definition of the instance's class. The location of storage for the slot is determined by the slot's allocation. A program retrieves the value of a slot by calling that slot's getter generic function, and, unless the slot is constant, it sets the value by calling the slot's setter generic function.

slot option

An option that specifies a characteristic of a slot, such as the default initial value or the init keyword. Slot options appear in the **`define class`** form.

source record

A unit that organizes a portion of the Dylan source code for a program. Different Dylan implementations divide code into source records differently, and store the source records differently. For example, an implementation might store source records in a database. Many implementations store source records in files, and typically each file contains one source record.

subclass

The subclasses of a class include the class itself, and all classes that inherit from the class (all the class's direct subclasses, and all their direct subclasses, and so on).

subtype

The subtypes of a type include the type itself, and all types that inherit from the type, directly or indirectly.

superclass

The superclasses of a class include all that class's direct superclasses, and all their direct superclasses, and so on, all the way to the root of class inheritance, which is the `<object>` class. You can use `all-superclasses` to find all the superclasses of a class.

supertype

The supertypes of a type include all the types from which the type inherits, directly or indirectly.

symbol

An instance of the `<symbol>` type. Symbols are much like strings. There are two reasons to use symbols in certain cases where you might consider strings. First, symbol comparison is not case sensitive. Second, comparison of two symbols is much faster than is comparison of two strings, because symbols are compared by identity, and strings are usually compared element by element., There are two equivalent syntaxes for referring to symbols: `north:` is an example of the keyword syntax, whereas `#"north"` is an example of the hash syntax.

#t

The canonical value of true. Note that any value other than `#f` is considered a value of true.

type

An object that describes the structure and behavior of its members. All classes are types, but not all types are classes. You can define new nonclass types with `limited`, `singleton`, and `type-union`.

type constraint

A type associated with a binding or slot that ensures that the value of that binding or slot can hold only objects of that type.

union type

A type whose members include all the members of one or more base types. Union types are created via `type-union`.

user-defined class

A class defined by a Dylan user, and not provided by Dylan itself.

virtual slot

A slot that does not occupy storage; instead, its value is computed. When you define a virtual slot, you need to define a getter method to return the value of the virtual slot, and you can optionally define a setter method to set the value of the virtual slot.

Index